MICROCOMPUTERS IN BUSINESS

WORDSTAR, dBASE II AND III, AND LOTUS 1-2-3

The Times Mirror/Mosby
Data Processing and Information Systems Series

Cohen-Alger-Boyd **Business BASIC for the IBM PC with Cases**

Dravillas-Stilwell-Williams **Power Pack for the IBM PC**

Floyd **Essentials of Data Processing**

Harpool-Culp-Galehouse **Systems Analysis and Design Projects**

Lientz-Rea **Data Communications for Business**

Spence-Windsor **Microcomputers in Business: WordStar, dBASE II and III, and Lotus 1-2-3**

Spence-Windsor **Using Microcomputers: Applications for Business**

Times Mirror/Mosby College Publishing **Microcomputer Applications Software: WordPerfect, dBASE III Plus, and SuperCalc4**

Whitten-Bentley **Using Excelerator for Systems Analysis and Design**

Whitten-Bentley-Ho **Systems Analysis and Design Methods**

The Spence-Windsor System of Instruction

- Instructor's Guide with Transparency Masters
- Student Laboratory Manual
- Data Diskettes
- Test Items
- Microtest Computerized Testing Package

All of these supplements were written by J. Wayne Spence and John C. Windsor. When combined with the **Using Microcomputers: Applications for Business** text, they provide a complete system of instruction for teaching introductory microcomputer applications. For more information see the Preface in this text or call Times Mirror/Mosby College Publishing at 800-325-4177.

MICRO COMPUTERS IN BUSINESS

WORDSTAR, dBASE II AND III, AND LOTUS 1-2-3

J. WAYNE SPENCE

JOHN C. WINDSOR

BOTH AT NORTH TEXAS STATE UNIVERSITY

Times Mirror/Mosby College Publishing
St. Louis Toronto Santa Clara 1987

To Jan, Pat, and Cari. Thanks for your help, interest, and patience. Now—how about a vacation?

J.W.S.

To Eileen, Laura, and Rachel. Thanks for all your encouragement and support. We will go fishing this weekend.

J.C.W.

Editor: Susan A. Solomon
Developmental Editor: Rebecca A. Reece
Editorial Assistants: Pamela Lanam and Lisa Donohoe
Text and Cover Designer: Nancy Benedict
Production Coordinator: Stacey C. Sawyer, Montara, California
Illustrator: Bob Haydock
Typesetting: Progressive Typographers Inc.

FIRST EDITION

A division of the C. V. Mosby Company
11830 Westline Industrial Drive,
St. Louis, MO 63146

Printed in the United States of America

Library of Congress Cataloging in Publication Data
Spence, J. Wayne.
Microcomputers in business.

Includes index.
1. Business—Data Processing. 2. Business—Computer programs. 3. Microcomputers. I. Windsor, John, 1946–
II. Title.
HF5548.2.S728 1987 650′.028′5536
86-30013
ISBN 0-8016-5030-5

PR/VH/VH 9 8 7 6 5 4 3 2 1 04/A/573

CONTENTS

Preface ix

Overview: Microcomputer Applications in Business 1

Historical Development of Software 2
Types of Software 5
  System Software 5
  Developmental Software (Programming Languages) 5
  Applications Software 6
Summary 9

1 Module One Word Processing: WordStar 10

Introduction to Word Processing 10
Definition of Word Processing 10

WordStar 13

Learning to Use WordStar 13
  Some Preliminaries About Working with Documents 17
  Getting Help from WordStar 20
Solving the Job Hunting Problem 21
  Entering Text 23
  Editing Text 26
  A Cut-and Paste Operation 27
  Page Formatting—Redefining the Page 28
  Enhancing the Letter for Effect—Output Specifications 29
  Checking for Spelling Errors 29
  Personalized Messages—Find and Replace Functions 35
  Printing Your Letter—The Print Function 36
  Printing Several Letters—The MailMerge Function 37
Uses of Word Processing 44
Summary 45
Guidelines for the Evaluation of Word Processing Packages 45

2 Module Two Database: dBASE II and III 49

Introduction to Databases 49
Defining Databases 49
  Data Management Systems (DMS) 50
  Data Views 50
Database Systems 54
  The Definition of a Database 54
  Relationships within a Database 54
Types of Database Structures 56
  Relational Structure 58

dBASE II and III 59

Learning to Use dBASE II and dBASE III 59
Solving the Job Hunting Problem 60
  Building a Database—The CREATE Command 61
  Starting and Stopping—The QUIT and USE Commands 67
  Keeping Track of Where You Are—The LIST and DISPLAY Commands 67

CONTENTS, continued

Changing the Contents of a Database —The BROWSE and EDIT Commands 71
Adding Records to a Database—The INSERT and APPEND Commands 75
Getting a Look at the Database—The LIST and DISPLAY Commands 77
Eliminating Records from the Database—The DELETE, PACK, and RECALL Commands 81
Building, Specifying, and Using Indexes—The INDEX, USE, and SET INDEX Commands 83
An Ordered Database from Old Data —The SORT Command 84
Building Readable Reports—The REPORT Command 87
Making One New Database from Two—The JOIN Command 91
Other Features of dBASE II and dBASE III 96
Special Features of dBASE III 98
Uses of Databases 98
Guidelines for the Evaluation of Databases 99
Summary 102

3 Module Three Spreadsheet, Database, and Graphics: Lotus 1-2-3 116

Introduction to Lotus 1-2-3 116
Introduction to Spreadsheets 116
Definition of Spreadsheets 117
Matrix Terminology 118
Arithmetic Operations 119
There Are Different Kinds of Data—Data Types 119
Character Data 119
Numeric Data 121

Lotus 1-2-3 Spreadsheet 122

Learning to Use Lotus 1-2-3 122
The Arrangement—What a 1-2-3 Spreadsheet Looks Like 122
Learning About Your Keyboard—Cursor Movement and Function Keys 126
Trying to Remember—The Help Function 128
Solving the Job Hunting Problem 128
What's in a Name?—Entering Headings and Labels 130
Too Large or Too Small?—Changing Column Widths 131
Creating a New Look!—Formatting Cells for Text 132
A View with Numbers—Formatting Cells for Numeric Values 134
Entering the Company Names—Another Example of Entering Text 137
Two Views of the Spreadsheet—Using the Window Function 137
What Is Your Offer?—Placing Numeric Values in the Spreadsheet 139
Holding on to What You've Got—Saving the Spreadsheet 140

A Spreadsheet with Room to Grow—The Insert Function 141
Figure It This Way—Using Formulas 143
Duplicating—The Copy Function 144
Providing a Visual Break—The Copy Function Again 146
Letting 1-2-3 "Compute"—Using Functions 147
New Information on a Job Offer—Adding a New Row 151
Putting Rows in Order—The Sort Function 153
Calculations Without Changing the Spreadsheet—The Table Function 156
Showing Off Your Spreadsheet—The Print Function 160
Getting Out of Lotus—The Quit Function 161
Other Features of Lotus Spreadsheets 161

Lotus 1-2-3 Database 163
Learning to Use Lotus 1-2-3 Database 163
Solving the Job Hunting Problem 163
Loading Data into a Lotus Database 165
Performing Search Operations in the Database—Finding Rejected Companies 167
Producing a Report Containing Only Offered Jobs 172
Producing a Report for Companies Offering More Than $19,000 175
Other Features of Lotus Database 178
Automating Lotus Commands—Keyboard Macros 178

Introduction to Graphics 183
Defining Business Graphics 183
Charting and Chart Selection 183

Lotus 1-2-3 Graphics 186
Learning to Use Lotus 1-2-3 Graphics 186
Solving the Job Hunting Problem 186
What Is the Distribution of Job Status Values?—Producing a Pie Chart 187
Titles for the Pie Chart—An Initial Look at Labeling 188
Chart Manipulations—Viewing, Clearing, and Saving 188
How Do the Offers Measure Up?—Producing a Bar Chart 188
Titles for the Bar Chart—More on Labeling 188
Looking at the Actual Offers—Creating a Stacked Bar Chart 189
Comparing Actual Offers with the Average Offer—Creating a Line Chart 189
Printing Your Charts 190
Summary 190
Uses of Spreadsheets 191
Uses of Graphics 196
Movies 197
Industry 197
Business 197

CONTENTS, continued

Guidelines for the Evaluation of Spreadsheet Packages 197
Guidelines for the Evaluation of Graphics Packages 199

Appendix A Job Hunting Data 217
Appendix B Questions and Activities 220
Index 222

PREFACE

The Intended Audience for This Book

We wrote *Microcomputers in Business: WordStar, dBASE II and III, and Lotus 1-2-3* for a practical, hands-on, first course on how to use the microcomputer as a business problem-solving tool. This course is typically taught at the freshman or sophomore level in two- or four-year colleges and is typically aimed at business majors, information systems majors, and MBAs. Our book assumes no previous knowledge of the three software packages.

Why We Wrote This Book

Several years ago our consulting work indicated increasing demand for microcomputer application systems and for instruction on microcomputers and software packages. In response to this trend, we developed one of the first college-level courses designed to provide students with hands-on use of computers.

A book was originally written for our course to fill the void that the then-available books couldn't fill. It began as a locally produced software manual, and, through extensive class testing and marketing-based development, it evolved into a business-oriented microcomputer concepts and specific applications textbook, *Using Microcomputers: Applications for Business.* For those courses that teach only WordStar, dBASE II and III, and Lotus 1-2-3, we wrote this text, *Microcomputers in Business.*

While we were writing our book, a number of competing books were published. We've taken great care to ensure that our book does not have the deficiencies present in these currently available competitors. We specifically note the following:

Some Books Don't Address Specific Packages

A generic approach is fine for nonbusiness majors who need to "get their feet wet." Most businesses, however, now expect prospective employees to know how to use the popular packages to solve business problems.

Few Books Have a Business Orientation

When they do have any, it's "tacked on" in the form of exercises or boxed features. In general, our competitors do not integrate a business problem-solving theme, but instead concentrate on package commands.

Why We Think You Should Use This Book

Put quite simply, it works! The materials in our book have either been directly classroom tested or based on a classroom-tested model. Furthermore, much of this text has been used at North Texas State and in seminars for business professionals, employees of governmental agencies, and members of professional associations. We have taught from this material, located its weaknesses, and altered its presentation so that it meets the following educational objective:

To Emphasize Business Applications and a Problem-solving Orientation

Each Module focuses on solving a problem associated with searching for and finding a job. The strength of this approach is that students see how business problems are solved, rather than simply learning a list of commands.

How to Use This Book

The Modules are self-contained and as such may be taught in any order without loss of continuity. We do recommend, however, that Module Two be taught before Module Three.

Modules

The Modules provide a step-by-step approach to solving business problems. Each software package presentation is preceded by background information and an *Introduction* that identifies the details of the business problem to be solved. Each Module can be discussed in the classroom (ideally with a live demonstration), or students can work through each Module in the lab. Each Module concludes with a *Summary,* which contains a general review of package features, a discussion of uses, and a checklist for evaluating software of that application type. Appendix B contains questions and problems that test students' knowledge of the specific commands of each software package and students' ability to use the software to solve business problems.

The Job Hunting Problem

As mentioned above, realistic business examples are found throughout the book. The Job Hunting Problem is used throughout the Modules. Solving the same problem with different packages offers a building-block approach not found in other texts.

Additional business problems to solve can be found in the Student Lab Manual that accompanies our text. These problems encourage student interest, reinforce concepts, and promote a problem-solving approach.

Additional Options

Microcomputer concepts are often taught in combination with computer concepts and/or BASIC programming. Thus this text may be used with:

- A computer concepts text
- A BASIC programming text

Times Mirror/Mosby's two offerings in this area are Floyd, *Essentials of Data Processing* (1987), and Cohen-Alger-Boyd, *Business BASIC for the IBM PC with Cases* (1987).

Long Version of Our Text

A version of our text that contains generic chapters and additional modules for operating systems, word processing, spreadsheets, database, graphics, and integrated software is available from Times Mirror/Mosby.

Supplements

This text has a direct, practical approach. Likewise, our supplements package reflects a clear, useful business-oriented theme. The supplements can be used with both versions of our book.

Instructor's Manual

Our Instructor's Manual provides the most complete assistance currently available to instructors of introductory microcomputing courses. Further, this guide was designed to allow instructors to add their own teaching notes and so tailor it for their use. It includes:

- Notes on establishing and managing a microcomputer laboratory facility.
- A series of course syllabus suggestions for:
  —semester/quarter-oriented courses
  —courses with limited/extensive software use
  —courses to be supplemented by other material
- Approximately 100 Transparency Masters, which include:
  —key graphics that appear in the book
  —adaptations of text graphics
  —completely new illustrations
- Chapter components include:
  —teaching tips and notes
  —Transparency Master guide for each chapter
  —answers to all Chapter Questions
- Module components include:
  —teaching tips and notes
  —Transparency Master guide for each Module
  —answers/solutions to all Module Questions and Problems
  —additional Module Problems with solutions
- Sign-up sheet for those instructors wishing to be notified of Module Updates

Student's Laboratory Manual

This supplement, designed to facilitate students' use of the laboratory, is composed of:

- Hardware configuration guide—to record the types and locations of hardware available
- Software inventory—to keep track of the software packages and versions
- Restatement of all Module Problems with the appropriate data for each exercise
- "Test Yourself"—fill-in-the-blank and matching review questions and answers
- Quick response form—to be completed and submitted to the instructor for each exercise solved (minimizes amount of printout produced)
- Additional Module exercises, with the accompanying data for each exercise

- "Where do I find?" guide—to identify where items such as microcomputer magazines, hardware vendors, software vendors, and so on may be found
- Software summary sheets for each of the software packages presented in the text indicating the organization and structure of menus and commands (reduces the need to have both text and lab manual in the lab at the same time)

Data Diskettes

A set of three data diskettes contains data sets for the Module Job Hunting Problem and the four additional problems in the Student Lab Manual as well as solutions for all Module exercises.

Testbank and Computerized Testing Package

This includes over 1000 items with an average of over 50 items for each Chapter, an average of 20 items for each Module, and an average of 20 items that require knowledge of multiple Modules. The questions are predominately multiple choice, with the remainder distributed between true/false and matching. The testbank includes correct answers keyed to the appropriate Chapter or Module. This supplement is available to adoptors in printed and diskette version.

Acknowledgments

We are indebted to the many reviewers and market research telephone survey and personal interview respondents. Their input assisted us greatly.

Reviewers

Sarah Baker
Miami University of Ohio

Patricia Boggs
Wright State University

Samuel Coppage
Old Dominion University

Marilyn Correa
Polk Community College

Gary Erkes
Western Washington State

Sue Finch
Pima Community College

Al Garfinkel
Bergen Community College

Darrell Gobel
Catonsville Community College

George Grill
University of North Carolina

Don Henderson
Mankato State University

Russell Hollingsworth
Tarrant County Junior College

John Huhtala
Ferris State College

Santiago Ibarreche
University of Texas, El Paso

Richard Jarka
Oakton Community College

Donna Kizzier
Kearney State University

Buddy Krizan
Murray State University

Patrick Lamont
Western Illinois University

Jim LeBarre
University of Wisconsin, Eau Claire

Len Lindenmeyer
Anne Arundell Community College

Gary Marks
Austin Community College

Gerald Meyer
LeGuardia Community College

Micki Miller
Skyline College

Steve Murtha
Tulsa Community College

William O'Brian
Florida International University

William O'Hare
Prince Georges Community College

J. B. Orris
Butler University

Linda Rice
Saddleback Community College

Douglas Rippy
University of Dayton

Paul Ross
Millersville State College

Mark Sabet
California State University, Los Angeles

Al Schroeder
Richland College

Richard Smith
Oregon State University

Tim Sylvester
College of DuPage

Linda Taylor
Consultant

John Tower
Oakland University

Richard White
University of California, Berkeley

Dean Whittaker
Ball State University

Market Research Respondents

Alabama: Steve Zimmerman. **Arizona:** Sue Finch. **California:** Ronald Cerruti, Jason Frand, Vivian Frederick, Professor Gessford, Shepperd Gold, Ko Isshiki, Bob Jones, David Patterson, Kevin Shannon, Bob Van Spyke, Gerald Wagner, Richard White. **Florida:** Bruce DeSautel. **Georgia:** Rod O'Connor. **Illinois:** Beverly Bilshausen, Jim Boyd, John Chandler, Janet Cook, Paul Dravillas, Dr. Duffy, Richard Jarka, Jean Longhurst, Linda Salchenburger, John Schrage, Richard Sosnowski, George Warren, Kurt White. **Indiana:** Tom Harris, Ruth Lankford, Dean Orris, Gloria Wagoner, Jeff Whitten, Jim Wilson. **Iowa:** Jerry Fottrah, Curtis Rawson. **Kentucky:** Bonnie Bailey. **Maryland:** Mike Ball, Al Hebner. **Michigan:** Randy Cooper, Clyde Hardman, Hans Lee, Al Polish, Dennis Severance, Sid Sysma, Donald Weinshank, Dave Wilson. **Minnesota:** Bernice Folz, Layne Hopkins. **Missouri:** David Bird. **New Jersey:** Al Garfunkel. **New Mexico:** James Menching. **New York:** William Hillman, Professor Minena. **North Carolina:** Rob Adler, John Gallagher, Richard Kerns, James Teng, Dale Williams, Don Williams. **Ohio:** Sarah Baker, Don Brazelton, Kenneth Dunning, Miles Kennedy, Ed Kosiewicz, Kathryn Murphy, Art Polan, Kathleen Preem, Clyde Randall, James Schefler, Thomas Schraber, Glenn Thomas, Professor Vernon. **Oklahoma:** Dr. Ackerman, Darryl Nord. **Oregon:** William Harrison, Mike Johnson, Jeanne Sloper, Rick Smith, David Sullivan. **Pennsylvania:** Darrell Craig, Ron Teichman, Clinton White. **South Carolina:** C. Brian Honess. **Tennessee:** Mohammed Ahrandi. **Texas:** Carl Ahlers, Maryam Alavi, Professor Friedich, Rod Hustenberg, Gary Marks, Mike Parks, Professor Ricketts, Dr. Les Rydl. **Virginia:** Sam Coppage, Bob Gray, Art Hodge, Professor Pope, Rich Redmond, Howard Wilson, Jim Wynne. **Wisconsin:** Hank Bell, Susan Haugen, Robert Horton, Arthur Larson, Steve Ross.

We also wish to thank our colleagues and College of Business students at North Texas State, Nancy Benedict (Designer), Stacey Sawyer (Production Coordinator), Lisa Donohoe and Pam Lanam (Editorial Assistants), Rebecca Reece (Developmental Editor), and Susan Solomon (Executive Editor).

J. Wayne Spence

John C. Windsor

OVERVIEW: MICROCOMPUTER APPLICATIONS IN BUSINESS

Welcome to the world of computers, especially microcomputers! You are about to learn how to use a computer to solve problems.

In the following modules, you will become familiar with three of the most popular microcomputer packages available today.

Module 1 covers the **word processing** program WordStar. If you have to write textual material and want to be able to change it easily, a word processing program can solve the problem. As a student, you might want to use word processing to write letters, prepare class papers, or create outlines to assist you in studying for an exam.

dBASE II and III, database software, is covered in Module 2. If you find it necessary to keep a list of many items and then search that list for particular entries (or combinations of entries), a database program can help you. For example, you could create a list containing all of your credit card accounts and names and addresses of persons to notify in case the cards are lost or stolen. You could create a household inventory that could be reported to an insurance company in the event of theft or damage by fire. You could record expenses in particular categories to assist you in preparing your federal or state income tax.

Module 3 explores Lotus 1-2-3, a **spreadsheet** program. Spreadsheets are used to solve problems dealing with sets of interrelated numbers. For example, you might want to keep track of your progress in the courses you are taking by creating a spreadsheet that computes course averages based on exam scores and grades on other assignments. You could also use a spreadsheet to maintain a personal budget and keep track of expenses. Thus, whereas word processing deals with words, spreadsheets generally deal with numbers.

Sometimes "a picture is worth a thousand words"; therefore, it is often better to use a visual representation of data that words or numbers cannot adequately describe. Lotus 1-2-3 has the capability of presenting information pictorially — by the use of charts. Perhaps you want a visual representation of how you spend your money each month. You could produce a spreadsheet table that shows you, with numbers, where your money went, or you could produce a pie chart that demonstrates how your money was used. Perhaps you want to track your total income from year to year. One way of illustrating this type of comparison is to use a line or bar chart.

We have already identified a few personal uses of microcomputers and computer programs. Table 1 illustrates these and more. You will notice that the table lists a number of occupations or professions. Although the list is not exhaustive, see if your planned profession is in the list. Whether it is or not, you should examine the complete table; not only will you get an idea of how computers are being used in other occupations or professions, you might also get some new ideas about how computers could be used in your chosen career.

A computer program is a piece of software or a instruction set that tells the computer hardware what to do. In other words, computers are made to work for you through the use of software. For this reason, no introduction would be complete without a quick overview of computer software.

Historical Development of Software

Starting with the abacus, **software** was being developed along with calculating and computing equipment. During the early years, software was the set of procedures or instructions followed by the individual using a machine. [As advances were made in the design of these machines, more of the instruction processing was shifted from the individual (user) to the machine.] However, no major advances were made in software until 1804, when Joseph Jacquard transformed some of the instructions for a weaving loom into punched holes in paper cards.

Jacquard's punched cards were the first example of instructions put on a medium (or device) usable by a machine; by changing the program, one could change what the machine did. The principles behind the punched cards were used by Augusta Ada Byron, Countess of Lovelace, in the early 1840s to code the instructions for Charles Babbage's Analytical Engine, which was capable of doing certain types of mathematical computations. Lady Lovelace has since become known as the world's first programmer, and the codes she developed have been called the first software.

No further advances were made in software development until John von Neumann published his paper detailing the theory needed for the stored-program concept. The idea was to store instructions in the machine and change those instructions directly rather than write a new set each time the desired function changed. As the stored-program concept became better un-

TABLE 1 Using Microcomputers: A List of Occupations or Professions and Possible Uses of Application Programs

Occupation or Profession	Word Processing (Using Words)	Spreadsheets (Manipulating Numbers)	Database (Maintaining Lists)
Auto service/repair	Customer service report	Repair estimates	Appointment list, common problems list
Broadcasting (radio and TV)	Script preparation	Projecting advertising revenues	Advertising client list
Commercial and residential construction	Project description and specifications	Project cost estimates	Project materials requirements list ordering
Country club or pro shop	Member newsletter	Golf handicap computation	Membership list
Educator	Preparing exams, lesson plans, student worksheets	Analysis of grades	Classroom inventory, assignment of textbooks
Engineer	Project reports	Structural stress analysis	Parts list, bill of materials
Entertainment (movie production)	Script preparation and modification	Project cost estimates	Prop management, scene requirements
Equipment rental services	Customer contracts	Project cost estimates	Link to other rental services
Farmer	Financial report to bank	Crop rotation and planting mix analysis	Acreage inventory and historical crop performance
Health and fitness studio	Membership renewal notices, advertising	Member performance analysis	Member profiles, membership list
Hotel/motel management	Registration confirmations	Conference/banquet cost projections	Reservations, property inventory
Investments and financial consultant	Investment portfolio	Analysis of investment performance	Client investment portfolio management

Using Microcomputers *(continued)*

Occupation or Profession	Word Processing (Using Words)	Spreadsheets (Manipulating Numbers)	Database (Maintaining Lists)
Janitorial service	Advertising, brochures	New client cost estimates	Type of services by client
Journalist or reporter	Story preparation and production	Numerical analysis, expense reporting	Story-line items
Law enforcement	Neighborhood Watch program preparation	Call frequency analysis	Crime incidence data
Legal	Contracts, wills, brief preparation	Client charges	Case disposition, client list
Limousine or taxi service	Vehicle operators guide book	Fleet cost analysis	Client list, reservations
Medical	Patient charts	Office budget	Diagnostic codes, insurance payment history
Preschool and day care center	Report to parents	Operating cost analysis	Client medical and emergency data
Property management	Tenant contracts	Utility usage tracking per unit	Occupancy information
Real estate sales	Property description	Estimating client costs	List of available properties
Religious organization	Member newsletters, special program announcements	Operating budget analysis	Membership list
Social worker	Case reports	Client financial needs analysis	Case assignment list and history
Travel/tourism agency	Tour package preparation and advertising	Package cost projection, cost per party member	Customer contact

derstood, and as computer hardware improved, modern software evolved.

Types of Software

We have already used several terms in referring to software: **program, instructions,** and **code.** Several other names may also be used, including **language, package,** and **application.** All these terms refer to the same concept: a set of instructions used to make the computer perform a specific task. Although these terms may be interpreted somewhat differently, the name *software* covers all of them. Software can be divided into three groups, **system software, developmental software** (programming languages), and **applications software (packages).**

System Software

System software runs the computer; applications software and programming languages cannot be used without it. Sometimes these programs are on disk, but some newer computers may have all or part of the system software built in and stored in ROM. This is called **firmware.**

The collection of programs used by the computer to run the supervisor and control the flow of other programs and data is called **operating system software** (see Figure 1). The operating system integrates the computer hardware with other software. It reduces the amount of user action required to perform specific tasks on the machine and allows the user to concentrate on the task to be performed, rather than on the internal workings of the computer.

Developmental Software (Programming Languages)

Humans have a great deal of difficulty communicating with a computer in machine language, and computers cannot yet speak a human language, so several "intermediate" languages have been developed to allow humans to "converse" more easily with computers. These intermediate languages are called **developmental languages** because they are used to develop specific computer programs that apply to particular problem-solving situations. In other words, these are the languages most frequently associated with the term computer **programming.** Because they use more easily recognized symbols, **programming languages** are easier to use than assembly languages. Programming languages, also known as **procedural languages,** represent a substantial improvement over assembly language—therefore, they are sometimes referred to as *third-generation languages.*

Each language has its own structure and set of rules. Instructions written in a particular language must follow those rules. In any computer language, a typical program statement or instruction is made up of two parts: an **operation code (op code)** and **operands.** The op code, sometimes called a **reserved word,** tells the computer what operation to perform (for example, add, subtract, multiply, divide). The operands tell the computer what data to use when performing the operation.

Some computers and computer languages (particularly assembly languages) may use many different operation codes in their instruction set. Although this may lead to some confusion, op codes consist of four general command types:

1. **Input-output:** reading or writing data
2. **Arithmetic:** using data in a calculation
3. **Branching:** going from one place in a program to another
4. **Logic:** making decisions based on data

The developmental languages used by a

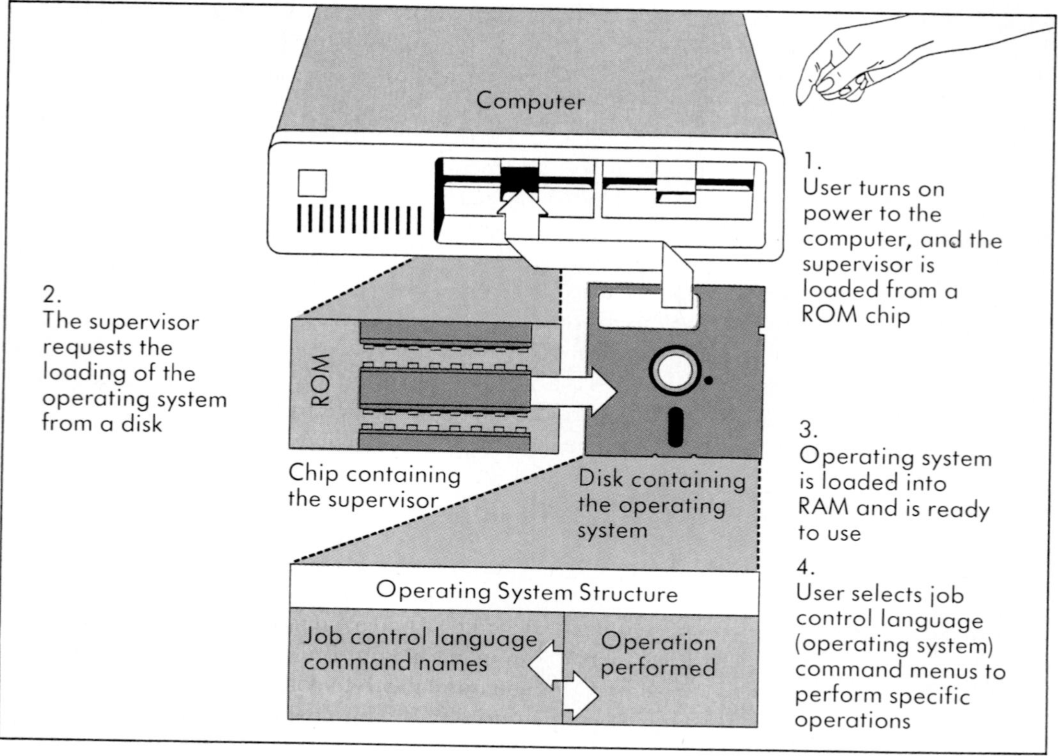

FIGURE 1
How system software works

programmer will generally depend on the type of application being implemented. Because developmental languages were created with particular types of tasks in mind, they each have specific strengths that programmers use to solve specific problems. Some popular programming languages are BASIC, FORTRAN, COBOL, Pascal, PL/I, and C.

Applications Software

The term **applications software** refers to programs designed to accomplish a particular task for an individual user or a specified group of users. They are written in a developmental or assembly language, and they provide the user with the full power of the computer without requiring that he or she go through the laborious process of developing the program. The modules that follow show you how to use this power.

How Does Software Work? Applications software comes in one of two forms on disk: **source code** or **object code.** Figure 2 shows the relationship between source code and object code. *Source code* is another name for a program written in a developmental language. It allows a user who is familiar with the language to read and understand the program's logic and to modify the program. For an applications program in this form to work on the computer, it first must be translated into machine language. This is done through either a **compiler** or an **interpreter.** A compiler translates the program into machine language all at once. An interpreter translates one statement at a time into machine language, allowing the user to check each statement for errors as it is executed. Although interpreters are slower than compilers, they are generally easier to use—they note errors for the

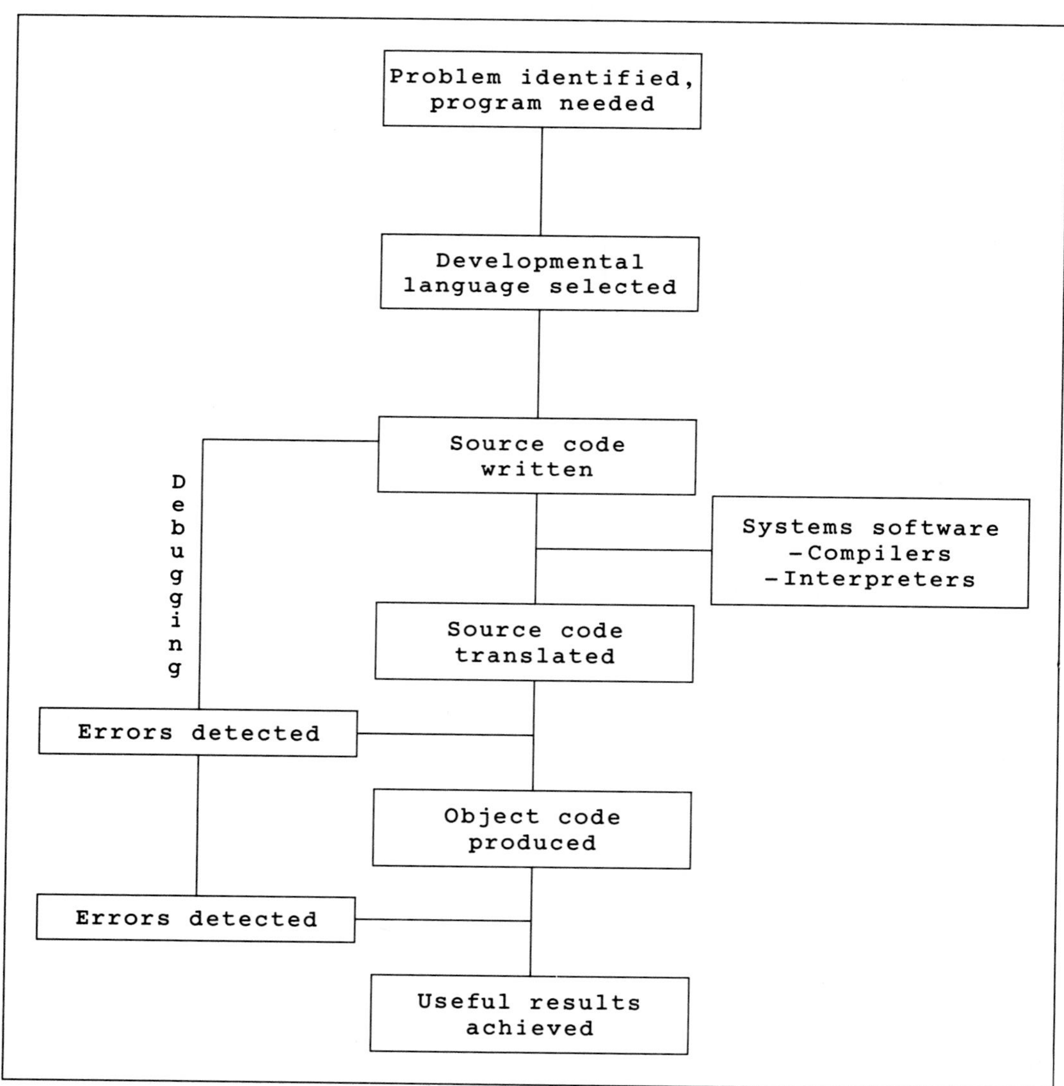

FIGURE 2
Relationship between source code and object code

user. Some developmental languages such as BASIC have both compilers and interpreters, although only one per language is more typical.

Object code is the machine language version of a program—in other words, the compiled version. Object code works faster than source code, and it usually requires less internal memory to store. However, the user cannot read it or modify the program to meet any special needs.

Who writes applications software? Perhaps you will some day. However, this can be a long and tedious process, especially if the problem is very complex. In some cases, the need for the program may have disappeared long before the program is completed. Your company may have programmers who can develop programs for you, you may hire a consultant to develop programs, or you may buy *packaged* applications programs sold by a **software house** (a company specializing in software development) or a computer manufacturer.

No matter who develops the applications software, the steps involved in developing a program are the same:

1. **Plan the task solution**—identify the task and determine how to do it
2. **Prepare the program**—determine the logic and steps needed to make the computer perform the desired task in the chosen language
3. **Code the program**—write the program in the chosen language
4. **Make the program work (debugging)**—make sure the program is free of any errors
5. **Document the program**—finish writing the instructions for running and applying the program
6. **Implement the program**—make the applications software available to whoever is going to use it

Packaged Software Sometimes called **user friendly** software, **packaged software** is the name given to software sold by software houses or other software suppliers. It is applications software that is produced for a general audience and can be used for a variety of tasks. Packaged software is the topic of this text. The types of **packages** to be discussed include: word processing, spreadsheets, and databases.

Software packages are typically **protected** (something is done to the software to prevent the user from copying it) and come in object code to speed their execution time. Because the packages are generally in object code, they are also somewhat machine dependent. To bypass this problem and make the packages work on as many different types of computers as possible, the packages frequently contain an **install program** (a special program that accompanies many software packages and that allows the user to tailor other programs in the package to the individual needs of the user or the user's equipment) that must be executed before the package will work on the computer being used.

Package Command Languages Every software package comes with a set of commands needed to use it. These command languages have been called many names, including **command language, macro language,** and **meta language.** They are usually fairly easy to use, and a single command accomplishes a lot (as you will see). Sometimes a set of instructions in these languages can be saved, producing a "program." This process might be more appropriately called **activity specification** rather than *programming* because it does not require extensive user training to perform.

To illustrate the concept of a command language, suppose you have entered a column of numbers—say, grades—in a spreadsheet package. To find the average of these grades manually, you would need to perform the following steps:

1. Add the numbers
2. Count how many numbers have been added
3. Divide the sum of the numbers by the count of the numbers
4. Display the results

In a spreadsheet package, all you would need to do is place the cursor where you want the results shown and type *average* (B3 . . . B40) (you'll learn why later). When you press the RETURN key, the average of the grades would be displayed—the computation is automatic. Similarly, rows or columns of numbers, such as stock prices, could be summed or otherwise manipulated.

The structure of the command language instruction in the example is the same as for all the other languages discussed. There is an *op code* (or *reserved word*) that tells the computer what to do (calculate the average) and one or more *operands* telling the computer what to operate on (the numbers in rows 3 through 40 in column B3 . . . B40). Although not all command language instructions are this obvious, they are structured similarly.

Sometimes the op code or the operands are *implied,* which makes the package easier to use. Although they may not be visible, they are present. For example, if you are using a word processing package, you wouldn't want "background" operations to display on the screen as you type each letter. The package would then be hard to use, and nobody would want to buy it. Therefore, whenever you type a letter, the display command is "implied" at the cursor location.

A **menu** is another approach that is frequently used to facilitate the ease of use of a package. A menu is a list of functions that are displayed on the screen, from which the user makes a selection. Thus packages that require the user to enter the command to be executed are referred to as **command driven,** whereas packages that rely exclusively on menus for specification of activity are usually referred to as **menu driven.**

Packaged software is a rapidly growing part of the computer industry. Increasing competition is forcing manufacturers to lower the cost of software packages, sometimes dramatically, and motivating them to produce packages that are easier to use and more efficient. Packages are gradually bringing the full power of the computer to people who do not have the time or desire to learn a developmental language or programming.

Summary

The choice of computer software depends on the knowledge and the type of applications required by the user. Users familiar with programming languages, or developmental software, will select a language according to its strengths and weaknesses. If they choose not to develop their own program, they can select packaged software specific to their needs. Users must first identify the task to be done and then select the appropriate software, rather than selecting the software and then figuring out what can be done.

Module One Word Processing: WordStar

Introduction to Word Processing

Suppose you are working in the Dallas office of a company based in Chicago. The district manager is asked to prepare a sales analysis report for the local office to be presented to the president at the annual sales meeting in Chicago. The district manager then asks the sales manager to prepare the report, and he gathers all the information and hands it to you. Once you have written and typed the report, the sales manager will read it, make corrections, and give it back to you to correct and retype. When you have finally typed a version that the sales manager is happy with, the whole process will start again with the district manager making the corrections. When the report is finally ready, it is sent to Chicago, but it gets lost in the mail, and you are asked to take your notes and retype the entire report, starting the process over again. Of course, you have only two weeks to complete the report.

There should be an easier way to complete this report, and there is. If you had used **word processing,** you could have simply made the necessary changes and printed a new copy instead of retyping the entire report every time there was a correction or change to make. When the report was lost, you could have simply pressed a few keys on your microcomputer and printed a new copy. Two weeks is plenty of time to write a report using word processing.

Definition of Word Processing

Data processing systems are designed to manipulate data. Manipulation of data may include a variety of operations, such as classifying, calculating, summarizing, sorting, and storing. Data processing systems most frequently operate on numeric data. Word processing systems generally deal with alphabetic and alphanumeric data; that is, the data for a word processing system is words!

Some of the characteristics of data processing systems do not necessarily apply to word processing systems (for example, how do you "calculate" words?). Therefore, it is more meaningful to establish a new set of characteristics related to word processing systems. These characteristics include:

- **Word origination**—creating textual "data"
- **Editing**—correcting or otherwise modifiying text
- **Formatting**—arranging text in a useful and meaningful form
- **Printing**—producing a hard-copy version of electronic text

Although many word processing systems have capabilities that are superior to these, all word processing systems, regardless of how limited, have at least these capabilities.

The hierarchical structure used in word processing (see Figure 1.1) should be familiar to you already. At the highest level is the file. It is used to store a large body of text, such as a business letter, a project report, or a term paper. In some word processing systems, a file is also called a **document.** Thus, in the "creation" mode, you develop and save a file or document. In the processing mode, you retrieve a file or document. In fact, if any part of the text is known to the operating system, it would be the file or document name.

The second level in the word processing hierarchy is the **page.** This may be the same amount of text as the file for a single-page business letter; however, longer documents would consist of a number of pages. Depending on the word processing system, you will be given access to either the entire file at one time or a single page at a time. (Single-page-oriented word processing sys-

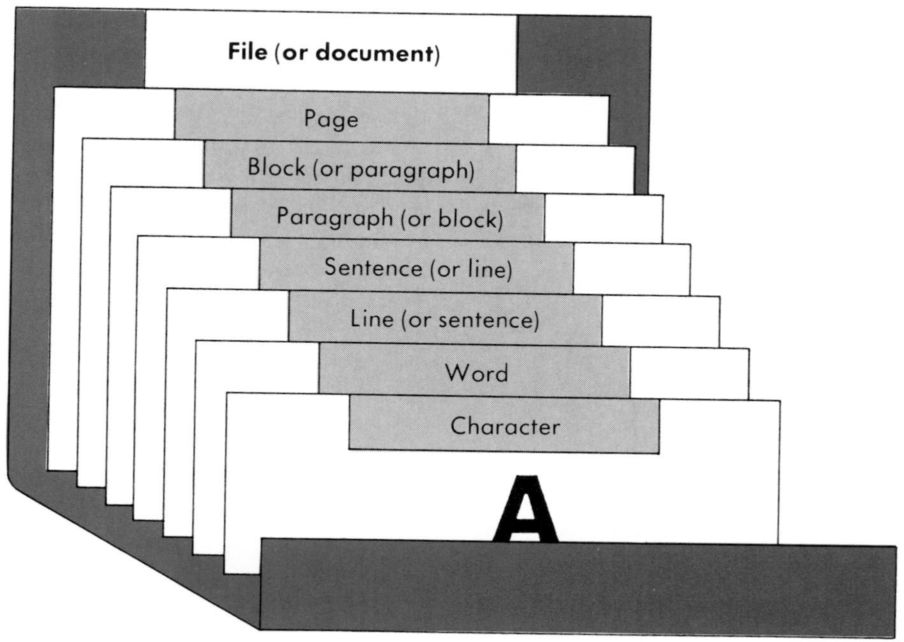

FIGURE 1.1
The word processing hierarchy

tems allow a single file to be larger than the amount of internal memory available on the computer, since only a small portion of the file is placed into memory at one time.) The third level of text is the **block.** A block is typically an amount of text defined by the person using the word processing package. It could be as large as several pages or as small as a few characters. A block is usually thought of as text that has the same format (for example, indented paragraphs versus paragraphs using regular spacing).

Each page is usually composed of a series of **paragraphs.** The paragraph level is one of the most significant levels associated with a file. Paragraphs will appear in a traditional form on a display screen or in a printed form, but they are generally stored as a continuous string of characters—from the first character of the paragraph to the end of the paragraph. In other words, a paragraph is composed of the characters entered between two RETURN keys. The reason for storing a paragraph in this manner, rather than as a series of lines, is fundamental to the way word processing works. When text changes are made within a paragraph, they typically affect all the text in the paragraph from the point of the change to the end of the paragraph, but they do not cause the format of the paragraph to change. Thus, regardless of the changes that may be made within a paragraph, it will continue to look like a paragraph and not a series of lines that are not associated with each other. The result is that when paragraphs are produced (either on the screen or on the printer), they are relatively well blocked; that is, they do not have severely jagged right margins.

Paragraphs are composed of one or more **sentences.** Each sentence may be composed of one or more **lines.** Almost all word processing systems permit some manipulation of sentences, and some systems even permit the manipulation of individual lines (regardless of whether they include complete sentences). The difference between sentences and lines is that a sentence is concluded with some form of punctuation (for example, a period or a question mark), whereas a line is the sequence of characters on one line display within a paragraph.

Sentences are composed of **words.** Words are one or more characters surrounded by spaces or some form of punctuation. Some word processing systems are capable of checking the spelling accuracy of words that appear in a file.

Finally, the last level of the word processing hierarchy is the **character.** The term *character* has its usual meaning. Words are made up of characters that may be alphabetic or numeric or of special characters (for example $, %, or &). Even a blank is a character, in this sense. In addition, some word processing systems use **control characters.** These are not characters as you usually think of them, but rather characters that can be used to control special features of the word processor, either in the way text is presented on the display screen or in the printed version of the text. An example of the use of control characters is at the beginning of this paragraph. The first sentence of this paragraph contains the word "character." Note that it looks different from the other words in the sentence: it is boldface. Control characters are often used to achieve this effect, as well as to do underlining.

WordStar

Learning to Use WordStar

WordStar is one of the most popular word processing packages. In part, this stems from the fact that WordStar has been around for a while. However, its popularity is probably due more to the fact that WordStar is among the most versatile word processing packages. It is available on a wide variety of microcomputer hardware and can be used with a variety of operating systems, including CP/M and MS-DOS.

Once you have started your computer and the operating system is ready to go, all you have to do to load WordStar is enter the command WS. WordStar will respond with the log-on screen, as shown in Figure 1.2. The version of WordStar used in this module is one that can be used with the IBM PC and IBM-PC compatible microcomputers.

Momentarily, the log-on screen will disappear and will be replaced with the WordStar OPENING MENU, or general command menu, as shown in Figure 1.3. At this point, you can begin working on a document file. Note that the command screen is arranged in sections. You may select any of the commands on the screen by simply pressing the letter associated with the indicated function. You do not have to press the RETURN key to complete the entry. If you find you have selected the wrong function, press the ESCape key, and you will be returned to the previous command screen.

In the Preliminary Commands section, you may change the currently logged disk drive. The typical default disk drive is A, but it can be changed with the L command. Unless you specify otherwise, WordStar will use this disk drive when retrieving and saving documents. If the File directory option is ON, WordStar will display the directory of the default disk drive at the bottom of the command screen. Thus, if you are unsure of the names of the documents on the disk in drive B, you need only change the default drive to view the directory. Among the WordStar Options shown in the lower right corner of the screen are MailMerge and CorrectStar. These options will be discussed later.

The final option available from Preliminary Commands is the one that selects the help level (H). WordStar, like many software packages, has a built-in way of assisting you to use the package. This is usually called a *Help function.*

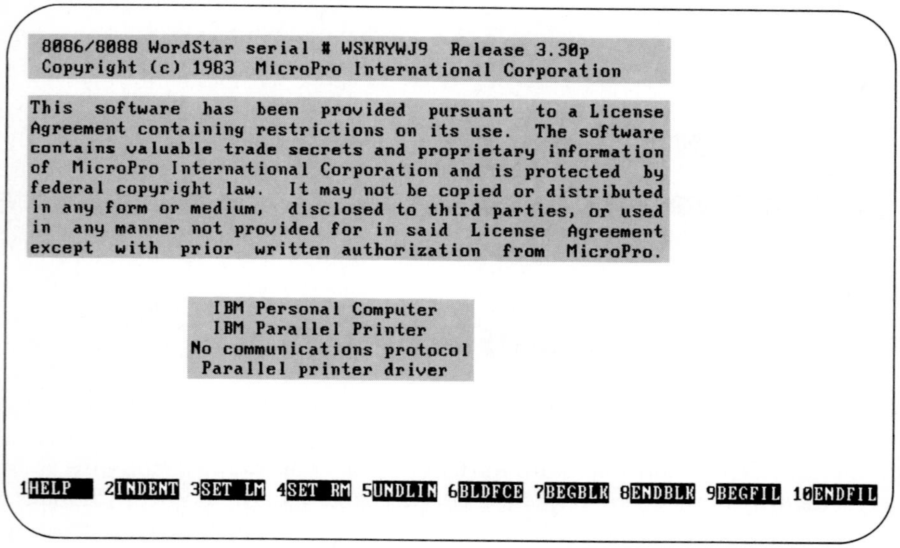

```
8086/8088 WordStar serial # WSKRYWJ9  Release 3.30p
Copyright (c) 1983  MicroPro International Corporation

This  software  has  been  provided  pursuant  to a License
Agreement containing restrictions on its use.  The software
contains valuable trade secrets and proprietary information
of  MicroPro International Corporation and is protected  by
federal copyright law.  It may not be copied or distributed
in any form or medium,  disclosed to third parties, or used
in  any manner not provided for in said  License  Agreement
except  with  prior  written authorization  from  MicroPro.

               IBM Personal Computer
               IBM Parallel Printer
              No communications protocol
               Parallel printer driver

1HELP  2INDENT 3SET LM 4SET RM 5UNDLIN 6BLDFCE 7BEGBLK 8ENDBLK 9BEGFIL 10ENDFIL
```

FIGURE 1.2
The WordStar log-on screen

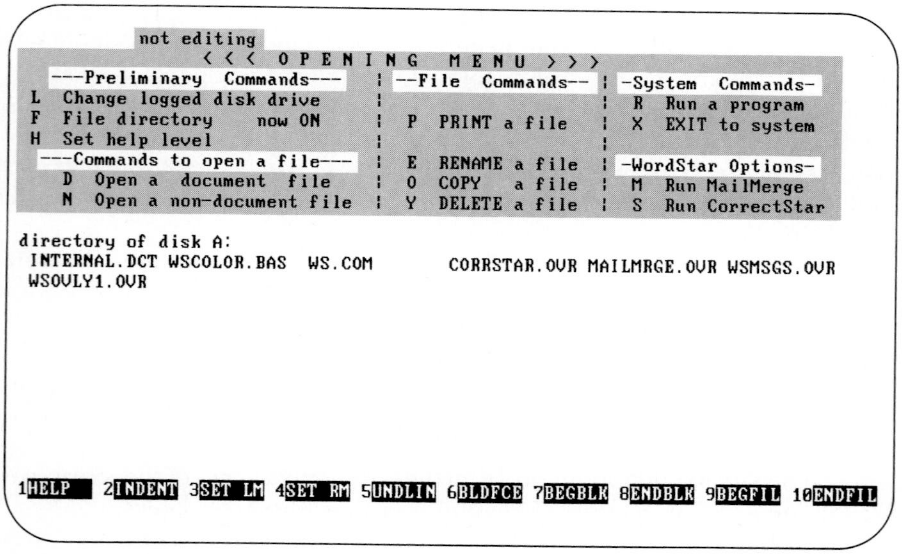

```
          not editing
                  < < <  O P E N I N G   M E N U  > > >
  ---Preliminary  Commands---   |  --File  Commands--  | -System  Commands-
L  Change  logged disk drive    |                      |  R  Run a program
F  File directory    now ON     |  P  PRINT a file     |  X  EXIT to system
H  Set help level               |                      |
 ---Commands to open a file---  |  E  RENAME a file    | -WordStar Options-
   D  Open a  document  file    |  O  COPY   a file    |  M  Run MailMerge
   N  Open a non-document file  |  Y  DELETE a file    |  S  Run CorrectStar
directory of disk A:
 INTERNAL.DCT WSCOLOR.BAS  WS.COM       CORRSTAR.OVR MAILMRGE.OVR WSMSGS.OVR
 WSOVLY1.OVR

1HELP  2INDENT 3SET LM 4SET RM 5UNDLIN 6BLDFCE 7BEGBLK 8ENDBLK 9BEGFIL 10ENDFIL
```

FIGURE 1.3
WordStar OPENING MENU

However, unlike most software packages, WordStar permits you to establish the level of help that you desire. If you press the H key, you will see the screen shown in Figure 1.4. Normally, WordStar begins with a help level of 3, the level that provides you with the most information. However, as you become more familiar with using WordStar, you may decide you want less help. Later, you will see that the help level can be changed as you are working on a document. This is done to provide you with "less visible help" and "more visible document."

The File Commands section of the screen permits you to perform manipulations of complete documents (see Figure 1.3). You can print a document (P), create a new name for a document (E), make a copy of an existing file (O), or delete a file from a disk (Y). Of these options, Print and Copy are probably the most used. The P option will be discussed after you have had a chance to build your document.

The Copy option, however, is worth talking about now. If you have a document with which you want to "experiment," you might decide to save a copy of the original document in case the one you are experimenting with is lost or altered to the extent it cannot be recovered. If your work pattern involves repeated modifications of existing documents, you can use the WordStar Copy option to make a duplicate of the document. (However, you could always use the operating system's copy function to make a duplicate of a file on your data disk before you load WordStar.)

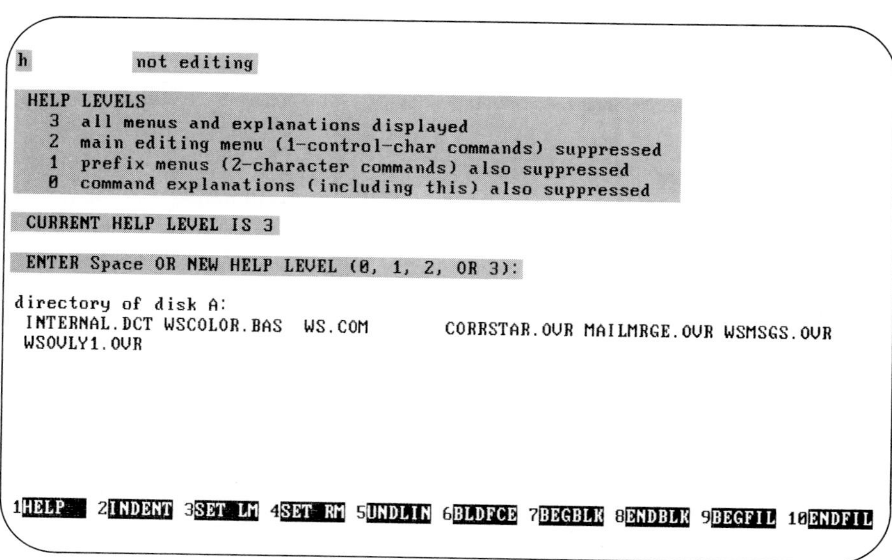

FIGURE 1.4
Setting the help level

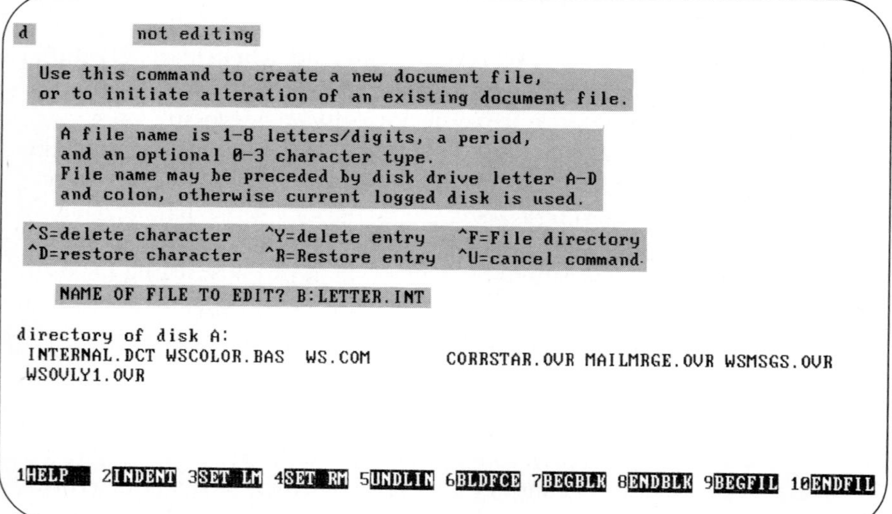

d not editing
Use this command to create a new document file,
or to initiate alteration of an existing document file.
A file name is 1-8 letters/digits, a period,
and an optional 0-3 character type.
File name may be preceded by disk drive letter A-D
and colon, otherwise current logged disk is used.
^S=delete character ^Y=delete entry ^F=File directory
^D=restore character ^R=Restore entry ^U=cancel command.
NAME OF FILE TO EDIT? B:LETTER.INT
directory of disk A:
INTERNAL.DCT WSCOLOR.BAS WS.COM CORRSTAR.OVR MAILMRGE.OVR WSMSGS.OVR
WSOVLY1.OVR
1HELP 2INDENT 3SET LM 4SET RM 5UNDLIN 6BLDFCE 7BEGBLK 8ENDBLK 9BEGFIL 10ENDFIL

FIGURE 1.5
Opening a document file

The System Commands section of the screen (Figure 1.3) permits you to run a program (R) or to exit WordStar (X) and return to the operating system. Among other functions, the R option will permit you to execute operating system commands without leaving WordStar. The X option gets you out of WordStar.

The final section of the WordStar OPENING MENU deals with opening files. (The terms *file* and *document* may be used interchangeably.) To begin the manipulation of a document in WordStar, you would normally select the D option (Figure 1.3). This means either that you are going to work on a document that WordStar has built or that you wish to create a new document. However, WordStar is capable of manipulating documents that have been created by other packages; so long as the document has been saved as a text (ASCII) file, the file can be retrieved by WordStar using the N option.

Figure 1.5 shows the screen after using the D option. WordStar will prompt you with information at this point that should enable you to create a valid document name. For the job hunting problem, you may want to create a file called B:LETTER.INT. This document will be placed on drive B and will be called LETTER.INT—the letter that is used to establish an interview date. The same process is also used to retrieve an existing document when you are using the OPENING MENU screen.

Some Preliminaries About Working with Documents

If you have set help to the highest level, you will see a screen like the one in Figure 1.6 when you enter the document mode. This is called the MAIN MENU, and it will stay on the screen as you work with a document. The MAIN MENU is divided into four parts. The first part appears across the top of the screen and might be called a "status area." It identifies the current document name, page number, line number, and column position. The document name will be fixed while working on a document; however, the page number, line number, and column position will change as you move about the document. The page number identifies a page for printing purposes. The line number indicates the line position on a page. The column number indicates which character position you are addressing on the indicated line. Any character typed on the keyboard exists at the indicated page, line, and column position.

The second part of the MAIN MENU screen might be called the "available operations area" (left section of Figure 1.6), because it identifies the types of operations that can currently be performed. All of the operations shown in this area require a two-key combination. The symbol ^ indicates that the CTRL key must be used in conjunction with the associated character. For example, the first combination shown at the upper left corner of the screen is ^S. This means

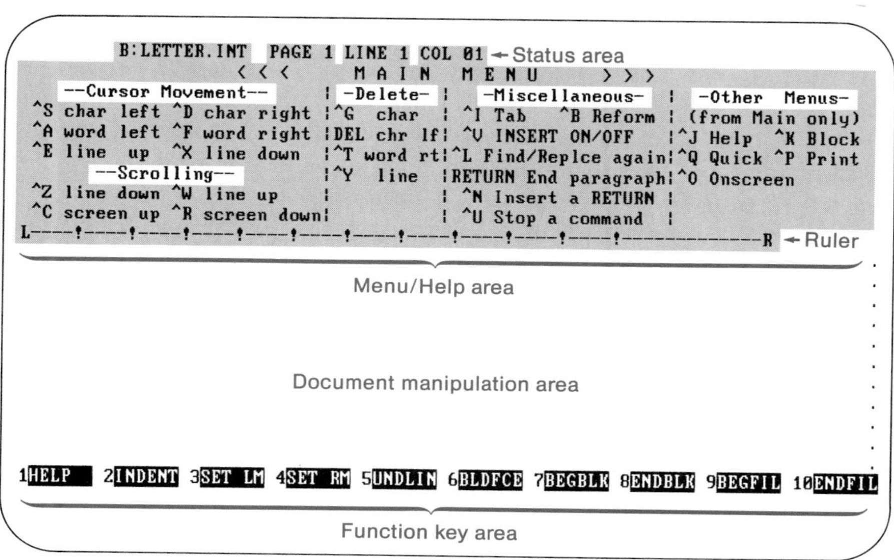

FIGURE 1.6
WordStar's MAIN MENU

that to perform this function you must press the CTRL key and, while holding it, press the S key. (Hereafter, unless stated to the contrary, it will be assumed that the CTRL key is also pressed when selecting a particular operation.)

The first section of the operations area is labeled Cursor Movement. For example, ^S is used when you want to move one character position to the left. Cursor movement operations such as this (using the CTRL key in combination with another key) may be a bit tedious and unnatural. However, if arrow keys are available on your keyboard, you may find that they are much more convenient to use to perform the same function. The cursor control operations that are possible with WordStar are summarized in Table 1.1, but because there are a number of varieties of WordStar, you should check your version to determine which "control code" (control key combination) to use to perform a particular operation. The second section of the MAIN MENU, Scrolling, also deals with cursor movement, but in larger "jumps."

The third section, Delete, allows you to delete text on the screen. ^G deletes the current character (the character in the same position as the cursor). The DEL key can be used to delete the character immediately to the left of the current cursor position. (It can also be used to eliminate paragraph markers, as will be discussed shortly.) ^T deletes the word immediately to the right of the cursor, and ^Y deletes the entire line in which the cursor appears. ^QY deletes all characters from the cursor position to the right end of the line. ^Q DEL deletes all characters from the cursor position to the left end of the line. (All ^Q functions are a part of the QUICK MENU, identified in the right corner of the OPENING MENU shown in Figure 1.3.)

The fourth section of the MAIN MENU is called *Miscellaneous.* It indicates that ^I may be used to tab from one tab marker to another. However, the TAB key can also be used for this purpose. ^B is used to reformat a paragraph. Reformatting means to manipulate the text, usually after a modification, so that it fits within the left and right margin positions. ^V is a "toggle switch" that turns the text insertion mode on or off (this can also be accomplished by using the INS key). ^L is used to indicate whether the last find or replace operation is to be continued to the next occurrence or whether Spell Check is to continue. The RETURN key is used to mark the end of paragraphs. ^N is used to insert a RETURN (end of paragraph marker) within currently existing text. ^U or the BREAK key is used to interrupt an operation that is in progress.

The final section of the operations area identifies Other Menus that may be selected from the MAIN MENU. The first of these is the HELP MENU selected by pressing ^J. The HELP MENU provides additional information on a wide variety of topics and may be used to determine how a particular function works or to learn about other functions. By pressing ^Q, the QUICK MENU is presented. The general functions associated with the QUICK MENU are moving through blocks of text (for example, a few words or several paragraphs of text) and performing find and replace operations. The ONSCREEN MENU is selected by pressing ^O. The Onscreen functions control the appearance of

TABLE 1.1 WordStar Cursor Movements (IBM-PC and IBM-PC Compatibles)

Operation or Function	Control Key Combination	Other Key Combinations
Move left one character	^S	Left Arrow
Move right one character	^D	Right Arrow
Move up one line	^E	Up Arrow
Move down one line	^X	Down Arrow
Move left one word	^A	
Move right one word	^F	
Move display screen up one line	^W	
Move display screen down one line	^Z	
Move to previous display screen	^R	Pg Up
Move to next display screen	^C	Pg Down
Move to the top of the screen	^QS/^QE*	Home
Move to the bottom of the screen	^QX*	End
Move to the right end of the current line	^QD*	
Move to the beginning of the document	^QR*	
Move to the end of the document	^QC*	

* Available through the QUICK MENU. Check your version of WordStar for other useful key combinations; some versions may differ.

the document, both on the screen and in terms of what is printed. Onscreen functions include such operations as setting left and right margins, centering text, setting line spacing (for example, single-space or double-space), and so on. ^K is used to select the BLOCK MENU. The BLOCK MENU deals with functions such as saving a document, cut-and-paste operations, and merging other documents into the current file. Finally, the PRINT MENU is selected by pressing ^P. The Print functions generally specify special printing effects, such as boldface and underline.

The next major area indicated on the MAIN MENU screen is called a *ruler*. It begins with the character L (Figure 1.6), which indicates the position of the left margin. The character R on the other end shows the position of the right margin. Along the line between the left and right margins are hyphens and exclamation points. The position of each ! marks the position of a tab stop.

The final area of the MAIN MENU screen is currently blank. It is the area of the screen where your document will be shown. It could be called the document manipulation area or text area, because most changes to the document will be shown here. Note that each of the lines of the text area ends with a period—indicating that no text has been entered on these lines—you are at the bottom of the document area. Other symbols that might appear in this area are :—lines preceding the document, <—paragraph marker, +—line exceeds screen width, and ---, current line to overprint previous line. Thus, when you view your document through the document manipulation area, you will see more than just the document itself. You will also see certain control symbols, such as the markers at the ends of lines and special printing symbols.

Getting Help from WordStar

Depending on your hardware and the version of WordStar you are using, the bottom line on your screen may show function key designations (Figure 1.6). If your system does not show this line, you will have room for an extra line of text in your document manipulation area. In addition, your function key designa-

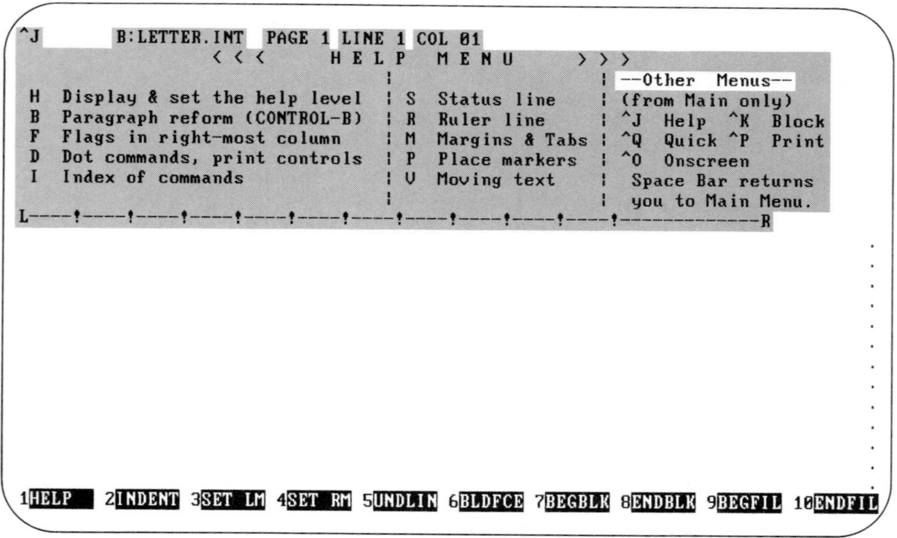

FIGURE 1.7
The HELP MENU

tions may be different from those shown in Figure 1.6 because the functions these keys control can be selected when WordStar is installed. The function key designations, although present on the initial WordStar screen, are not usable until you enter a document. The function keys and the designations shown in Figure 1.6 specify functions that select the HELP MENU (F1), indent or reformat a paragraph (F2), set the left margin (F3), set the right margin (F4), underline (F5), boldface (F6), mark the beginning of a block (F7), mark the end of a block (F8), go to the beginning of the file (F9), and go to the end of the file (F10).

Select ^J from the MAIN MENU (or press F1). As previously indicated, this key sequence selects the HELP MENU, as shown in Figure 1.7. Note that even though you leave the document manipulation area when you get help (or perform other functions), the status line remains unchanged, the Other Menus area is presented, the ruler is visible, and perhaps a portion of your document is shown. When you select certain functions, your document may totally disappear from view. However, after the function has been completed, you will return to the MAIN MENU and the document manipulation area. In other words, even though your document may momentarily disappear, WordStar is saving it for you until you return to the MAIN MENU.

Solving the Job Hunting Problem

The remaining sections in this module are devoted to solving a job hunting problem. The data in Appendix A reveals that you are in contact with a number of companies. The status of this contact varies depending on how far the contact process has progressed. In some cases, you have not yet established a date for an on-site interview (for example, with Champion Cowboy Supply). You will eventually want to write letters to the companies confirming the interview date, so you have decided to develop a business letter that can be modified for each company. The initial draft of this letter is as follows:

```
                    Letterhead
                  (Your Address)


                                     Letter Date

Company Address

Salutation

    According to your (telephone call on or
letter dated) (response date), it appears that
```

```
(interview date) is an acceptable date for my
visit to your company. Thank you very much for
expressing an interest in my qualifications
for your job position at (company name).

     I look forward to visiting you at your
company. I am excited about the prospect of
being employed by a company with such an
excellent reputation.

     Again, let me express my apprecaition for
your interest and prompt reply to my job
inquiry. If you need to contact me before our
meeting, please feel free to call me at
427-1964.

                                   Closing
```

With this draft in hand, you are ready to start working on your word processing package to produce a business letter that can be used repeatedly. The following list represents the types of operations you may use in the development and production of this letter.

1. Load the word processing package and enter the letterhead information. This information should consist of:

   ```
   (Your Name)
   1427 Shannon Lane
   Carrolton, TX 75343
   ```

   Once the text for the letterhead has been entered, center the lines.
2. Enter the general information related to the date, company address, and salutation. The date entry should begin in a column position that is at least halfway across the page.
3. Enter the text of the letter and the closing, as shown earlier.
4. After examining the structure of the letter, you decide that the first and second paragraphs should be joined and that the first paragraph should begin with what is currently the second sentence. Thus, you need to alter the separation of the first and second paragraphs and move the second sentence so that it becomes the first sentence. You will probably have to adjust the text afterward to make the letter more visually appealing. You also decide to modify the line margins to produce a 65-character space line.
5. You want the letterhead to stand out, so you decide to boldface it.
6. To verify your spelling, use the spelling checker.

7. Now that the general format of the letter has been established, customize the letter for sending to Champion Cowboy Supply. Their address is:

   ```
   Mr. Joe Garcia
   Champion Cowboy Supply
   126 Hollyhill Road
   Garland, TX 75342
   ```

8. After you print the letter to Champion Cowboy Supply, prepare letters to the Mosteq Computer Company and the Kelly Construction Company.

Entering Text

When you begin the problem (creating your interview letters), the MAIN MENU should be visible. Enter your name on the first line and press the RETURN key to indicate that the line has been completed. Note that the < symbol appears at the end of the line. Continue the process by entering your address on the next line, and your city, state, and zip code on the third line. Then press the RETURN key twice and enter your phone number. Be sure to complete the last line by pressing the RETURN key. You now have your letterhead at the top of the document. However, each of these lines begins at the left margin. To center the text of each of these lines, first move the cursor to the line to be centered and press the key sequence ^OC. This selects the ONSCREEN MENU, and, as you can see from Figure 1.8, the character C performs the centering function. Repeat the cursor movement and ^OC key sequences for each of the remaining lines to be centered.

Next, you need to specify the location for the date. Move the cursor to the line after your phone number. You need a couple of blank lines before you enter the date, so press the RETURN key twice. Since you want the date to appear toward the right side of the line, press the TAB key (or use ^I) to move across the line to approximately column 45. (Watch the status line, and you will see the column position indicator change each time you perform the tab operation.)

Since you are creating a general letter, you have decided to use brackets ([ ]) to enter all information that will be changed. This will make these items easier to find and replace later on when you get ready to send the letter to different companies on a specific date. Thus, you should enter the characters [Date].

Continue the letter by entering a general reference (in brackets) for the contact name, company name, company address, city, state, and zip code and a salutation. Make sure you press the RETURN key an extra time between the date and the contact name and between the city, state, and zip code and the salutation. Now, your letter should look like Figure 1.9. Note that as you have entered these lines, your name has disappeared from the document manipula-

```
^O        B:LETTER.INT  PAGE 1 LINE 2 COL 01
                      < < <  O N S C R E E N   M E N U  > > >
 -Margins & Tabs-  | -Line  Functions- |  --More Toggles--  |  -Other  Menus-
 L Set left margin |C Center text      |J Justify    now OFF | (from Main only)
 R Set right margin|S Set line spacing |V Vari-Tabs  now ON  |^J Help   ^K Block
 X Release margins |                   |H Hyph-help  now OFF |^Q Quick  ^P Print
 I Set  N Clear tab|   ---Toggles---   |E Soft hyph  now OFF |^O Onscreen
 G Paragraph tab   |W Wrd wrap now ON  |D Prnt disp  now ON  |Space Bar returns
 F Ruler from line |T Rlr line now ON  |P Pge break  now ON  |you to Main Menu.
L----!----!----!----!----!----!----!----!----!----!----!----!-----------R
                          (your name)                                        <
1427 Shannon Lane                                                            <
Carrolton, TX 75343                                                          <
                                                                             <
Phone:  (214) 427-1964                                                       <

1HELP  2INDENT 3SET LM 4SET RM 5UNDLIN 6BLDFCE 7BEGBLK 8ENDBLK 9BEGFIL 10ENDFIL
```

FIGURE 1.8
The ONSCREEN MENU and centering text

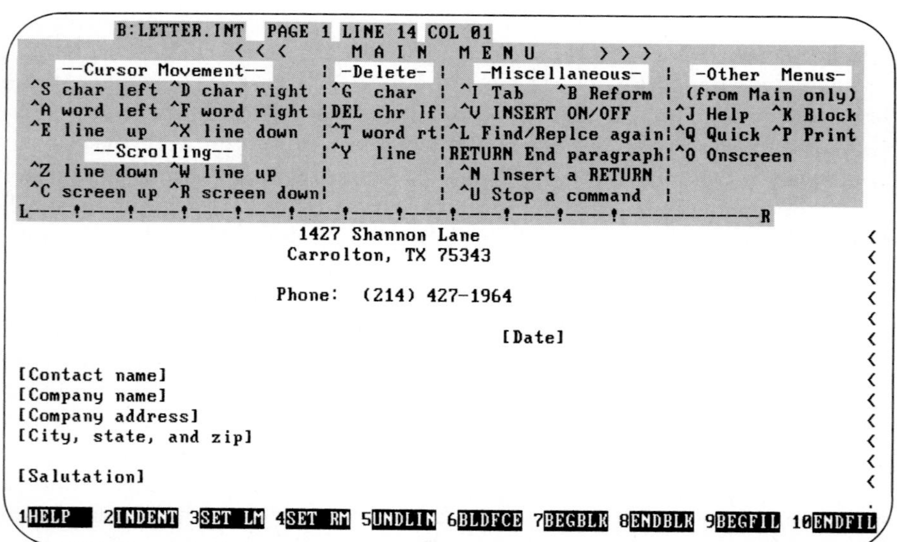

```
          B:LETTER.INT  PAGE 1 LINE 14 COL 01
                    < < <     M A I N   M E N U     > > >
   --Cursor Movement--     | -Delete- |  -Miscellaneous-   |  -Other  Menus-
^S char left ^D char right |^G  char |  ^I Tab   ^B Reform | (from Main only)
^A word left ^F word right |DEL chr lf|  ^V INSERT ON/OFF  |^J Help   ^K Block
^E line  up  ^X line down  |^T word rt|^L Find/Replce again|^Q Quick  ^P Print
     --Scrolling--         |^Y  line  |RETURN End paragraph|^O Onscreen
^Z line down ^W line up    |          |  ^N Insert a RETURN |
^C screen up ^R screen down|          |  ^U Stop a command  |
L----!----!----!----!----!----!----!----!----!----!----!----!-----------R
                      1427 Shannon Lane                                  <
                     Carrolton, TX 75343                                 <
                                                                         <
                    Phone:  (214) 427-1964                               <
                                                                         <
                                         [Date]                          <
                                                                         <
[Contact name]                                                           <
[Company name]                                                           <
[Company address]                                                        <
[City, state, and zip]                                                   <
                                                                         <
[Salutation]                                                             <

1HELP  2INDENT 3SET LM 4SET RM 5UNDLIN 6BLDFCE 7BEGBLK 8ENDBLK 9BEGFIL 10ENDFIL
```

FIGURE 1.9
Working on the interview letter — the initial heading

tion area. It has not been lost, it has simply disappeared from view. You may want to make sure that your name is still present by moving the cursor to the top of the document. It would be quicker to do this by entering ^R (or pressing F9)—previous screen. However, to continue with your letter, remember to move back to the bottom again—possibly by using ^C a few times (or pressing F10).

Now that the heading for your letter has been completed, continue with the body of the letter. Move to the second line below the salutation area and begin to type the remaining text. Remember, cursor movement will take you only to the bottom of the existing text. You will need to add a blank line between the salutation and the body by pressing the RETURN key.

As you type, mistakes can be corrected by using a series of keys. For example, you may delete characters by using the ^G and DEL keys. You may also use the BACKSPACE key to move backward and then overtype existing characters or use the ^V or INS keys to turn the insertion mode on and off. This will allow you to insert characters between existing characters on a line. However, remember to turn the insertion mode off after you have completed the operation by pressing ^V or the INS key again.

Start the first paragraph with a tab operation. This will cause the first line of the paragraph to be indented. Then continue by simply typing the text of the first paragraph. As you approach the end of the first line of the paragraph, your screen will look similar to the one in Figure 1.10. As you approach the end of

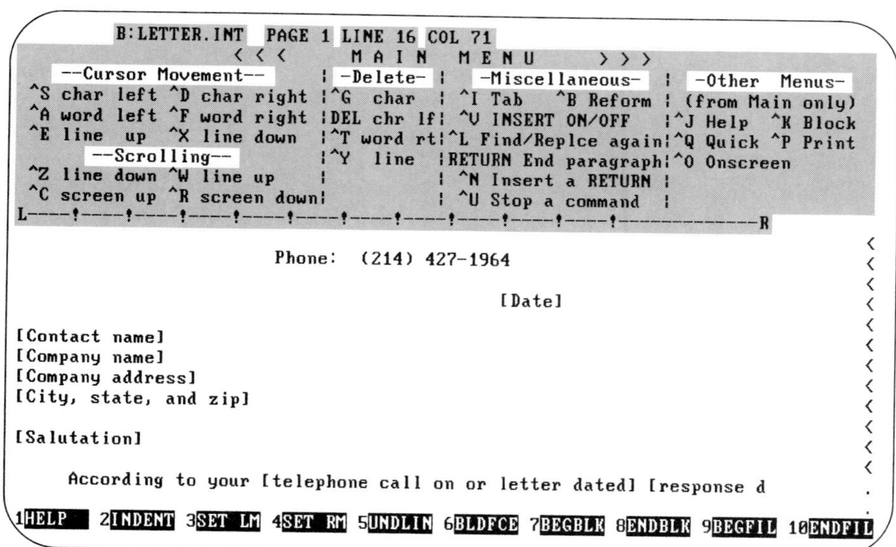

FIGURE 1.10
The word wrap feature on paragraphs

```
      B:LETTER.INT  PAGE 1 LINE 29 COL 56
                 < < <     M A I N   M E N U      > > >
  --Cursor Movement--     | -Delete- |  -Miscellaneous-  |  -Other Menus-
^S char left ^D char right |^G  char  | ^I Tab    ^B Reform | (from Main only)
^A word left ^F word right |DEL chr lf| ^V INSERT ON/OFF    |^J Help   ^K Block
^E line  up  ^X line down  |^T word rt|^L Find/Replce again|^Q Quick ^P Print
      --Scrolling--        |^Y  line  |RETURN End paragraph|^O Onscreen
^Z line down ^W line up    |          | ^N Insert a RETURN |
^C screen up ^R screen down|          | ^U Stop a command  |
L----!----!----!----!----!----!----!----!----!----!----!--------------R
date], it appears that [interview date] is an acceptable date for my
visit to your company.  Thank you very much for expressing an interest
in my qualifications for your job position at [Company name].              <
                                                                           <
     I am looking forward to visiting you at your company.  I am
excited about the prospect of being employed by a company with such an
excellent reputation.                                                      <
                                                                           <
     Again, let me express my apprecaition for your interest and
prompt reply to my job inquiry.  If you need to contact me before our
meeting, please feel free to call me at 427-1964.                          <
                                                                           <
                                          Sincerely,                       .
                                                                           .
1HELP  2INDENT 3SET LM 4SET RM 5UNDLIN 6BLDFCE 7BEGBLK 8ENDBLK 9BEGFIL 10ENDFIL
```

FIGURE 1.11
Completing the first draft of the interview letter

the line, resist the temptation to press the RETURN key. WordStar is equipped with a word wrapping function, and it will automatically break each line of text as you enter a paragraph so that it fits within the specified margins. Thus, you should continue typing as though all of the text of the paragraph were a single line—WordStar will fit it within the margins. When you reach the end of the first paragraph, press the RETURN key twice. This will end the current paragraph and will produce a blank line between the first and second paragraphs. Continue typing the remainder of the text, using a similar mode of operation, until you reach the closing area of the letter. Place the closing toward the right end of the line by using the tab operation to move the text over so that it is aligned with the date entry. Now your letter should look like Figure 1.11.

Editing Text

Now that you have written the letter, you decide to make a few changes. First, you think the letter would read better if the first and second paragraphs were joined. Move the cursor to the beginning of the second paragraph, and begin pressing the DEL key. You will notice that the < paragraph-marker character disappears and the first line of the second paragraph is joined to the last line of the first paragraph. You may need to turn the insertion mode on and add a couple of blanks between the sentences after you have joined the paragraphs (depending on where you started the cursor at the beginning of the second paragraph).

Now that the paragraphs have been joined, note that the + symbol appears at the end of the line where the two paragraphs were merged (see Figure 1.12). This means that the current text does not fit within the existing margins. To correct this problem, make sure the cursor is on this line and press ^B (or press F2). This function reformats the text of the paragraph to conform to the current margin settings. You may use this operation at other times, such as when you add or delete words or sentences within a paragraph.

A Cut-and-Paste Operation

Now you decide that the new first paragraph would flow better if it began with the second sentence. It is quicker to perform a cut-and-paste operation than to delete and retype the sentence. To cut and paste, move the cursor to the first character of the second sentence and press ^K to enter the BLOCK MENU. Press the letter B to mark the beginning of the block to be manipulated at this position (or press F7). Now the symbol <B> will appear in your document to mark the location of the beginning of the block (see Figure 1.13). Move the cursor to the first letter of the next sentence and press the ^K key again. To

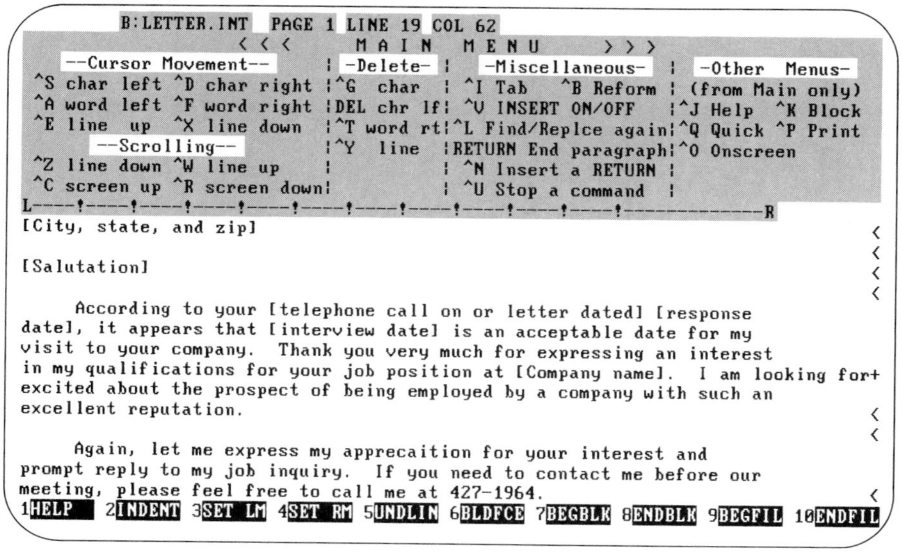

```
        B:LETTER.INT  PAGE 1 LINE 19 COL 62
                    < < <     M A I N   M E N U      > > >
   --Cursor Movement--      | -Delete- |   -Miscellaneous-   |  -Other  Menus-
 ^S char left ^D char right |^G  char  | ^I Tab    ^B Reform | (from Main only)
 ^A word left ^F word right |DEL chr lf| ^V INSERT ON/OFF    |^J Help   ^K Block
 ^E line  up  ^X line down  |^T word rt|^L Find/Replce again|^Q Quick ^P Print
     --Scrolling--          |^Y  line  |RETURN End paragraph|^O Onscreen
 ^Z line down ^W line up    |          | ^N Insert a RETURN |
 ^C screen up ^R screen down|          | ^U Stop a command  |
L----!----!----!----!----!----!----!----!----!----!----!-------------R
[City, state, and zip]                                                       <
                                                                             <
[Salutation]                                                                 <
                                                                             <
     According to your [telephone call on or letter dated] [response
date], it appears that [interview date] is an acceptable date for my
visit to your company.  Thank you very much for expressing an interest
in my qualifications for your job position at [Company name].  I am looking for+
excited about the prospect of being employed by a company with such an
excellent reputation.                                                        <
                                                                             <
     Again, let me express my apprecaition for your interest and
prompt reply to my job inquiry.  If you need to contact me before our
meeting, please feel free to call me at 427-1964.                            <
1HELP   2INDENT 3SET LM 4SET RM 5UNDLIN 6BLDFCE 7BEGBLK 8ENDBLK 9BEGFIL 10ENDFIL
```

FIGURE 1.12
Joining paragraphs

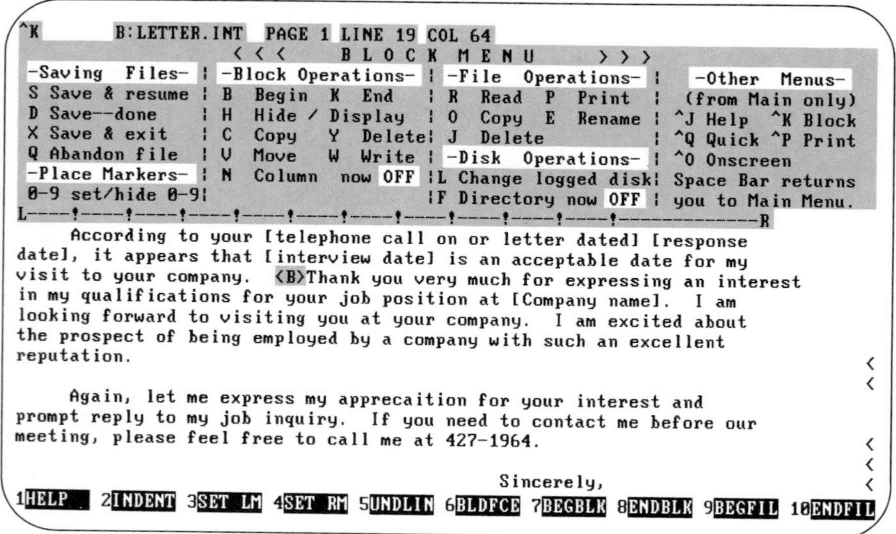

FIGURE 1.13
Moving the second sentence to the beginning of the letter

mark the end of the block at this position, press the letter K (or press F8). You will immediately be returned to the MAIN MENU, and the entire block will be highlighted. The highlighted area marks the text to be manipulated—in this case, the second sentence of the letter. To move this sentence to the beginning of the letter, move the cursor to the first letter of the first sentence. Now press the key sequence ^KV—perform a block move. The highlighted text will disappear from its original position and will reappear at the location of the cursor. To remove the highlighting, simply press the key sequence ^KH—hide block. The first paragraph is again a bit ragged, so press ^B to reformat it. This should result in the text shown in Figure 1.14.

Page Formatting—Redefining the Page

Your letter has only about 20 lines of text, and it looks too short. Rather than adding more text, reformat the document so that it appears to be longer. One means of performing this alteration is to change the margins. As shown in Figure 1.14, you enter the ONSCREEN MENU by pressing ^O and select R—set right margin. Note that the new right margin is to be set at column 65. After you press the RETURN key to enter the right margin, the right margin marker in the ruler will move to column 65. (You may also move the cursor to column 65 of any existing line of text and press F4). However, you still need to reformat the existing paragraphs to conform to this new line format. Thus, move to the beginning of each paragraph and press ^B; each paragraph will be restructured to conform to the new line length.

Enhancing the Letter for Effect — Output Specifications

Now that you have changed the line length, recenter the text of the letterhead to conform to the new format. To enhance the letterhead, print it in boldface. To do this, move to the first character of your name, turn the insertion mode on, and press ^P. You will be provided with the PRINT MENU; the letter B signifies boldface. After pressing B (or F6) to indicate where boldface printing is to begin, move the cursor to the end of your phone number and enter the PRINT MENU again (see Figure 1.15). ^B appears before your name to indicate that boldface is now on. By entering B again, you indicate where boldface printing is to end.

Checking for Spelling Errors

Now that all of the modifications have been made, it is time to save the work you have done. By entering ^KD, you indicate that you have finished the document

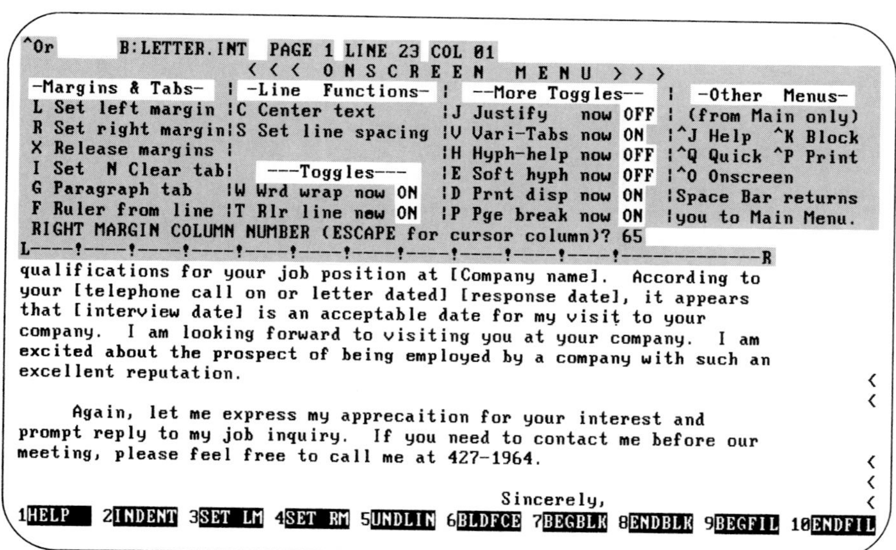

FIGURE 1.14
Resetting the right margin — making the letter longer

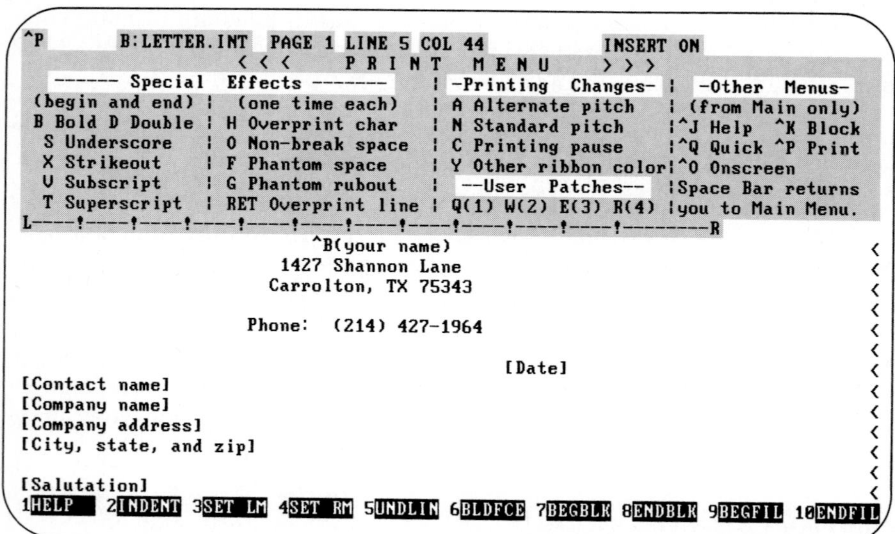

FIGURE 1.15
Boldfacing the letterhead

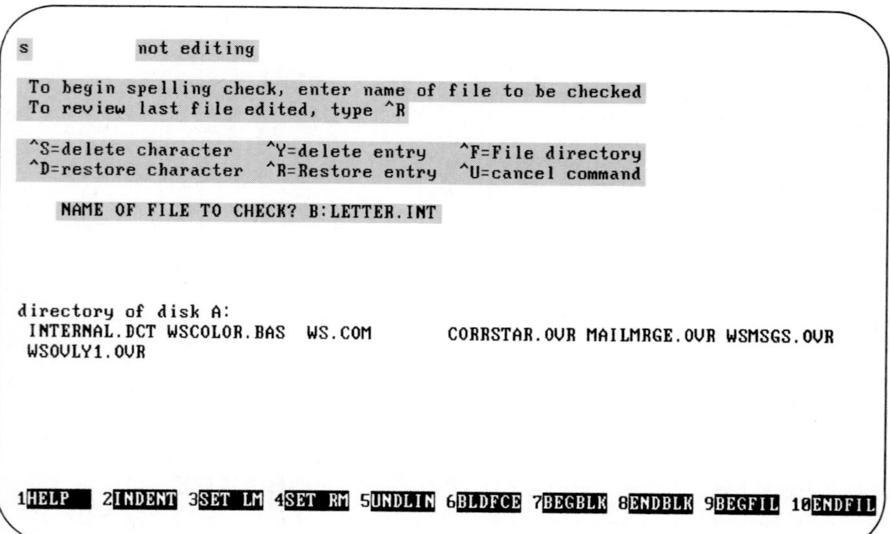

FIGURE 1.16
Entering CorrectStar

```
            CorrectStar      Release 3.30   I.D. # 26334204-001
     Copyright (c) 1983, 1984,   MicroPro International Corporation.
                         All Rights Reserved

              (c) Copyright 1983, 1981, Houghton Mifflin Company.
                Based upon The American Heritage Dictionary.

Please check your CorrectStar options

 <ESC>=start spelling check   ^S=delete character      ^Y=delete entry
 ^U=cancel spelling check     ^D=restore character     ^R=restore entry

Document: B:LETTER.INT
Personal Dictionary:
 A:PERSONAL.DCT
Auto Reform (Y/N):
 Y
Soft Hyphen Insertion (Y/N):
 N
<RET> - to begin:

Please wait...loading internal dictionary
```

FIGURE 1.17
Selecting spell checking options

and you wish to save it. This will also return you to the OPENING MENU. (There are other means of ending a work session. For example, you may enter a document and later decide you don't want to work on it or save any changes you might have made. You can abandon changes made to a file by using ^KQ to terminate a session.)

Now that your document is saved, it is time to verify the accuracy of your spelling. From the OPENING MENU, select the S option—Run CorrectStar. As shown in Figure 1.16, CorrectStar will request the name of the document to be checked. You should enter B:LETTER.INT. CorrectStar will then ask you to specify the options to be used during the spell checking operation (see Figure 1.17). The first option, which has a default value of A:PERSONAL.DCT, is to specify the disk drive and the file name containing your personal dictionary. CorrectStar actually uses three dictionaries—a personal dictionary containing a list of words that you may frequently use that are not in the other CorrectStar dictionaries, an internal dictionary (INTERNAL.DCT) that contains approximately 30.000 commonly used words, and a main dictionary (MAIN.DCT) that contains approximately 100,000 words (see Figure 1.18). The personal dictionary is tailored to your use; the internal dictionary is placed directly into memory, and it contains words like *it, the, and,* and so on. The main dictionary is used when a word is not found in either the personal or the internal dictionary.

The other options you control from the screen (shown in Figure 1.17) are automatic reformatting and hyphenation. If you use the default value of Y for

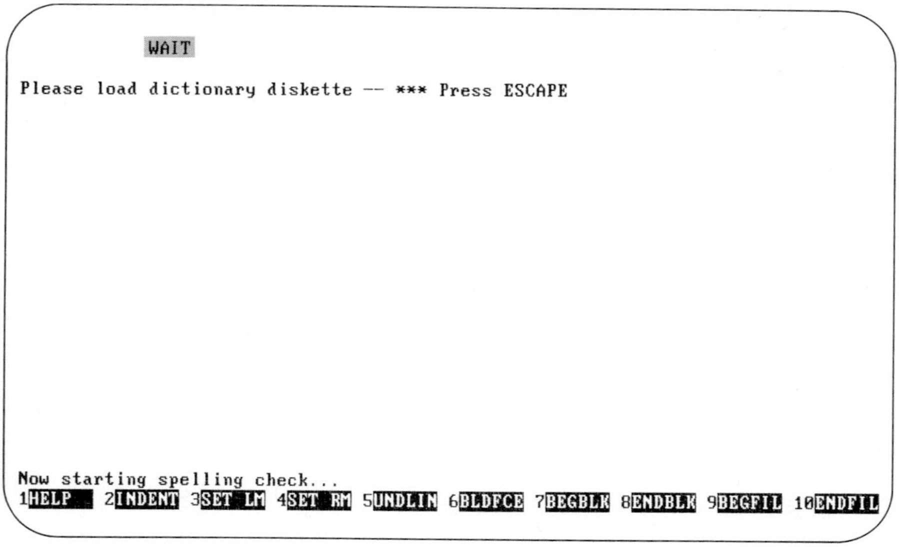

WAIT

Please load dictionary diskette -- *** Press ESCAPE

Now starting spelling check...
1HELP 2INDENT 3SET LM 4SET RM 5UNDLIN 6BLDFCE 7BEGBLK 8ENDBLK 9BEGFIL 10ENDFIL

FIGURE 1.18
Loading the main dictionary

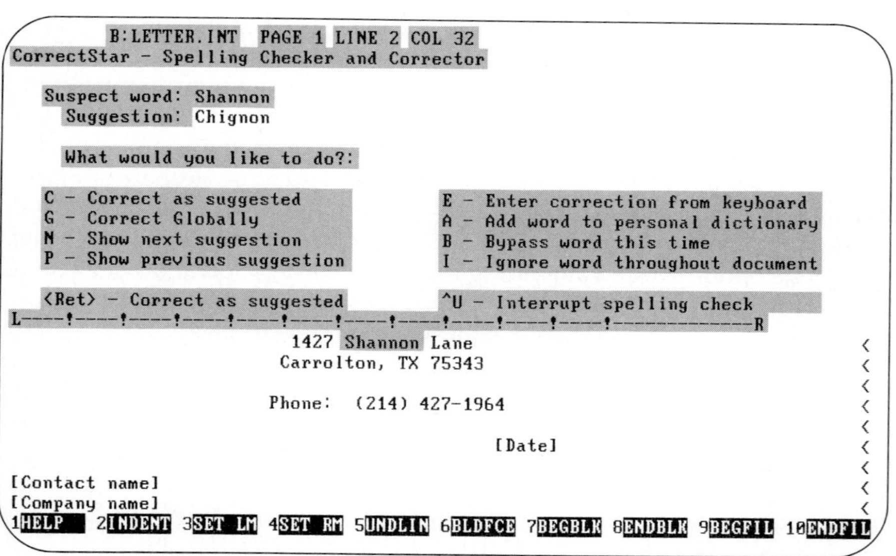

FIGURE 1.19
When CorrectStar makes a spelling suggestion

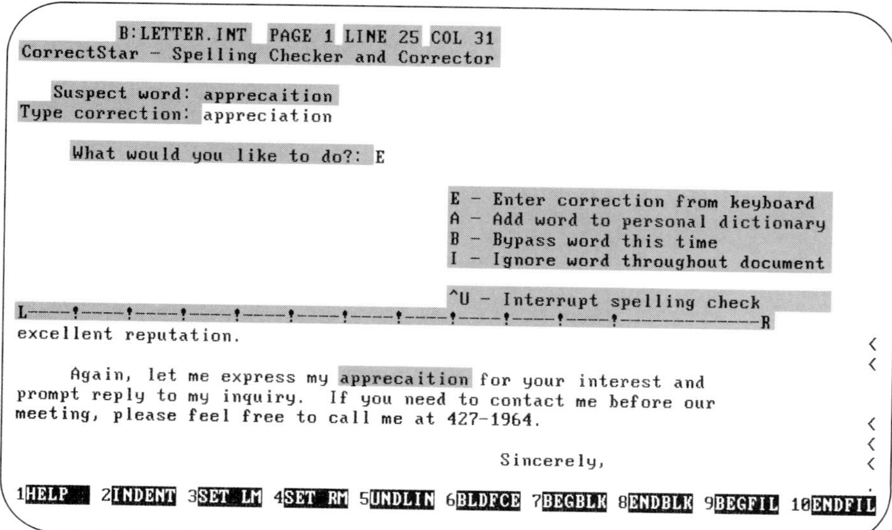

FIGURE 1.20
***Correcting** apprecaition*

Auto Reform, CorrectStar will adjust the text of a paragraph so that it fits between the margins when spelling corrections result in either longer or shorter words. Otherwise, line lengths are not adjusted. When the Soft Hyphen Insertion is selected, words at the end of each line will automatically be hyphenated in such a way that the maximum line length is used. If the default value of N is used, only full words will appear at the end of each line.

Once you have selected the CorrectStar options, your screen will look like the one in Figure 1.18. At this point, CorrectStar verifies the presence of the main dictionary. If you are working on a microcomputer that has only floppy disk drives, you will find it necessary to remove the WordStar disk from drive A and replace it with the main dictionary disk.

After a momentary pause, your screen will look like Figure 1.19. You are now ready to begin correcting the spelling in your document. The first word that is marked by CorrectStar is *Shannon,* which is not included in the personal, internal, or main dictionaries. However, for many words, CorrectStar will search dictionaries and suggest other words with similar spellings or sounds—one such suggestion is *Chignon.*

Once a dictionary search has been completed, you are provided with a list of actions, including the following: use the suggested correction for the current word (C or the RETURN key), use the suggested correction for the current word wherever it appears in the document (G), select another suggestion (N), recall a previous suggestion (P), enter a correction from the keyboard (E), add

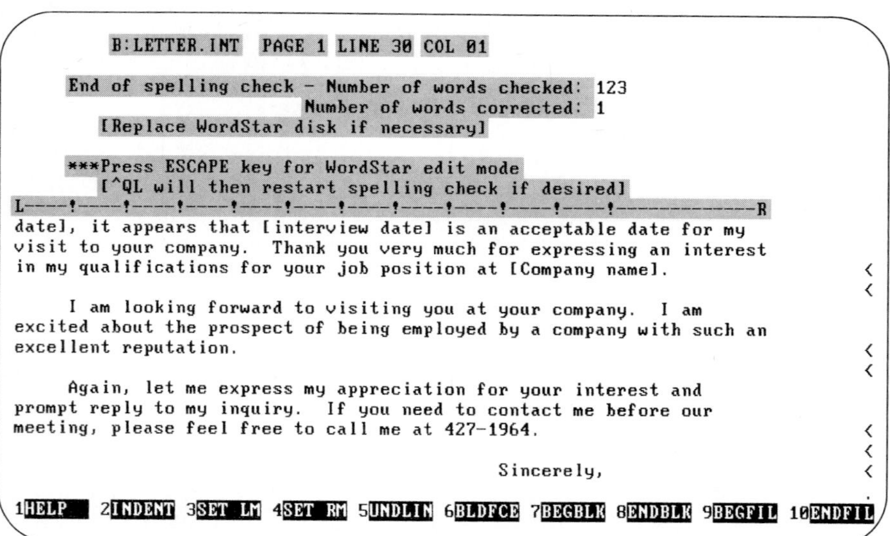
```
B:LETTER.INT  PAGE 1 LINE 30 COL 01

End of spelling check - Number of words checked: 123
                        Number of words corrected: 1
   [Replace WordStar disk if necessary]

***Press ESCAPE key for WordStar edit mode
   [^QL will then restart spelling check if desired]
L----!----!----!----!----!----!----!----!----!----!------------R
date], it appears that [interview date] is an acceptable date for my
visit to your company.  Thank you very much for expressing an interest
in my qualifications for your job position at [Company name].           <
                                                                        <
     I am looking forward to visiting you at your company.  I am
excited about the prospect of being employed by a company with such an
excellent reputation.                                                   <
                                                                        <
     Again, let me express my appreciation for your interest and
prompt reply to my inquiry.  If you need to contact me before our
meeting, please feel free to call me at 427-1964.                       <
                                                                        <
                                          Sincerely,                    <

1HELP  2INDENT 3SET LM 4SET RM 5UNDLIN 6BLDFCE 7BEGBLK 8ENDBLK 9BEGFIL 10ENDFIL
```

FIGURE 1.21
Returning to normal WordStar operations

the word to the personal dictionary (A), ignore the occurrence of the word (B), and ignore all occurrences of the word (I). CorrectStar can be interrupted by using ^U, should you find the need to make other changes to a document while checking for correct spelling. To restart CorrectStar, enter ^L. For the suspect word in Figure 1.19, you could select the A, B, or I option. (If this were your actual street name, you would probably want to add it to your personal dictionary rather than ignore it.)

Other words that do not appear in any of CorrectStar's dictionaries are "Carrolton," "TX," and "apprecaition." You would probably choose to bypass corrections for Carrolton and TX. However (as shown in Figure 1.20), *appreciation* is misspelled. Furthermore, CorrectStar provides no suggestion for a correction. As a result, the first four choices (C, G, N, and P) are not shown on the screen. In this case, enter the correction from the keyboard (E). Simply type the correction and press the RETURN key.

Since *appreciation* is the last suspect word in the letter, the next step is to return to the WordStar edit mode (see Figure 1.21). If you are using a floppy disk system, you will have to replace the CorrectStar disk in drive A with the WordStar disk. Once this is done, press the ESC key, and you will continue in the normal WordStar mode. Remember to save the corrected document if you made any corrections.

Personalized Messages—Find and Replace Functions

Your next task is to prepare your general letter so that it can be sent to Mr. Joe Garcia at Champion Cowboy Supply. First, go to the [Date] area of the letter and enter the appropriate date. Then change [Contact name] to Mr. Joe Garcia. Next, change [Company name] to Champion Cowboy Supply. However, this name appears both in the address area and within the body of the letter. Thus, it might be quicker to find each reference to [Company name] and replace them all at once. To perform this operation, enter the QUICK MENU by pressing ^Q and select the A option—find and replace.

Figure 1.22 illustrates how this process works. First, WordStar will ask for the character string you wish to find. You should supply the exact text—[Company name]. Next, WordStar will ask for the replacement: all occurrences of [Company name] are to be replaced with Champion Cowboy Supply. Finally, the find and replace operation needs information on how the operation is to be handled through a request for options. Note that NG has been specified in Figure 1.22, which means "perform the operation without stopping each time to ask if the replacement is correct in this circumstance" (N) and "perform the operation for the entire file" (G). Once the RETURN key is pressed, all of the occurrences of [Company name] are replaced.

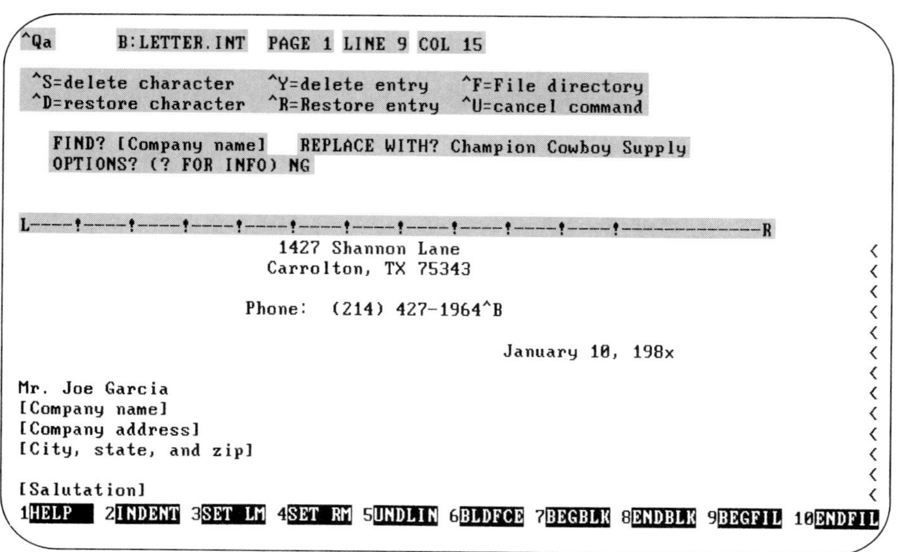

FIGURE 1.22
Using the find and replace functions

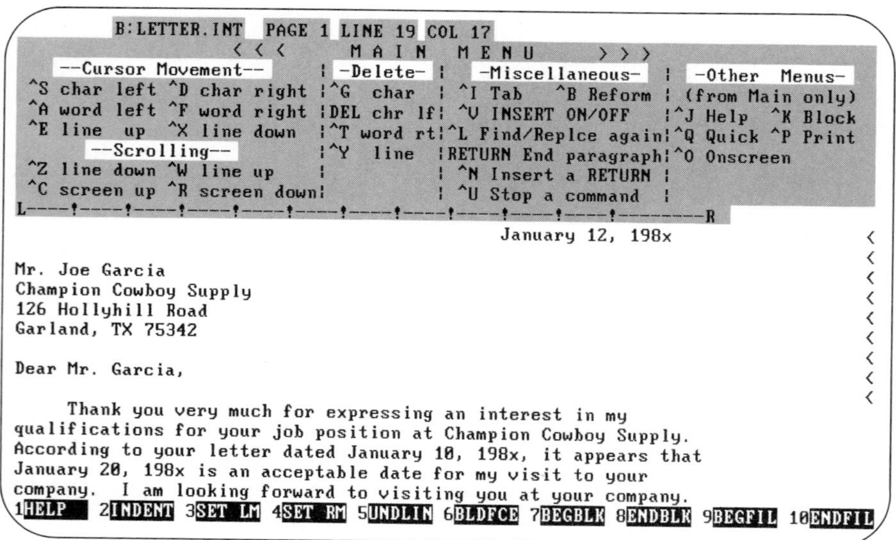
```
        B:LETTER.INT  PAGE 1 LINE 19 COL 17
                    < < <      M A I N   M E N U        > > >
 --Cursor Movement--       | -Delete- |  -Miscellaneous-   | -Other Menus-
^S char left ^D char right |^G  char  | ^I Tab   ^B Reform | (from Main only)
^A word left ^F word right |DEL chr lf| ^V INSERT ON/OFF   |^J Help  ^K Block
^E line  up  ^X line down  |^T word rt|^L Find/Replce again|^Q Quick ^P Print
   --Scrolling--           |^Y  line  |RETURN End paragraph|^O Onscreen
^Z line down ^W line up    |          | ^N Insert a RETURN |
^C screen up ^R screen down|          | ^U Stop a command  |
L----!----!----!----!----!----!----!----!----!----!----!----!--------R
                                             January 12, 198x

Mr. Joe Garcia
Champion Cowboy Supply
126 Hollyhill Road
Garland, TX 75342

Dear Mr. Garcia,

     Thank you very much for expressing an interest in my
qualifications for your job position at Champion Cowboy Supply.
According to your letter dated January 10, 198x, it appears that
January 20, 198x is an acceptable date for my visit to your
company.  I am looking forward to visiting you at your company.
1HELP  2INDENT 3SET LM 4SET RM 5UNDLIN 6BLDFCE 7BEGBLK 8ENDBLK 9BEGFIL 10ENDFIL
```

FIGURE 1.23
The interview letter after the find and replace operation

After this operation has been completed, continue to make changes for other items contained in brackets ([ ]). You may find it more convenient to use the find operation than looking for them yourself. This can easily be done by entering ^QF and entering [as the text to be found. The finding operation can be easily repeated by entering ^L for the next occurrence of the character string [. (The ^L operation also works for the replacing function when you have not specified G—global—as one of the options.) After all the substitutions have been made, your letter should look like the one in Figure 1.23.

Printing Your Letter—The Print Function

Once you have modified the letter, save it and return to the OPENING MENU. Once this is done, select P—the print function. As shown in Figure 1.24, you will be asked a series of questions, beginning with "Which document do you want to print?" You should enter B:LETTER.INT. You will be asked a number of additional questions, including "Do you want the output to be placed on a disk file rather than printed?" This option allows you to save the document as a print (ASCII) file in addition to a WordStar document. This might be a desirable format for interfacing with other applications packages. In addition, you will be asked to supply the beginning page number and the ending page number. On a long document, you could select only a portion of the file—particular page ranges—for printing.

Other questions include the use of form feeds (control of vertical printing, suppression of page formatting) automatic formatting to a saved description of individual pages, and stopping between individual pages—so that single sheets of paper may be fed into the printer. As shown in Figure 1.24, each of these questions has a default response generated by pressing the RETURN key. (If you press the ESCape key after entering the document name, WordStar will immediately begin printing your document using the default values without asking you additional questions.)

Align the printer to the top of the page before the document begins printing. If for some reason you want to stop the printing function, press the letter P, which halts the printing process and asks you what you want to do next. (These prompts will appear on your screen after printing begins.) The result of printing the document B:LETTER.INT is shown in Figure 1.25.

Printing Several Personal Letters — The MailMerge Function

In addition to sending a letter to Champion Cowboy Supply, you are also to send letters to Kelly Construction Company and Mosteq Computer Company.

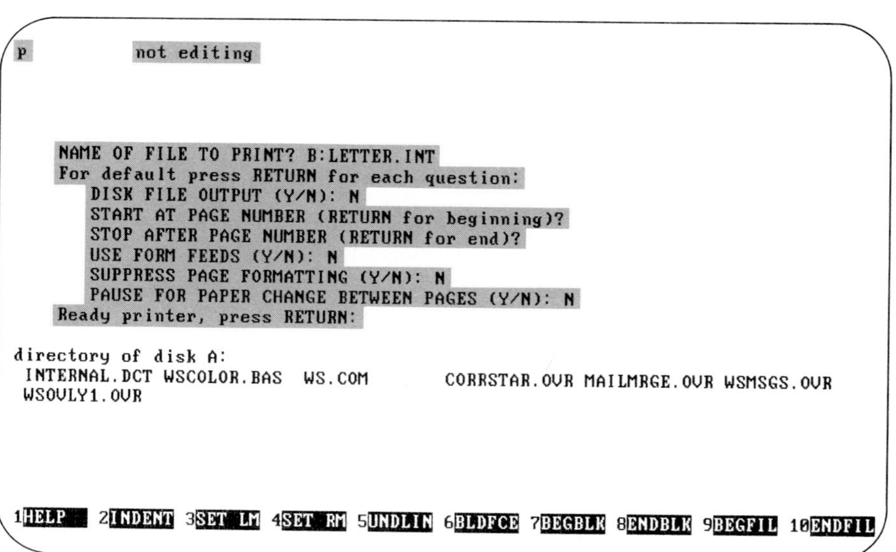

FIGURE 1.24
Entering the print function

```
                         (your name)
                      1427 Shannon Lane
                     Carrolton, TX 75343

                  Phone:  (214) 427-1964

                                      January 12, 198x

Mr. Joe Garcia
Champion Cowboy Supply
126 Hollyhill Road
Garland, TX 75342

Dear Mr. Garcia,

     Thank you very much for expressing an interest in my
qualifications for your job position at Champion Cowboy Supply.
According to your letter dated January 10, 198x, it appears that
January 20, 198x is an acceptable date for my visit to your company.
I am looking forward to visiting you at your company.  I am excited
about the prospect of being employed by a company with such an
excellent reputation.

     Again, let me express my appreciation for your interest and
prompt reply to my job inquiry.  If you need to contact me before
our meeting, please feel free to call me at 427-1964.

                                      Sincerely,
```

FIGURE 1.25
The interview letter to Champion Cowboy Supply

You could repeat the find and replace and printing operations just described, but you might find it easier to use the MailMerge function of WordStar. To use this function, you must alter the interview letter. As shown in Figure 1.26, B:LETTER.INT has been altered to include a number of new lines. The top three lines now contain what are known as *dot commands*—each of these lines begins with a period in column 1.

Dot commands are used to control the printing and MailMerge functions. For example, .HE at the beginning of a line is used to specify a page heading; .FO designates a page footing. Additional text would accompany each of these dot commands to specify the content of the page heading or the page footing.

In Figure 1.26, the first dot command is .OP, which means that page numbers are to be omitted. The second dot command is .DF—define file. This command indicates that when the document is printed, it should use the contents of B:JOBS.DTA in the process. For your problem, the file B:JOBS.DTA will contain the company information (names, addresses) necessary to print all three interview letters. The third dot command is only partially visible. The .RV command indicates that a list of variables (for example, Date, Contact-name, Company-name) are to be read during the printing process. Each of these names appears later in the document and is used in a kind of "fill in the blank" operation. For example, when the letter is being printed, a certain value will be retrieved from B:JOBS.DTA for Date, and it will be substituted for each entry in the letter marked &Date&. The locations of data values that match the list provided in the .RV command are marked by field names beginning and ending with the & symbol. Furthermore, these field names do not have to be listed in the same order in the .RV command as they are used in the document. (Note that the &Company-name& field appears twice in the letter.)

The last dot command goes at the bottom of the page, as shown in Figure 1.27. The .PA indicates that a new page is to begin at this position. This ensures that each letter will begin on a new page when multiple copies of it are printed. Remember to save this version of the letter before continuing.

The next step is to create the B:JOBS.DTA file (see Figure 1.28). This file must be created using the nondocument (ASCII) mode. Thus, you must select N, rather than D, from the OPENING MENU when creating or editing this file. Also, it is recommended that the .DTA file extension be used. This will avoid any conflict between this file and any other WordStar-related file.

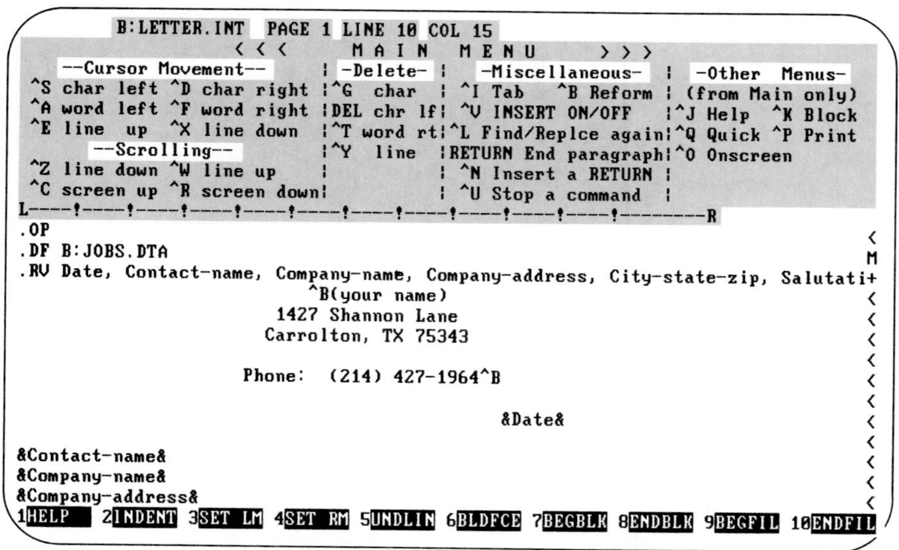

```
      B:LETTER.INT  PAGE 1 LINE 10 COL 15
                    < < <      M A I N   M E N U       > > >
   --Cursor Movement--      | -Delete- |    -Miscellaneous-   |  -Other  Menus-
^S char left ^D char right |^G  char  | ^I Tab     ^B Reform | (from Main only)
^A word left ^F word right |DEL chr lf| ^V INSERT ON/OFF     |^J Help   ^K Block
^E line  up  ^X line down  |^T word rt|^L Find/Replce again|^Q Quick ^P Print
      --Scrolling--        |^Y  line  |RETURN End paragraph|^O Onscreen
^Z line down ^W line up    |          | ^N Insert a RETURN |
^C screen up ^R screen down|          | ^U Stop a command  |
L----!----!----!----!----!----!----!----!----!----!----!---------R
.OP                                                                  <
.DF B:JOBS.DTA                                                       M
.RV Date, Contact-name, Company-name, Company-address, City-state-zip, Salutati+
                         ^B(your name)                               <
                       1427 Shannon Lane                             <
                      Carrolton, TX 75343                            <
                                                                     <
                    Phone:  (214) 427-1964^B                         <
                                                                     <
                                         &Date&                      <
                                                                     <
&Contact-name&                                                       <
&Company-name&                                                       <
&Company-address&                                                    <
1HELP  2INDENT 3SET LM 4SET RM 5UNDLIN 6BLDFCE 7BEGBLK 8ENDBLK 9BEGFIL 10ENDFIL
```

FIGURE 1.26
Setting up the letter for a MailMerge operation

```
        B:LETTER.INT  PAGE 1 LINE 29 COL 04
                          < < <      M A I N   M E N U     > > >
   --Cursor Movement--       | -Delete- |  -Miscellaneous-  |  -Other Menus-
^S char left ^D char right |^G  char  | ^I Tab    ^B Reform | (from Main only)
^A word left ^F word right |DEL chr lf| ^V INSERT ON/OFF    |^J Help  ^K Block
^E line  up  ^X line down  |^T word rt|^L Find/Replce again|^Q Quick ^P Print
      --Scrolling--        |^Y  line  |RETURN End paragraph|^O Onscreen
^Z line down ^W line up    |          | ^N Insert a RETURN |
^C screen up ^R screen down|          | ^U Stop a command  |
L----!----!----!----!----!----!----!----!----!----!----!--------R
According to your &Telephone-call-on-or-letter-dated& &Response-
date&, it appears that &Interview-date& is an acceptable date for
my visit to your company.  I am looking forward to visiting you
at your company.  I am excited about the prospect of being
employed by a company with such an excellent reputation.              <
                                                                      <
     Again, let me express my appreciation for your interest and
prompt reply to my job inquiry.  If you need to contact me before
our meeting, please feel free to call me at 427-1964.                 <
                                                                      <
                                        Sincerely,                    <
.PA                                                                   <
----------------------------------------------------------------------P
1HELP  2INDENT 3SET LM 4SET RM 5UNDLIN 6BLDFCE 7BEGBLK 8ENDBLK 9BEGFIL 10ENDFIL
```

FIGURE 1.27
Forcing an end-of-page

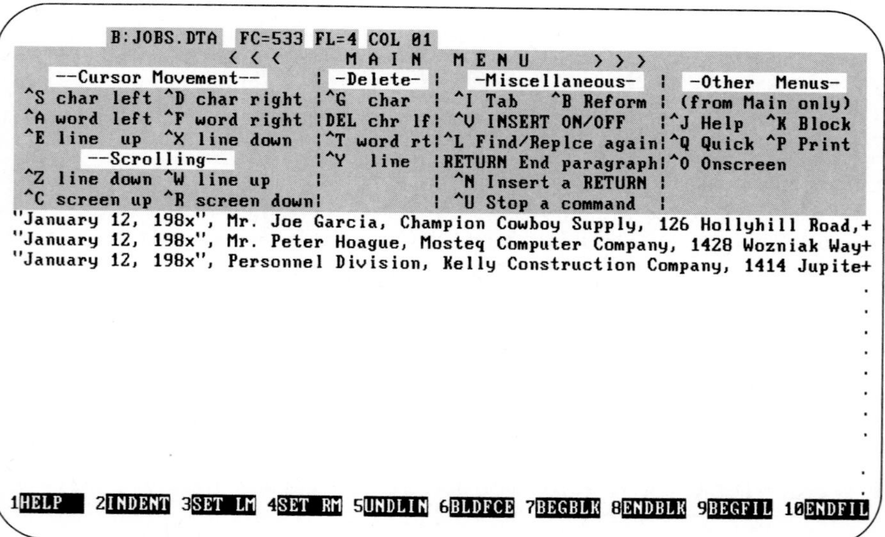

```
        B:JOBS.DTA  FC=533 FL=4 COL 01
                          < < <      M A I N   M E N U     > > >
   --Cursor Movement--       | -Delete- |  -Miscellaneous-  |  -Other Menus-
^S char left ^D char right |^G  char  | ^I Tab    ^B Reform | (from Main only)
^A word left ^F word right |DEL chr lf| ^V INSERT ON/OFF    |^J Help  ^K Block
^E line  up  ^X line down  |^T word rt|^L Find/Replce again|^Q Quick ^P Print
      --Scrolling--        |^Y  line  |RETURN End paragraph|^O Onscreen
^Z line down ^W line up    |          | ^N Insert a RETURN |
^C screen up ^R screen down|          | ^U Stop a command  |
"January 12, 198x", Mr. Joe Garcia, Champion Cowboy Supply, 126 Hollyhill Road,+
"January 12, 198x", Mr. Peter Hoague, Mosteq Computer Company, 1428 Wozniak Way+
"January 12, 198x", Personnel Division, Kelly Construction Company, 1414 Jupite+
1HELP  2INDENT 3SET LM 4SET RM 5UNDLIN 6BLDFCE 7BEGBLK 8ENDBLK 9BEGFIL 10ENDFIL
```

FIGURE 1.28
Creating the JOBS.DTA file

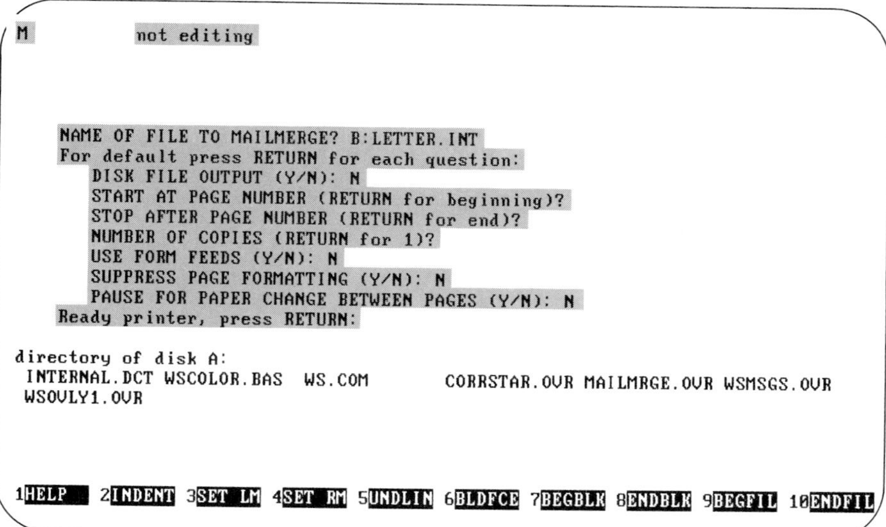

M not editing
NAME OF FILE TO MAILMERGE? B:LETTER.INT
For default press RETURN for each question:
DISK FILE OUTPUT (Y/N): N
START AT PAGE NUMBER (RETURN for beginning)?
STOP AFTER PAGE NUMBER (RETURN for end)?
NUMBER OF COPIES (RETURN for 1)?
USE FORM FEEDS (Y/N): N
SUPPRESS PAGE FORMATTING (Y/N): N
PAUSE FOR PAPER CHANGE BETWEEN PAGES (Y/N): N
Ready printer, press RETURN:
directory of disk A:
INTERNAL.DCT WSCOLOR.BAS WS.COM CORRSTAR.OVR MAILMRGE.OVR WSMSGS.OVR
WSOVLY1.OVR
1HELP 2INDENT 3SET LM 4SET RM 5UNDLIN 6BLDFCE 7BEGBLK 8ENDBLK 9BEGFIL 10ENDFIL

FIGURE 1.29
Entering the MailMerge function

The data values to be used in the B:LETTER.INT document must be in exactly the same order as specified in the .RV command. Thus, the Date value should be first, followed by the Contact name, Company name, and so on. Each data value should be separated by a comma (missing or omitted values should be accounted for by a comma indicating the location of the missing value). Any data value containing a comma should be enclosed within quotation (") marks, as in the Date field.

Finally, each line of a document or file cannot exceed 240 characters, and each data line should be terminated by pressing the RETURN key.

As shown in Figure 1.29, using the MailMerge function is similar to printing a document. Select the M—MailMerge—option from the OPENING MENU and supply B:LETTER.INT as the MailMerge file. Thereafter, you may either respond to the individual prompts for additional information or press the ESCape key to begin printing the documents immediately. The results of this operation are shown in Figure 1.30 on the next page.

Of course, WordStar has other means of performing merging operations. As illustrated in Figure 1.31, you can use the .AV dot command to insert data values into a document. The .AV command "ask for a value" is entered from the keyboard as the document is being printed. Thus, while printing B:LETTER.INT, the screen will appear as shown in Figure 1.32.

Finally, to complete your WordStar session, leave WordStar and return to the operating system by selecting X from the OPENING MENU screen.

(your name)
1427 Shannon Lane
Carrolton, TX 75343

Phone: (214) 427-1964

January 12, 198x

Personnel Division
Kelly Construction Company
1414 Jupiter Road
Garland, TX 75242

any.
t
pany.
ited

d
re

(your name)
1427 Shannon Lane
Carrolton, TX 75343

Phone: (214) 427-1964

January 12, 198x

Mr. Peter Hoague
Mosteq Computer Company
1428 Wozniak Way
Farmers Branch, TX 76331

y.
hat
mpany.
cited

nd
ore

(your name)
1427 Shannon Lane
Carrolton, TX 75343

Phone: (214) 427-1964

January 12, 198x

Mr. Joe Garcia
Champion Cowboy Supply
126 Hollyhill Road
Garland, TX 75342

Dear Mr. Garcia,

Thank you very much for expressing an interest in my qualifications for your job position at Champion Cowboy Supply. According to your letter dated January 10, 198x, it appears that January 20, 198x is an acceptable date for my visit to your company. I am looking forward to visiting you at your company. I am excited about the prospect of being employed by a company with such an excellent reputation.

Again, let me express my appreciation for your interest and prompt reply to my job inquiry. If you need to contact me before our meeting, please feel free to call me at 427-1964.

Sincerely,

FIGURE 1.30
Interview letters produced by MailMerge

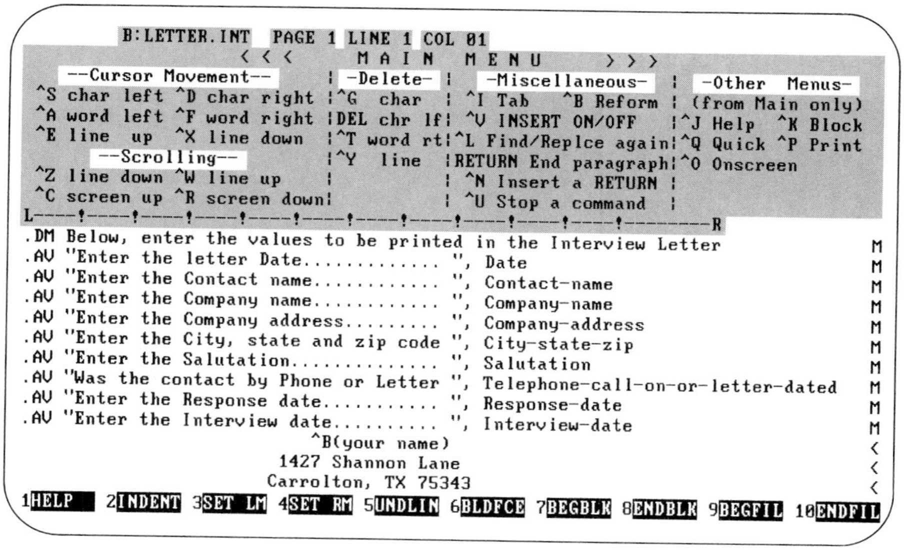

```
        B:LETTER.INT  PAGE 1 LINE 1 COL 01
                     < < <      M A I N   M E N U      > > >
   --Cursor Movement--      | -Delete- |  -Miscellaneous-   |  -Other Menus-
 ^S char left ^D char right |^G  char  | ^I Tab    ^B Reform | (from Main only)
 ^A word left ^F word right |DEL chr lf| ^V INSERT ON/OFF    |^J Help  ^K Block
 ^E line  up  ^X line down  |^T word rt|^L Find/Replce again|^Q Quick ^P Print
        --Scrolling--       |^Y  line  |RETURN End paragraph|^O Onscreen
 ^Z line down ^W line up    |          | ^N Insert a RETURN |
 ^C screen up ^R screen down|          | ^U Stop a command  |
L----!----!----!----!----!----!----!----!----!----!----!--------R
.DM Below, enter the values to be printed in the Interview Letter      M
.AV "Enter the letter Date............. ", Date                          M
.AV "Enter the Contact name............ ", Contact-name                  M
.AV "Enter the Company name............ ", Company-name                  M
.AV "Enter the Company address......... ", Company-address               M
.AV "Enter the City, state and zip code ", City-state-zip                M
.AV "Enter the Salutation.............. ", Salutation                    M
.AV "Was the contact by Phone or Letter ", Telephone-call-on-or-letter-dated M
.AV "Enter the Response date........... ", Response-date                 M
.AV "Enter the Interview date.......... ", Interview-date                M
                         ^B(your name)                                   <
                     1427 Shannon Lane                                   <
                   Carrolton, TX 75343                                   <
1HELP  2INDENT 3SET LM 4SET RM 5UNDLIN 6BLDFCE 7BEGBLK 8ENDBLK 9BEGFIL 10ENDFIL
```

FIGURE 1.31
Using the "Ask for Value" command

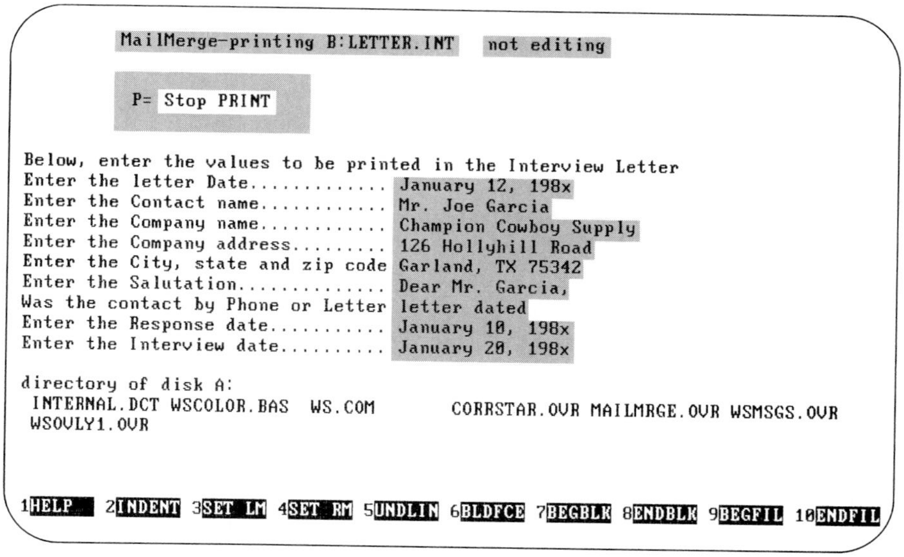

```
        MailMerge-printing B:LETTER.INT   not editing

        P= Stop PRINT

Below, enter the values to be printed in the Interview Letter
Enter the letter Date............. January 12, 198x
Enter the Contact name............ Mr. Joe Garcia
Enter the Company name............ Champion Cowboy Supply
Enter the Company address......... 126 Hollyhill Road
Enter the City, state and zip code Garland, TX 75342
Enter the Salutation.............. Dear Mr. Garcia,
Was the contact by Phone or Letter letter dated
Enter the Response date........... January 10, 198x
Enter the Interview date.......... January 20, 198x

directory of disk A:
 INTERNAL.DCT WSCOLOR.BAS  WS.COM       CORRSTAR.OVR MAILMRGE.OVR WSMSGS.OVR
 WSOVLY1.OVR

1HELP  2INDENT 3SET LM 4SET RM 5UNDLIN 6BLDFCE 7BEGBLK 8ENDBLK 9BEGFIL 10ENDFIL
```

FIGURE 1.32
Printing an interview letter containing "Ask for Value" commands

Uses of Word Processing

Many of the uses of word processing are obvious. Any secretary primarily responsible for maintaining correspondence with others could use this type of package. By using word processing software, a secretary could transcribe a dictated letter, transmit a draft copy of the letter to the boss, alter the letter on the basis of changes made by the boss, and produce a "letter perfect" copy for mailing. Furthermore, a copy of the letter could be stored electronically, rather than tying up file cabinet space. However, in some companies, even the boss produces letters and other documents such as memos, notices, and reports. The idea is for the document to be produced as quickly as possible. If the boss has the necessary keyboard skills, the document could probably be produced more quickly than if sent it to a secretary for typing and later review.

The necessity of producing printed reports is not unique to a business environment. For example, students write reports and résumés. Many people make shopping lists, Christmas card lists, insurance inventories, credit card accounts lists, personal financial statements for bank loan applications, and so on.

Some professions use word processing heavily. For example, the use of the boilerplating feature by the legal profession has been previously mentioned. In other areas of the legal profession, word processing is now being used to produce the final version of trial transcripts.

Most large news agencies use word processing to maintain notes about news events or stories. Many newspapers even have the ability to transmit word processing files directly into newsprint, thus shortening the time required to get the latest edition out. Many publishing firms also have this capability; that is, many authors now write on a word processor, and the publisher typesets the book from the electronic text (disks), thereby facilitating a quick and correct transcription process. This reduces both the number of typesetting errors and the necessity of proofreading the final product.

In the television and movie industries, writers are now using word processing systems to produce scripts. In fact, one writer for a television soap opera credits word processing for the improvement of scripts over the years. This is because scripts can now be rewritten and made available to the actors almost immediately.

In the advertising area, word processing is being used to produce catalogs and other advertising matter. In the mass mailing area, the mail merge feature of word processing systems is singularly responsible for making "personalized" contact possible with millions of potential customers annually. Using the same concept, country clubs can send lists of special events to members, political candidates can seek contributions from or send campaign literature to people in election districts, and amusement parks and tourist resorts can reach target markets for their services.

Word processing usually represents an improvement over any other method of dealing with words. Look around you. You can probably identify a dozen ways to use word processing that haven't yet been mentioned!

Summary

WordStar is a very powerful word processing package that can also be custom tailored to reflect your individual style. The availability of help menus makes the package easy to learn, and the ability to set the level of help provided allows the more experienced users to choose the amount of a document that is shown on the screen at any one time. Table 1.2 gives a summary of the commands available in the opening menu of the package, and Table 1.3 shows the commands available in each of the submenus, as well as the "dot commands" and Function Key setting.

Guidelines for the Evaluation of Word Processing Packages

Before you select a word processing package for your own use, answer the following questions:

- **Typing speed** Are special function and control character keys easy to reach? Does the package provide automatic word wrapping? Can you "get ahead" of the word processor during normal text entry? (You should not be able to.)
- **Automatic reformatting** Are paragraphs automatically reformatted when you make corrections, or must you reformat by hand? Can different paragraphs have different formats?
- **Copying text** How easy is it to mark the text to be copied and then move it to another location within the document?
- **Margin settings** How far can the right margin be moved? Does the package scroll to the right?
- **Cursor control** How easy is it to move around in the document? Is it possible to move directly from paragraph to paragraph? From page to page? Can you move directly to a specified page?

TABLE 1.2 WordStar Opening Menu Commands

WordStar Menus	
Opening Menu	Additional Messages
Preliminary commands	
L Change logged disk drive	THE LOGGED DISK DRIVE IS NOW _____ NEW LOGGED DISK DRIVE (letter, colon, RETURN)?
F File directory now _____	
H Set help level	CURRENT HELP LEVEL IS 3 ENTER Space OR NEW HELP LEVEL (0, 1, 2, OR 3):
Commands to open a file	
D Open a document file	NAME OF FILE TO EDIT? (see attached menus)
N Open a non-document file	NAME OF FILE TO EDIT? (see attached menus)
File commands	
P PRINT a file	NAME OF FILE TO PRINT? For default press RETURN for each question: DISK FILE OUTPUT (Y/N): START AT PAGE NUMBER (RETURN for beginning)? STOP AFTER PAGE NUMBER (RETURN for end)? USE FORM FEEDS (Y/N): SUPPRESS PAGE FORMATTING (Y/N): PAUSE FOR PAPER CHANGE BETWEEN PAGES (Y/N): Ready printer, press RETURN:
E RENAME a file	NAME OF FILE TO RENAME? NEW NAME?
O COPY a file	NAME OF FILE TO COPY FROM? NAME OF FILE TO COPY TO?
Y DELETE a file	NAME OF FILE TO DELETE?
System commands	
R Run a program	COMMAND?
X EXIT to system	
WordStar options	
M Run MailMerge	NAME OF FILE TO MAILMERGE? For default press RETURN for each question: DISK FILE OUTPUT (Y/N): START AT PAGE NUMBER (RETURN for beginning)? STOP AFTER PAGE NUMBER (RETURN for end)? NUMBER OF COPIES (RETURN for 1)? USE FORM FEEDS (Y/N): SUPPRESS PAGE FORMATTING (Y/N): PAUSE FOR PAPER CHANGE BETWEEN PAGES (Y/N): Ready printer, press RETURN:
S Run CorrectStar/SpellStar	NAME OF FILE TO CHECK?

TABLE 1.3 WordStar Menu Commands, Dot Commands, and Function Keys

MAIN MENU

Cursor Movement
- ^S char left
- ^D char right
- ^A word left
- ^F word right
- ^E line up
- ^X line down

Scrolling
- ^Z line down
- ^W line up
- ^C screen up
- ^R screen down

Delete
- ^G char
- DEL chr lf
- ^T word rt
- ^Y line

Miscellaneous
- ^I Tab
- ^B Reform
- ^V INSERT ON/OFF
- ^L Find/Replce again
- RETURN End paragraph
- ^N Insert a RETURN
- ^U Stop a command

Other Menus
(from Main only)
- ^J Help
- ^K Block
- ^Q Quick
- ^P Print
- ^O Onscreen

QUICK MENU

Cursor Movement
- S left side
- D right side
- E top scrn
- X bottom scrn
- R top file
- C end file
- B top block
- K end block
- 0-9 marker
- Z down
- W up
- P previous
- V last Find or Block

Delete
- Y Line rt
- DEL lin lf

Miscellaneous
- F Find text in file
- A Find & Replace
- L Find Misspelling
- Q Repeat command or key until space bar or other key

Other Menus
(See MAIN MENU)

ONSCREEN MENU

Margins & Tabs
- L Set left margin
- R Set right margin
- X Release margins
- I Set
- N Clear tab
- G Paragraph tab
- F Ruler from line

Line Functions
- C Center text
- S Set line spacing

Toggles
- W Wrd wrap now------
- T Rlr line now------
- J Justify now------
- V Vari-Tabs now------
- H Hyph-help now------
- E Soft hyph now------
- D Prnt disp now------
- P Pge break now------

Other Menus
(See MAIN MENU)

BLOCK MENU

Saving Files
- S Save & resume
- D Save — done
- X Save & exit
- Q Abandon file

Place Markers
- 0-9 set/hide 0-9

Block Operations
- B Begin
- K End
- H Hide/Display
- C Copy
- Y Delete
- V Move
- W Write
- N Column now ------

File Operations
- R Read
- P Print
- O Copy
- E Rename
- J Delete

Disk Operations
- L Change logged disk
- F Directory now ----

Other Menus
(See MAIN MENU)

PRINT MENU

Special Effects
(begin and end)
- B Bold
- D Double
- S Underscore
- X Strikeout
- V Subscript
- T Superscript

(one time each)
- H Overprint char
- O Non-break space
- F Phantom space
- G Phantom rubout
- RET Overprint line

Printing Changes
- A Alternate pitch
- N Standard pitch
- C Printing pause
- Y Other ribbon color

User Patches
- Q(1)
- W(2)
- E(3)
- R(4)

Other Menus
(See MAIN MENU)

HELP MENU ----------

- H Display & set the help level
- B Paragraph reform (CONTROL-B)
- F Flags in right-most column
- D Dot commands, print controls
- I Index of commands
- S Status line
- R Ruler line
- M Margins & Tabs
- P Place markers
- V Moving text

Other Menus
(See MAIN MENU)

Each dot command should be on a separate line with a "." in column 1.

Standard dot commands:

. PR	forced page break
. CP n	forced page break if current page has less than n lines
. OP	omit page numbers
. PN n	page numbers
. PC n	page number column
. PO n	page offset
.. text	comment
. HE text	page heading
. FO text	page footing
. PL n	paper length
. MT n	margin top
. MB n	margin bottom
. HM n	heading margin
. FM n	footing margin

Special dot commands for incremental printers:

. LH n	line height
. CW n	character width
. SR n	subscript/superscript roll
. UJ OFF/ON	microjustification

Special dot commands for MailMerge feature:

. DF filename	data file
. RV name,name,name, . . .	read variable
. AV "prompt",name	ask for variable
&name&	variable name
. FI filename	file insert
. DM text	display message

Special characters for headings and footings:

#	current page number
\	non-special character
^K	omit space if even-numbered page

Function Key	Default	Alternate Function
F1	^JH (Help)	----------------
F2	^OG (Paragraph Tab)	----------------
F3	^OL^[(Left Margin)	----------------
F4	^OR^[(Right Margin)	----------------
F5	^PS (Underline)	----------------
F6	^PB (Boldface)	----------------
F7	^KB (Begin Block)	----------------
F8	^KK (End Block)	----------------
F9	^QR (Top of File)	----------------
F10	^QC (End of File)	----------------

- **Search and replace** Can you replace parts of words as well as whole words? Can you control whether replacement is automatic or determined by you? Must you reenter the command every time a replacement is made? Can you search and replace from the bottom to the top of the document as well as from top to bottom?
- **Text editing** How easy is it to edit a document? (Remember, this is the true power of a word processor.) Are you required to switch modes in order to perform editing operations?
- **Type styles** Does the package provide the different type styles you need (for example, boldface, italic, underline, subscripts, superscripts)?
- **Text formatting** Is it easy to change the margins for the text? Can you easily change from single-spacing to double-spacing or triple-spacing? Does the package easily change between ragged, right-justified, and centered text?
- **Hardware compatibility** Will this word processor run on your microcomputer? Does it work with your brand of printer, and is it able to use the full capabilities of the printer?
- **Saving documents** Does the package automatically save documents before you quit? Does it automatically keep backups of the documents? What is the format used to save a file (ASCII or DIF)?

Module Two
Database: dBASE II and III

Introduction to Databases

Suppose you are given the problem of collecting and organizing all the data about players on a professional football team. For each player you would have to collect volumes of data—for example, the data illustrated in Figure 2.1.

Over the course of each player's career, you will need to produce many reports for the team. For example, each coach needs a player roster for his area of responsibility, the front office needs a list of contracts that expire in the coming year so that contract negotiations can be planned, the team physicians need a list of injuries resulting from last week's game, and so on; there are many more reports needed by the organization.

Putting all this collected data into filing cabinets is not a particularly efficient way of handling data. Going through all the records every time you need to prepare a report is not very efficient either. Instead, you can use a computer and a **database management system (DBMS)** to manage the data efficiently. A DBMS is a group of common utility programs designed to allow the user to interface with a vast collection of data, called a **database.**

Defining Databases

As shown in Figure 2.2, we have come a long way since the days when it was necessary to maintain the bulk of an organization's data in filing cabinets. However, even in the early days of computing, handling data was problematic; all file-handling operations (including input and output) were a direct consequence of programmer action, and not everyone possessed programming skills.

As programming became more sophisticated, procedures for handling large amounts of data were developed. In the 1960s, computer companies developed **file management systems (FMS)** to deal with the problems of large collections of data. The use of magnetic tape on early computers gave way to the **direct (random) access** approach using magnetic disk. It was during the 1960s that many business organizations put together huge information-handling systems. These information systems were built for individual functional

FIGURE 2.1 Data Required for a Professional Football Player

Social Security Number
Name
Street Address
City
State
Zip Code
Phone Number
Date of Birth
Height
Weight
Jersey Number
Years in Pro-Football
College Attended
College Position(s) Played

Expiration Date of Contract
Terms of Contract
Physical Performance:
- Time/10 Yards
- Time/40 Yards
- Time/100 Yards
- Weight/Dead Lift
- Weight/Bench Press
- Weight/Curl
- Weight/Squat Thrust
- .
- .
- .

Position(s) Played:
- Offense
- Defense
- Special Teams

Medical Data:
- Data of Last Physical
- Results of Physical
- Current Medical Status
- Injuries:
  - Head
  - Chest
  - Back
  - Arms/Shoulders
  - Wrists/Hands/Fingers
  - Upper Leg
  - Knee
  - Lower Leg
  - Ankles/Feet/Toes
  - Internal

Heart Rate/Blood Pressure:
- At Rest
- Mild Stress
- Playing Level
- Maximum Stress
- .
- .
- .

application areas, such as accounting, payroll, inventory, and personnel. What became very obvious was that there was significant duplication in the data, referred to as **data redundancy**, being stored. For example, both payroll and personnel files stored the names of all of an organization's employees.

Data Management Systems (DMS)

In the late 1960s, the use of large collections of data had increased so much that more advanced concepts of data storage and retrieval were needed. It was during this period that many vendors and large organizations began their development of the large-scale data-handling systems known as data management systems (DMS). These systems eventually came to be known as **database management systems (DBMS).** The early data management systems followed a very rigid design, known as a **hierarchical (tree) structure.** This structure (discussed later) is still used today, but it has given way to other structures, which, from a user's standpoint, are less formal and much easier to use.

Data Views

While companies were developing new and better ways to handle data, an important change was taking place: fewer programmers and more and more senior managers and office clerks were using the database management systems. However, the data had to be provided to these different types of users in different ways. Most users didn't want to know about the particular methods used in handling the data. In addition, all users didn't need the same data, and even if they did, they didn't want to examine the data in the same ways.

How can a database serve different functional areas? To answer this, look at the example of the football team: How can a database about the players serve different functions? The illustrations in Figure 2.3 show that each functional area of the franchise has access to the database for its own needs. This approach makes the database very effective. Because all the data is in one place, it is easier to control **data integrity** (the data is complete, accurate, and not misleading), reduce data redundancy, and share the data among all interested users (data independence).

In practice, you can view data in a database system in three ways: *conceptually, logically,* and *physically.* The diagram in Figure 2.4 and the following discussion will help you to understand the different ways of viewing data.

Conceptual View The **conceptual view** of data represents the general view of the overall flow of data within an organization such as a bank, hospital, farm, retail store, or football team. The purpose of this view is to identify all entities (record types) used in the organization and to identify the relationships among those entities. At the conceptual level, you are not concerned about which database management system to use, how the data itself will be used specifically,

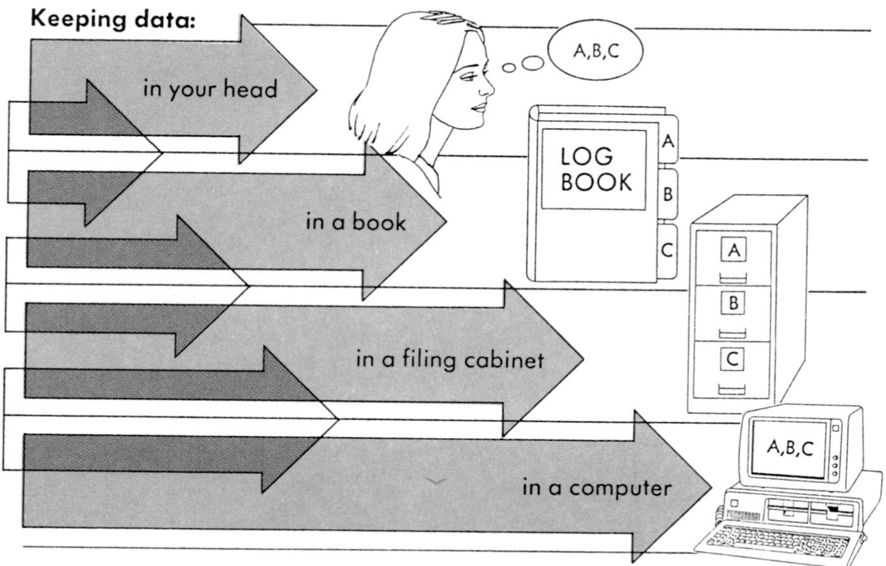

FIGURE 2.2
Developments in data storage and retrieval

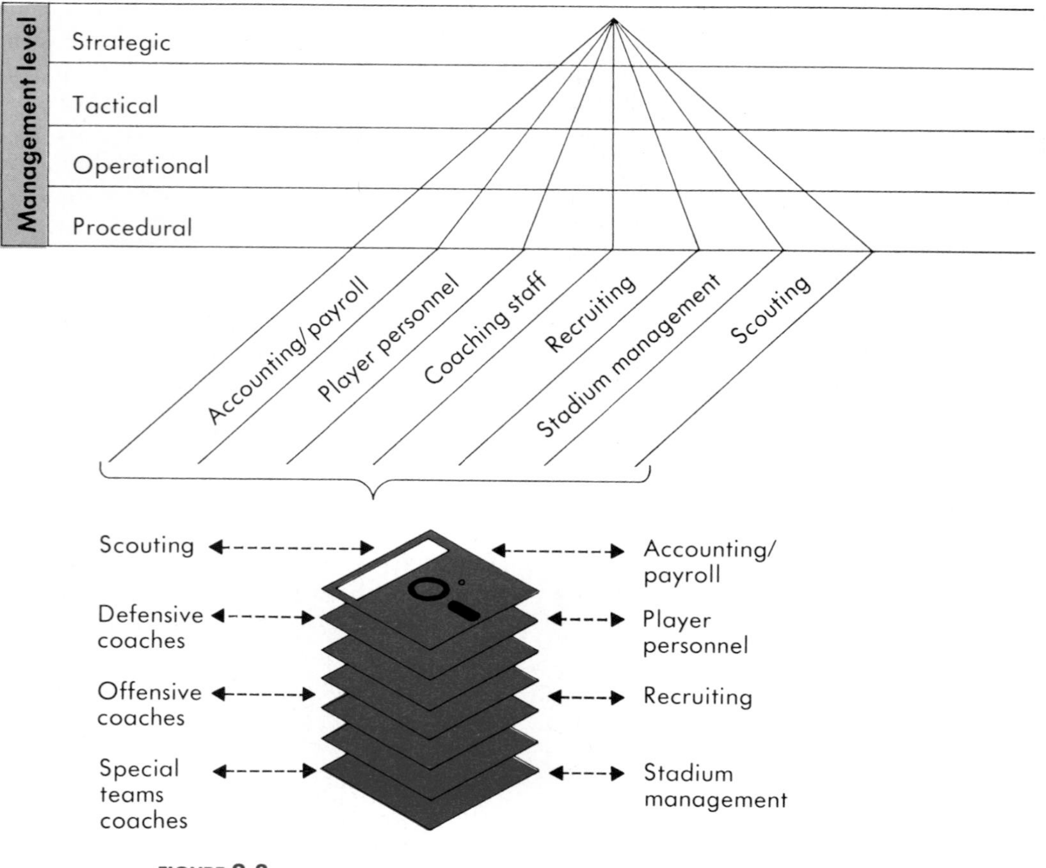

FIGURE 2.3
A football team database

or how the system will be implemented (placed into operation). Thus, the purpose of the conceptual view is to gain an overall grasp of the organization's data.

Logical View The **logical view** of data represents the application stage in the process of understanding the way data is organized and creating a database system. Thus, it represents the individual user's view of the database. (However, this view is always based on the conceptual view.) It is possible to have as many different logical views of a database as there are users.

For example, typical information needs of particular football franchise users of the database might be:

1. **Special teams coaches**—"Provide me with a list of players arranged according to their time over 40 yards who are not first string players on either offense or defense."

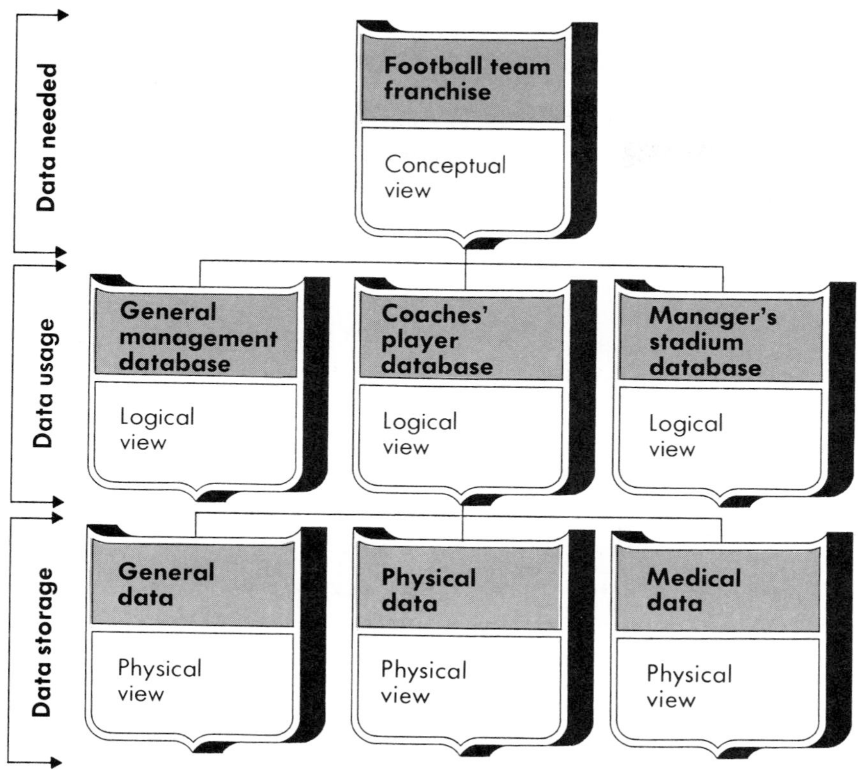

FIGURE 2.4
Different views of data

2. **Recruiting**—"What offensive team positions are currently manned by players who have been in professional football for more than five years?"
3. **Advertising and promotions**—"Which players have previously been involved in advertising or promotions for the franchise? Which players have been involved in commercial advertising?"

In each of these examples of database use, the player's name is used; however, in each case, it serves a different function, depending on the needs of the user.

Physical View The **physical view** of data represents the view that is closest to the actual machine representation of the data. It deals with the storage of data within the computer system—where the data is stored and what media are used, as well as the format of the stored data. The data is no longer described only in terms of concepts and logic; it can also be accessed and manipulated physically (or electronically). Generally speaking, the physical formats of the data are not important to the user or the programmer, but they are important to the computer system. What is important to the user is that the bridge or linkage between the logical view and the physical view is the database management system.

Database Systems

Before you proceed, you need more formal definitions of a database and its components. A database is an integrated collection of related computer data files. It is through integration that databases are able to solve two major problems normally associated with the more traditional data storage techniques of file processing: data independence and data redundancy. The goal of any database system is to increase data independence, reduce data redundancy, increase the speed of data handling, and improve the ease of data access.

The value of the database rests entirely on the quality of the data collected and stored. If you've been careless in the data collection operation, the data may contain errors, making the data worthless for use in future decision making. In the computer industry, this has been referred to as "**garbage-in, garbage-out**," GIGO for short.

The Definition of a Database

Databases are made up of entities, attributes, entity records, and keys. An **entity** is any identifiable object, concept, or activity belonging to an organization. Organizations can have many different entities. For example, if the organization is a football team, one of the entities within the football franchise structure is the PLAYER. Other entities could be COACHES, STADIUM SEATING, EQUIPMENT, BUDGETS, and so on. Thus, a database entity is similar to a record in a file management system.

An **attribute** (also referred to as a **field, data item,** or **data element**) is a property of an entity and is represented by a name and a set of values. Like an organization, an entity may have several attributes. For the football team example, the attribute POSITION could have several values, including QUARTERBACK, TIGHT END, OUTSIDE LINE BACKER, STRONG SAFETY, and so on. Thus, an attribute of an entity is similar to a field of a record in a file management system.

An **entity record** is a set of attributes and their associated values that describe a particular entity occurrence. If you have the entity called PLAYER with attributes of NAME, JERSEY NUMBER, POSITION, YEARS-PROFESSIONAL, and COLLEGE ATTENDED, three entity records could be

JAMES SMITH, 85, Flanker, 3, Baylor University
ROY O'NEILL, 54, Defensive Tackle, 2, University of Nebraska
LARRY HAND, 34, Running Back, 0, Miami (Florida)

A key, as mentioned previously, is an attribute that uniquely identifies the attribute values for that entity record. Keys can be thought of as being primary or secondary. Primary keys, such as JERSEY NUMBER, are considered the most important and are generally used to search for a particular entity record.

Relationships within a Database

A **relationship,** in database terms, represents the way two pieces of data—that is, entities and attributes—are tied together. This relationship can be one-to-one, one-to-many, or many-to-many.

One-to-One (1:1) Relationships When a single value in one entity can be related to only a single value in a second entity and a single value in the second entity relates to only one value in the first, it is called a **one-to-one (1:1) relationship.** For example, if a unique JERSEY NUMBER is assigned to each PLAYER NAME, the relationship between JERSEY NUMBER and PLAYER NAME is said to be one-to-one, as shown in Figure 2.5a.

One-to-Many (1:m) Relationships When a value in one entity relates to many values in the second entity but a value in the second entity can relate to only one value in the first, it is called a **one-to-many (1:m) relationship.** At any given point in time, zero, one, or many player names can be associated with a time over 40 yards. Thus, a given time over 40 yards can be assigned to many player names, and there is a "many" relationship between time and player names, as shown in Figure 2.5b.

Many-to-Many (m:m) Relationships When entity #1 references many values in entity #2, and a value in entity #2 relates to

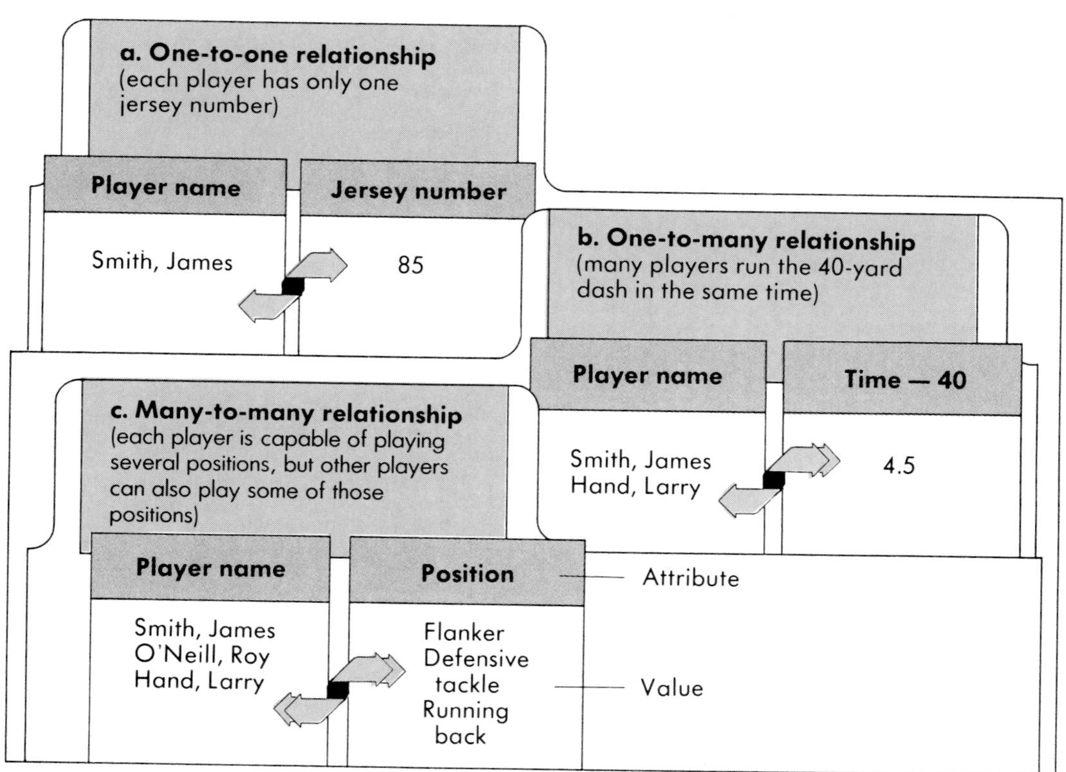

FIGURE 2.5
Relationships between attribute values (single arrowhead = one relationship; dual arrowhead = many relationships)

many values in entity #1, it is called a **many-to-many (m:m) relationship.** In the football team example, any PLAYER NAME could be associated with several different POSITIONs, and any POSITION could be performed by several PLAYER NAMEs. In this case, you have a many-to-many relationship between PLAYER NAME and POSITION, as illustrated in Figure 2.5c. For example, LARRY HAND is normally a RUNNING BACK but could also play as a PUNTER. However, he is not the only running back on the team, nor is he the only one capable of being a punter.

Types of Database Structures

There are three types of database structures in common use today: hierarchical, shown in Figure 2.6; network, shown in

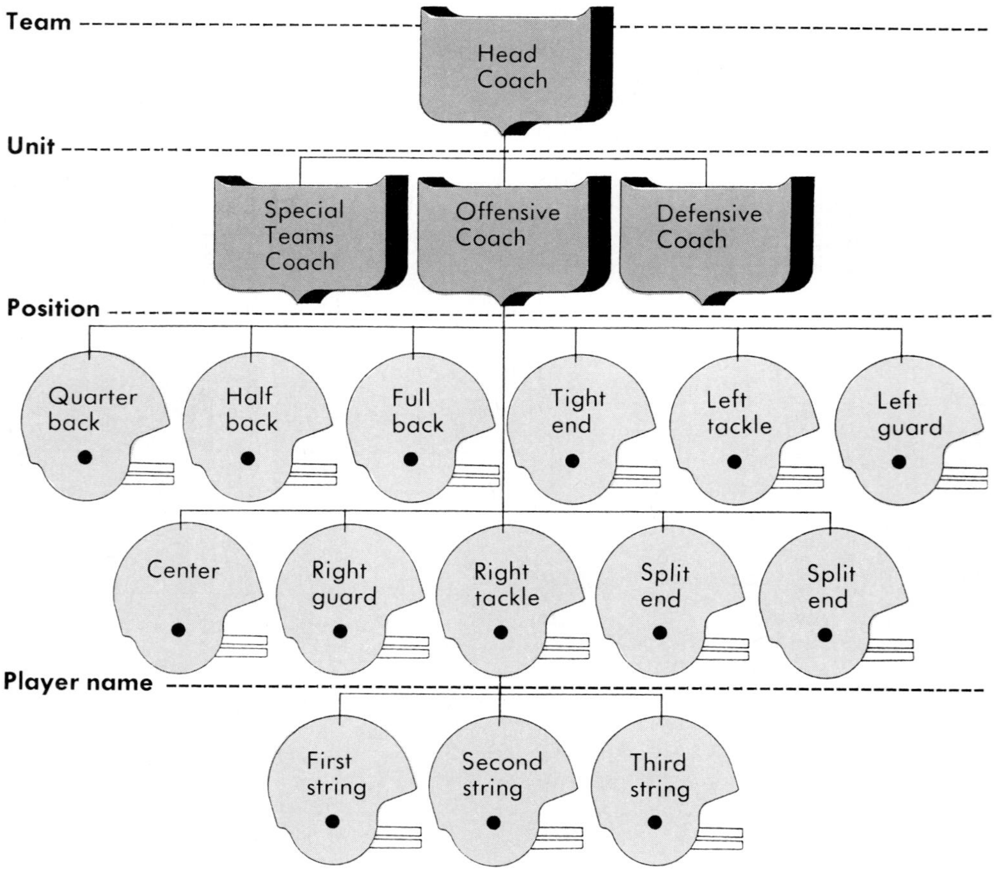

FIGURE 2.6
Hierarchy of a football team

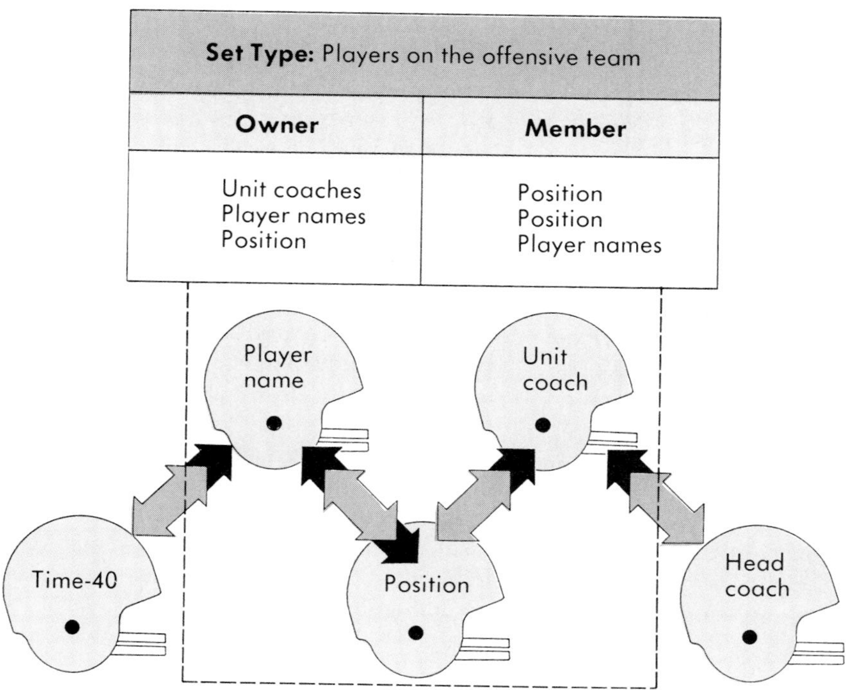

FIGURE 2.7
Network structure

			Player Database			
Player name	Position	Jersey number	College attended	Height	Weight	— — —

		Position Database			
Position	Minimum height	Minimum weight	Minimum speed	Minimum strength	— — —

FIGURE 2.8
Relationships within a relational database

Figure 2.7; and relational. The different structure types are referred to as *models* or *database models.*

Relational Structure

Software packages using the relational model are not only found on the large machines, but they are also the primary database model used on microcomputers. This type of structure is very easy to use, primarily because the relationships between entities are shown in table formats rather than organized like the diagrams shown for the hierarchical and network models. Tables like those illustrated in Figure 2.8 are common in relational models. Every table represents an entity type, every column represents an attribute of the entity, and every row represents an entity record. In more technical terms, rows are called **tuples.**

Relational models offer great flexibility in accessing data, because the relationship structure is flexible—it can be changed very easily. Records (rows) can easily be inserted or deleted, and complex relationships can be created and used. The only possible disadvantage is that data access may be slightly slower when compared to the other database models. Relational models also require that the primary keys used in the database uniquely specify each entity record. Relational databases that meet the unique-key criterion are said to be in **domain/key normal form**—there are no ambiguous record references.

dBASE II and dBASE III

Learning to Use dBASE II and dBASE III

dBASE II and its newer "big brother," dBASE III, are relational database packages that are available on a number of microcomputer systems using a variety of operating systems. dBASE II, one of the oldest microcomputer database packages, is very flexible and easy to use. dBASE III is a newer extension of dBASE II and includes additional powerful features. Although this module deals primarily with dBASE II, many of the functions of dBASE III are the same as or only slightly different from those of dBASE II. The differences between dBASE II and dBASE III will be presented as necessary when they reflect significant variations in the ways the packages work.

Before you start working with dBASE II and dBASE III, you need to become familiar with their terminology. First, a *database* is called a *file,* an *entity* is a *record,* and an *attribute* is a *field.* Thus, if you are familiar with the conventional terminology used in a file management system, you should be familiar with the terminology used in dBASE II and dBASE III.

When you are ready to begin running the package, place a dBASE disk in drive A, type DBASE, and press the RETURN key. When the package has been loaded into memory, it will respond with a "." (period) prompt character. Whenever dBASE is ready to accept a command (whether in the loading process or later on), it will respond with this prompt character.

As is the case with many of the commercially available software packages, dBASE is supported by a "help" function. In dBASE II, if you wish to receive assistance, enter the command HELP [topic], where HELP is the command name and the text enclosed within brackets represents an option. (In the remaining discussion, any text of a dBASE command within brackets can be considered optional.) If HELP is requested without a topic, a listing of the HELP text will begin. The total length of this text is about 65 pages when printed, so you will probably want to supply a topic when you use the help function. When the display screen is full of information, dBASE will pause and ask you to press the RETURN key to proceed with the next screen. If you wish to terminate the HELP function, press the ESCape key at any time and return to the "." prompt. You can use the ESCape key anytime a command is being executed to terminate the command and return to the "." prompt.

The HELP function has been completely revised in dBASE III. To enter the HELP function, you still enter the command HELP. However, dBASE III will respond with a menu of general "help" topics. When you select a general "help" topic, you will be provided with another menu of more specific topics. You may either select one of the indicated topics or return to the previous menu. This approach is much more user friendly, since you have to remember four instructions to receive assistance on any given topic. As long as you can remember "HELP," you should be able to determine quickly what you should do next.

Solving the Job Hunting Problem

The remaining sections of this module are devoted to solving a problem in job hunting. This problem will require you to build a database and maintain the contents of the database by adding new records, modifying attribute values, and deleting unwanted records. In addition, you will be required to query the database and produce reports based on the contents of the database.

As a job seeker, you are interested in keeping track of interviews and offers (or rejection letters) as they come in. Items to keep track of include company name and address, contact person within the company, date the company responded to the application, and the scheduled interview date or notice of "no openings." Once you get an interview, you want to be able to keep track of the salary offered, the amount of certain benefits (life insurance, health insurance, vacation days, and retirement contributions). You may also want to know the commuting distance to the job site and to order the job offers according to your personal job preferences.

Once you know what information you want to keep track of, you can build a database and use it to produce reports and comparisons. The data needed for this problem is presented in Appendix A. The following list represents the types of activities you will perform on the database once it has been built. (Note that some database packages permit the use of only one database at a time. Thus, steps 1 and 2 below may be combined because of this limitation.)

1. Build the structure of the COMPANY part of the database and enter the data.
2. Build the structure of the JOBS part of the database and enter the data.
3. You have just received a letter of rejection from WTBS Channel 5 TV. You need to enter the COMPANY part of the database and change the status of the offer from that company from "Ongoing" to "Rejected."
4. You have received a letter of acceptance from First State National Bank. You need to enter the COMPANY part of the database and change the

status of the offer from that company from "Ongoing" to "Offered." Enclosed with the letter of acceptance was a description of the job containing the following details:

Site: North
Amount of Offer: $22,000.00
Life Insurance: $210.00
Health Insurance: $325.00
Vacation: 14 Days
Retirement contribution: $2950.00

You have established that the commuting distance is 25 miles, and your preference for the job is 2. This information needs to be added to the JOBS database.

5. Find all companies that have rejected your employment application. You want to delete any job details that appear in the database for these companies.
6. Find all the jobs in the COMPANY part of the database for which offers have been extended. The report is to contain the company name, contact person, city, state, and zip code. You want the companies listed in order by zip code. You also want a count of the number of job offers.
7. Find all companies in the COMPANY part of the database for which you have an offer and for which the amount of the offer (from the JOBS database) is greater than $19,000. You want to produce a report containing the company name, the amount of the offer, your preference for the job, and the "net" offer (the amount of the offer plus life, health, and retirement contributions). You want these jobs listed by preference (and also by company name if the preferences happen to be the same for two or more jobs).

Building a Database — The CREATE Command

One of the first activities you will want to perform in any database package is to create your own database. To create a new database, enter the CREATE command. The format of this command is CREATE [filename], where the filename is any file name that is legitimate for the operating system in use. Note that only the file name need be specified. dBASE will add the extension ".DBF" (database file) to each file created. Also, unless the default disk drive has been altered, the disk drive should be indicated. In the examples that follow, drive B has been selected for the storage of data. If you do not enter the optional file name when using the CREATE command, dBASE will ask you to enter it. You can also create a new database by using the F8 key, which is usually the default key for the creation process. You should check your system to see if function keys are available and to determine the commands or operations associated with each of these keys. More will be said about function keys later.

To begin the job hunting problem, enter the command CREATE B:COMPANY to represent the company database. When you have finished, you will actually have constructed two separate databases—COMPANY and JOBS. This design was chosen to demonstrate the flexibility of dBASE and to illustrate the means by which the unnecessary duplication of data can be eliminated. (For example, duplication is eliminated by placing the Johnson Instruments, Inc., data in the COMPANY database once, while the JOBS database will contain three separate offers from this company.)

Next, dBASE will ask you to specify the structure for this new database. You will see the following headings produced on the display screen: FIELD, NAME, TYPE, WIDTH, and DECIMAL PLACES. dBASE will automatically number each field (from 1 through the maximum number of fields for each record), and the cursor will be moved under the NAME part of the heading. At this point, you need to supply a field name descriptive of the data it is to

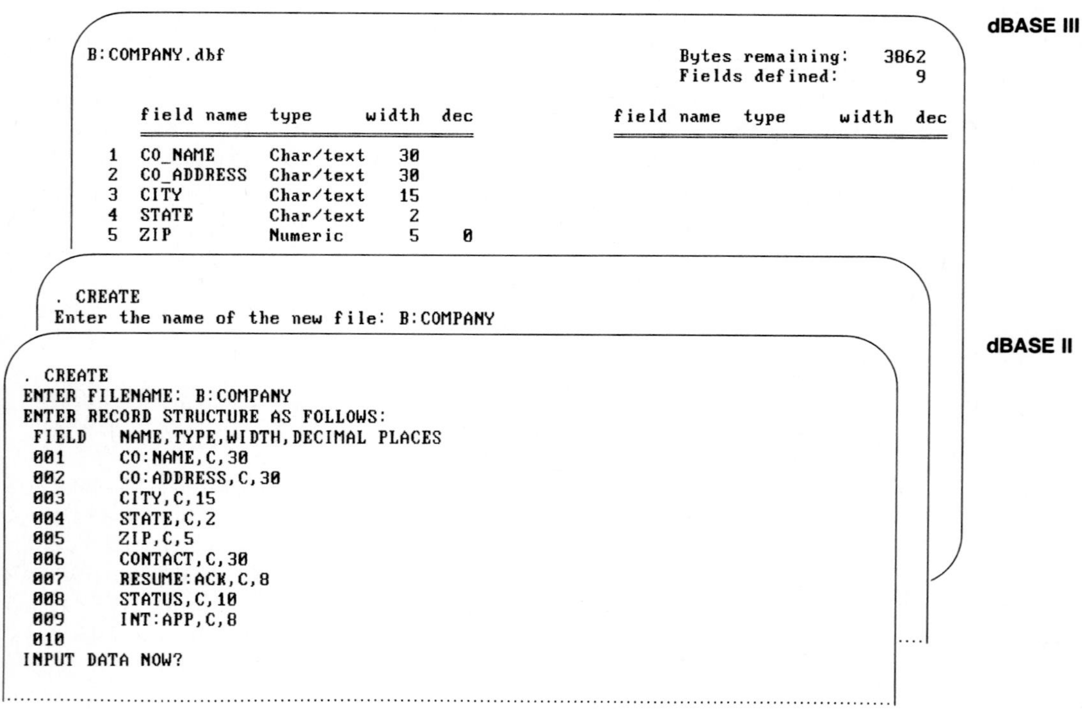

dBASE III

```
B:COMPANY.dbf                                   Bytes remaining:   3862
                                                Fields defined:       9

   field name  type       width  dec            field name  type      width  dec

 1 CO_NAME     Char/text    30
 2 CO_ADDRESS  Char/text    30
 3 CITY        Char/text    15
 4 STATE       Char/text     2
 5 ZIP         Numeric       5    0
```

```
. CREATE
Enter the name of the new file: B:COMPANY
```

dBASE II

```
. CREATE
ENTER FILENAME: B:COMPANY
ENTER RECORD STRUCTURE AS FOLLOWS:
 FIELD   NAME,TYPE,WIDTH,DECIMAL PLACES
 001     CO:NAME,C,30
 002     CO:ADDRESS,C,30
 003     CITY,C,15
 004     STATE,C,2
 005     ZIP,C,5
 006     CONTACT,C,30
 007     RESUME:ACK,C,8
 008     STATUS,C,10
 009     INT:APP,C,8
 010
INPUT DATA NOW?
```

FIGURE 2.9
Creating the COMPANY database with dBASE

represent. Each field name may be up to 10 characters long and may be composed of letters and digits. In dBASE II, a colon (:) symbol may also be used. [In dBASE III, an underline (_) should be used as a replacement for the colon symbol.] Spaces cannot appear in a field name—use a colon (or an underline) instead of a space to make the name more readable. Thus, as illustrated in Figure 2.9, enter each field name and other characteristics necessary to describe your file.

In the job hunting example, all the field names are composed of letters and colons (underlines for dBASE III); if you attempt to supply a field name that is not permitted, dBASE will respond with the message BAD NAME FIELD. If this should occur, the field number is repeated, and you are given another opportunity to specify the characteristics of the field. In fact, you will be given another chance, regardless of which of the characteristics you specify incorrectly.

Next you must supply the field TYPE. The allowable field types are presented in Table 2.1. On examining the structure of the example database in Figure 2.9, you will see that all the field names ("co:name," "co:address," "city," "state," "zip," "contact," "resume:ack," "status," and "int:app") are character fields. (Character is the default type for dBASE III.) They will never be used for computation purposes, and the data in these fields may contain any combination of letters, digits, and other characters. However, Figure 2.10 shows that the JOBS database indicates that several fields have been recorded

TABLE 2.1 Allowable Field Types

Field Type	Explanation
C	A character field; a field that will be any combination of letters, digits, and other characters with which no computation is planned.
N	A numeric field; a field composed totally of digits (and possibly a decimal point or minus sign) with which some form of computation may be performed.
L	A logical field; a field, of a length of one character, that is capable of retaining a "yes/no" type of data, where "T," "t," "Y," and "y" are treated as "true" and "F," "f," "N," and "n" are treated as "false."
D	A date field; a field, of a length of 8 characters, that is capable of retaining a date in a format of "MM/DD/YY," where "MM," "DD," and "YY" represent two-digit values of month, day, and year, respectively (available only with dBASE III).

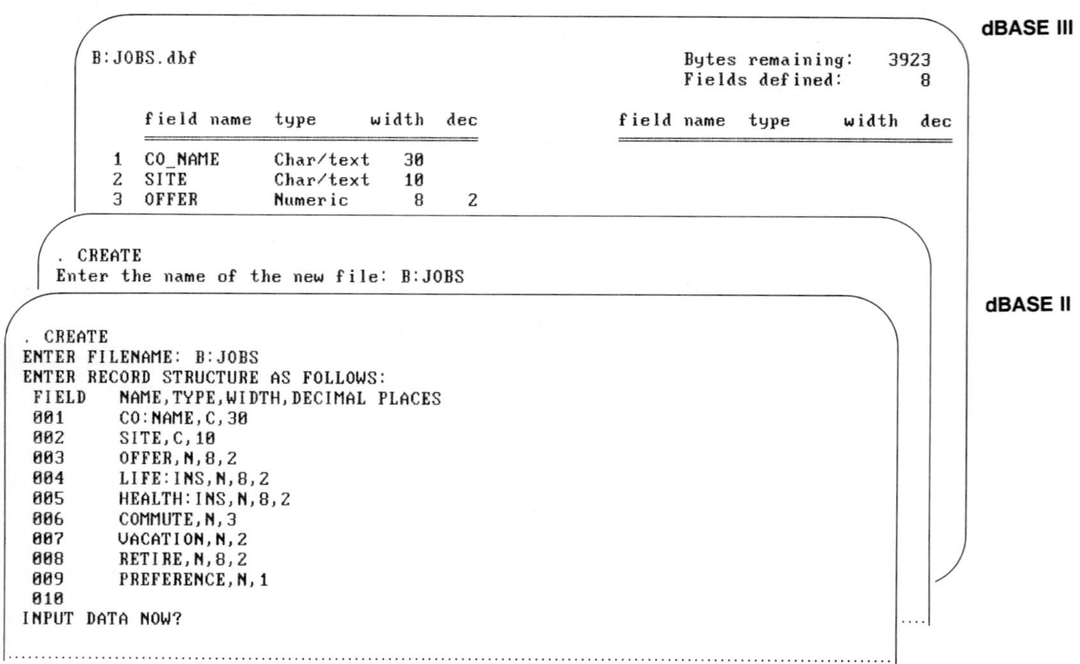

FIGURE 2.10
Creating the JOBS database with dBASE

as numeric field types. The field names "offer," "life:ins," "health:ins," "commute," "vacation," "retire," and "preference" are numeric fields, and the data in these fields will contain only numeric data. All of these fields *could* be used for computational purposes.

The field WIDTH must be supplied next. What is the maximum number of characters of data you plan to place in the field? dBASE must deal with the maximum field width to be able to store data, even if the field width is a "worst-case" situation. In Figure 2.9, "CO:NAME," "CO:ADDRESS," and "CONTACT" are all 30 characters long, even though you don't necessarily expect any of the data values to be that long. Specifying that they are 30 characters long allows you to enter a longer piece of data later. Some of the other fields and their widths are "CITY"—15 characters, "STATE"—a 2-character abbreviation, dates ("RESUME:ACK" and "INT:APP")—8 characters, "STATUS"—10 characters, and "ZIP"—5 characters.

Now you have to determine the number of any DECIMAL PLACES necessary in some of the numeric fields. If a numeric field is to contain a decimal fraction, how many digits in the field width follow the decimal point? Look at the field name "OFFER" in Figure 2.10. Note that the field WIDTH is 8 digits, of which 2 are DECIMAL PLACES. The result of such a definition is that numeric values may be placed into this field in the format of XXXXX.XX, where "X" represents a digit position. Furthermore, note that one position of the field is occupied by the decimal point. Thus, the maximum value that may be placed into this field is 99999.99, and the minimum is −9999.99. Next, look at the "COMMUTE" field. Note that it is also a numeric field but does not contain any decimal digits. Such a field definition indicates that only integers (whole numbers) are permitted in this field. Thus, the commuting distance will be recorded in whole miles.

After all the fields of the database have been entered, simply press the RETURN key when the next field number appears on the screen. When the field name position is blank, dBASE assumes you have completed the definition of the database structure. dBASE will then automatically store the database structure and produce the message ENTER DATA NOW:. If you respond with "N," dBASE will simply return to the "." prompt. If you respond with "Y," you will be presented with a record number and a screen format that identifies each field name specified in the database structure, as indicated in Figure 2.11. Two colons will follow each field name to indicate the maximum width of the field. This information will be shown in half-intensity (half the normal brightness) on the screen. As you enter data, the data will be shown in full-intensity (full brightness). As you are entering data, if you completely fill the field with characters, you will hear a "beep" tone, indicating the field is full. dBASE will then automatically proceed to the next field. If you are finished with the field but it is not completely filled with characters, proceed to the next field by pressing the RETURN key. If for some reason you need to return to a previous field, use the up-arrow key to go backward through the form. In fact, all the cursor control keys can be used. The left-arrow key can be used to back up within a field, the right-arrow key to go forward within a field, and the down-arrow key to go to the next field. These keys, in combination with the use of the BACKSPACE key, are extremely helpful when it is necessary to correct data. In dBASE III, you can even use the PgUp key to retrieve a previous record or the PgDn key to get the next record. In the case of numeric fields, if the field is not completely full when the RETURN key is pressed, dBASE will automatically right-justify the number(s) in that field. In the case of decimal fields, such as "OFFER," if only the integer portion of the numeric value is supplied, dBASE will automatically supply the decimal point and trailing zeros (".00").

After data has been placed in the last field of the first record, dBASE will clear the screen and automatically present the screen format for the next record. At this point, it is too late to modify the data in the previous record, because you are in the initial input mode. You will have to wait until later to make changes. If you wish to enter another record, proceed as before. If, however, you wish to terminate the input mode, do not enter any data into the first field. dBASE interprets an empty first field as a signal that you are ready to terminate the input operation and return to the "." prompt. All the data

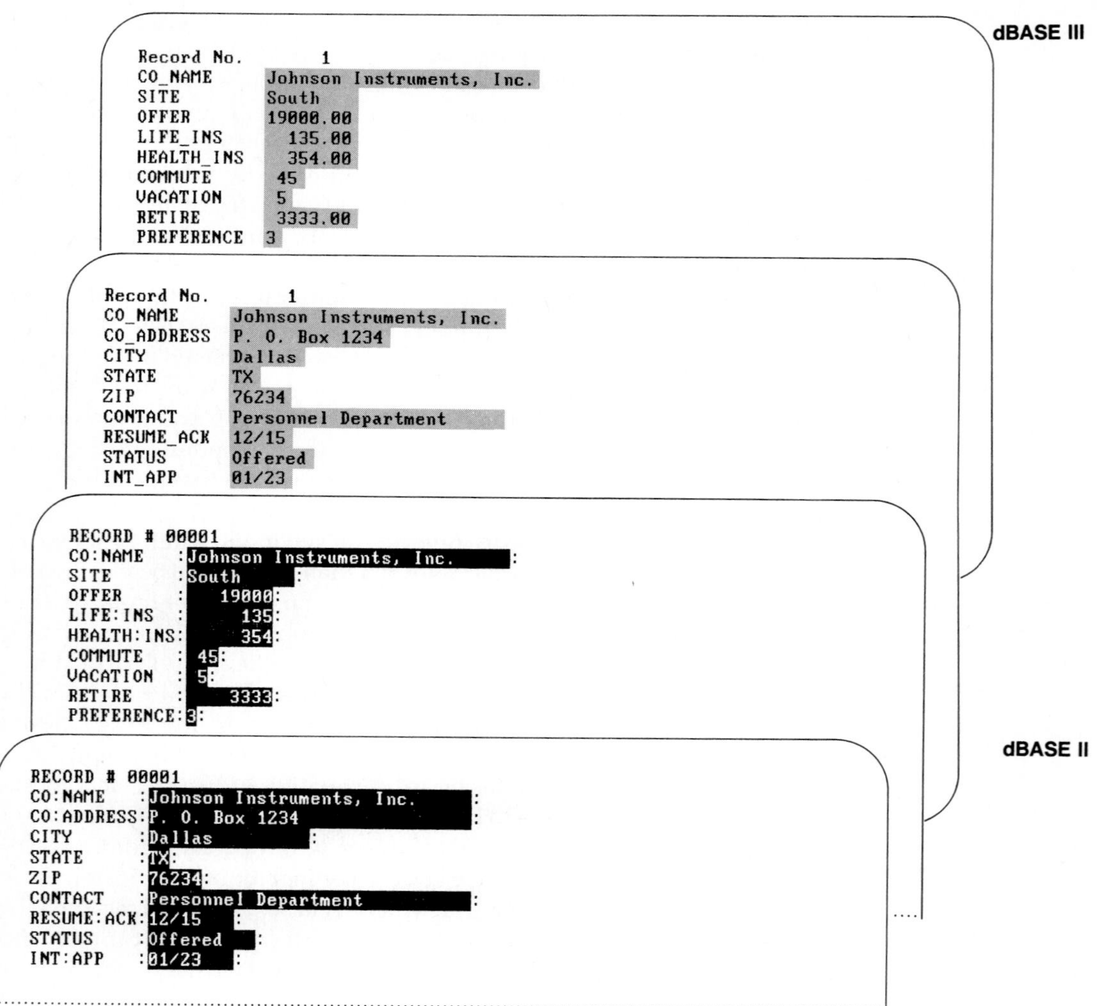

FIGURE 2.11
Input formats for dBASE

entered up to that point is automatically saved in the specified database—in this case, either COMPANY or JOBS.

Finally, suppose you had just finished the COMPANY database and you wished to start the JOBS database. Of course, you would use the CREATE command again, which closes all previously used databases. Thus, you cannot destroy the work you have already completed by getting part of one database into another by accident. However, you can use the commands that appear in the following discussion without creating another database.

Starting and Stopping—The QUIT and USE Commands

Assume that you are in a hurry and all that you have time for is to build your databases. To get out of dBASE and return to the operating system, all that is required is to enter the command QUIT.

When you come back later to use the databases that you have built, return to dBASE by entering the command DBASE. You will again see the "." prompt. To retrieve the previously generated databases, enter the command USE [filename] [INDEX indexfile1 [,indexfile2] . . .], where filename is the name of a previously created database. (The INDEX option will be described later.) Thus, to retrieve the company database, enter USE B:COMPANY. To retrieve the jobs database, enter USE B:JOBS. Each time a USE command is entered, any previously active databases are normally closed. Thus, it is a relatively simple matter to go from one database to another.

Keeping Track of Where You Are—The LIST and DISPLAY Commands

Now that you have two databases in storage (COMPANY and JOBS), it may be difficult to keep track of what you've done. You may not remember which database you are currently using, or you may not remember the structure of a database that was built a few days ago. Fortunately, there are a number of commands that will permit you to "recall" information about databases and other items.

Two commands, LIST and DISPLAY, are available for such purposes. The formats of the LIST command that are related to databases in general (rather than to fields) are LIST FILES [ON drive] [LIKE skeleton], LIST STATUS, and LIST STRUCTURE. Note that most of the words that appear in dBASE commands can be abbreviated by using the first four characters of the word. Thus, there is no abbreviation for LIST, but DISPLAY may be abbreviated DISP, STATUS may be abbreviated as STAT, STRUCTURE may be abbreviated as STRU, and so on.

The LIST FILES command is similar to the operating system command DIR. In fact, dBASE III permits the command: DIR[ectory] [drive] [LIKE skeleton] to be substituted for the LIST FILES command. These commands allow you to view files that exist on your disks. For example, suppose you forget the name of a database you wish to use. The command LIST FILES will list all the ".DBF" files on the default disk drive. The output from this command consists of the name of the databases, the number of records in each database, and the date each database was last updated. (dBASE III provides the names of the databases, the version of dBASE that created the files, the size of the files, and the amount of remaining space on the disk.) The same result can be achieved by pressing the F4 key, which usually defaults to a LIST FILES command.

If you wish to access the directory of a drive that is not the default disk drive, you can enter a command such as LIST FILES ON B:, which will list all ".DBF" files on drive B, as shown in Figure 2.12. If you wish to access files other than DBF files, you can use the skeleton option. For example, if you wished to know what index files are available, you would enter a command such as LIST FILES LIKE *.NDX, which would retrieve all file names on the default drive that have ".NDX" as an extension name. In addition, the "?" wildcard option that can be used with the operating system DIR command can also be used with the LIST FILES command. For example, suppose you know part of a database file name but are unsure of the exact spelling of that name: You could use a command like LIST FILES LIKE C??????.DBF, to which dBASE would respond with all database files on the default drive that contain the letter "C" as the first character.

The LIST STATUS command provides you with information about what activities are currently going on, as well as current settings of a number of default parameters. A sample of the output generated by entering this command (or by pressing the F6 key) is provided in Figure 2.13. Note that the output begins by identifying currently active databases (as well as indexes, if any are in use). The next information provided is related to usage characteristics that may be specified by SET commands. Thus, usage characteristics such as the data disk drive, bell sounding, and so on have certain default settings that can

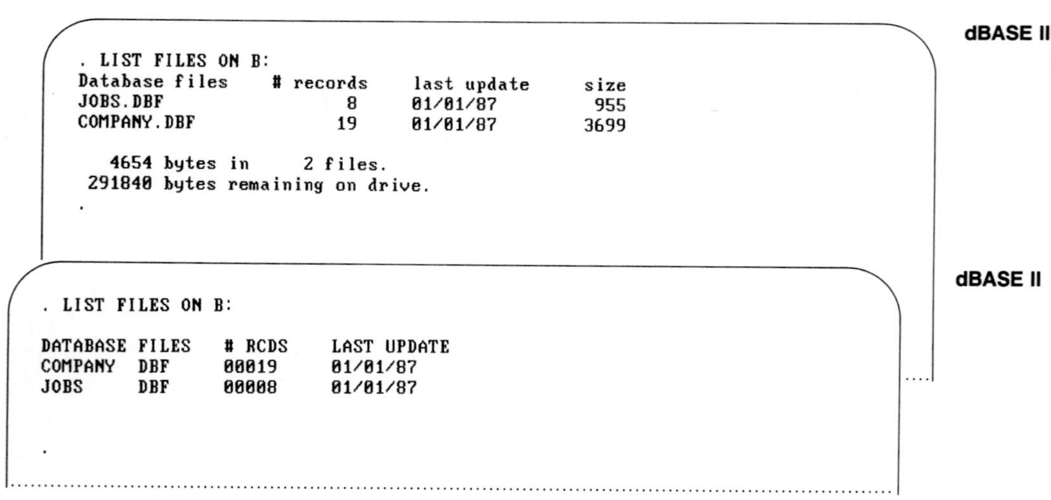

dBASE III

```
. LIST FILES ON B:
Database files    # records    last update    size
JOBS.DBF                  8    01/01/87        955
COMPANY.DBF              19    01/01/87       3699

   4654 bytes in      2 files.
 291840 bytes remaining on drive.
.
```

dBASE II

```
. LIST FILES ON B:

DATABASE FILES    # RCDS    LAST UPDATE
COMPANY   DBF     00019     01/01/87
JOBS      DBF     00008     01/01/87

.
```

FIGURE 2.12
Identifying the DATABASE—the LIST FILES command

dBASE III

```
File search path:
Default disk drive: B:
ALTERNATE    - OFF  DEBUG        - OFF  ESCAPE       - ON   MENU         - OFF
BELL         - ON   DELETED      - OFF  EXACT        - OFF  PRINT        - OFF
CARRY        - OFF  DELIMITERS   - OFF  HEADING      - ON   SAFETY       - ON
CONFIRM      - OFF  DEVICE       - SCRN HELP         - OFF  STEP         - OFF
CONSOLE      - ON   ECHO         - OFF  INTENSITY    - ON   TALK         - ON
UNIQUE       - OFF

Margin =      0

Function key  F1  - help;
Function key  F2  - assist;
Function key  F3  - list;
Function key  F4  - dir;
Function key  F5  - display structure;
Function key  F6  - display status;
Function key  F7  - display memory;
Function key  F8  - display;
Function key  F9  - append;
Function key  F10 - edit;

.
```

```
TODAYS DATE          - 01/01/87
DEFAULT DISK DRIVE - C:
ALTERNATE - OFF    BELL       - ON
CARRY     - OFF    COLON      - ON
CONFIRM   - OFF    CONSOLE    - ON
DEBUG     - OFF    DELETE     - OFF
ECHO      - OFF    EJECT      - ON
ESCAPE    - ON     EXACT      - OFF
INTENSITY - ON     LINKAGE    - OFF
PRINT     - OFF    RAW        - OFF
STEP      - OFF    TALK       - ON

FUNCTION KEY ASSIGNMENTS
KEY      ASSIGNMENT
F1       HELP;
F2       DISP;
F3       LIST;
F4       LIST FILES;
F5       LIST STRU;
F6       LIST STATUS;
F7       LIST MEMO;
F8       CREATE;
F9       APPEND;
F10      EDIT #;
.
```

dBASE II

```
. LIST STATUS

DATABASE SELECTED - B:COMPANY .DBF
PRIMARY USE DATABASE

WAITING
```

FIGURE 2.13
Determining current settings and defaults —the LIST STATUS command

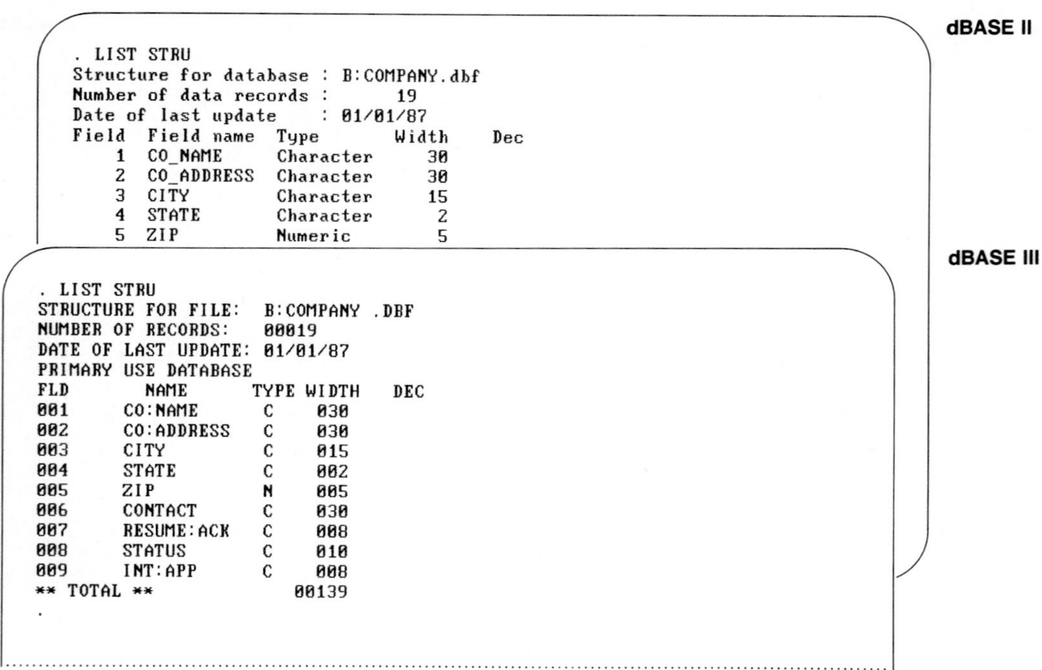

dBASE II

```
. LIST STRU
Structure for database : B:COMPANY.dbf
Number of data records :       19
Date of last update    : 01/01/87
Field  Field name  Type        Width    Dec
    1  CO_NAME     Character     30
    2  CO_ADDRESS  Character     30
    3  CITY        Character     15
    4  STATE       Character      2
    5  ZIP         Numeric        5
```

dBASE III

```
. LIST STRU
STRUCTURE FOR FILE:  B:COMPANY .DBF
NUMBER OF RECORDS:   00019
DATE OF LAST UPDATE: 01/01/87
PRIMARY USE DATABASE
FLD       NAME      TYPE WIDTH   DEC
001      CO:NAME      C    030
002      CO:ADDRESS   C    030
003      CITY         C    015
004      STATE        C    002
005      ZIP          N    005
006      CONTACT      C    030
007      RESUME:ACK   C    008
008      STATUS       C    010
009      INT:APP      C    008
** TOTAL **              00139
.
```

FIGURE 2.14
Now what was the structure of the database?—the LIST STRUCTURE command

be modified by a SET command. Finally, the LIST STATUS command provides the default setting of all function keys. (*Note:* The default function key settings are slightly different for dBASE III.) These defaults can also be altered by using the SET command.

The final form of the LIST command shown here displays the structure of the current database. By entering the command LIST STRUCTURE (or by pressing the F5 key), the output illustrated in Figure 2.14 is generated. Not only can you determine which database is currently active, you can also determine other characteristics of the database structure. These characteristics include the date last updated, the number of records in the database, how the database is used (PRIMARY or SECONDARY), and the characteristics of each field—its field number, name, type, width, and number of decimal places. Finally, you are provided with an indication of the total length of records in the database based on maximum field widths.

Each function of the LIST command is also supported by the DISPLAY command. Thus, you have your choice of wording—LIST or DISPLAY. (Other differences between LIST and DISPLAY are more fully discussed later.)

Changing the Contents of a Database— The BROWSE and EDIT Commands

Among the most important functions of a database is the capability of changing the contents of existing records. After all, it is unlikely that the situations represented by the data will always remain the same. Both the BROWSE and the EDIT commands permit the user to examine, and if necessary modify, the contents of records in the database.

The BROWSE command is perhaps the more versatile of the two commands. The format of this command is BROWSE [FIELDS fieldlist]. The simplest form of this statement is BROWSE. The result of entering this command while you are in an active database is illustrated in Figure 2.15. The BROWSE command is sensitive to the current record position; that is, the

dBASE III

```
Record No.        1     company
CO_NAME---------------------- CO_ADDRESS------------------- CITY----------
Johnson Instruments, Inc.     P. O. Box 1234                Dallas
Champion Cowboy Supply        126 Hollyhill Road            Garland
General Electronics, Inc.     87634 Dynamics Way            Ft. Worth
First State National Bank     302 Central Expressway        Dallas
Lewis & Melts Mortgage Co.    1 Bank Plaza                  Denton
Ethyl & Jung, DDS             23 Molar Hill Lane            Dennison
Aerospace Education Center    1423 Jupiter Road             Garland
ABC Stereo Warehouse          3434 Sound Place              Dallas
```

dBASE II

```
RECORD # :00001
CO:NAME---------------------- CO:ADDRESS------------------- CITY----------
Johnson Instruments, Inc.     P. O. Box 1234                Dallas
Champion Cowboy Supply        126 Hollyhill Road            Garland
General Electronics, Inc.     87634 Dynamics Way            Ft. Worth
First State National Bank     302 Central Expressway        Dallas
Lewis & Melts Mortgage Co.    1 Bank Plaza                  Denton
Ethyl & Jung, DDS             23 Molar Hill Lane            Dennison
Aerospace Education Center    1423 Jupiter Road             Garland
ABC Stereo Warehouse          3434 Sound Place              Dallas
WTBS Channel 5 TV             9826 Neonoise Court           Plano
Hormell Texas Chili Company   1 Hots Place                  Ft. Worth
Children's Museum             Look Out Point                Ft. Worth
FBI                           10-20 Parole Street           Arlington
Mosteq Computer Company       1428 Wozniak Way              Farmers Branch
Nephi's Hopi Crafts           16 Alma, Suite 34             Tulsa
Kelly Construction Company    1414 Jupiter Road             Garland
Jana's Management Consultants 2323 Beltline Road            Irving
Bar Four Ranch                P. O. Box 92341, Rt. 11       Denton
Matt's Films, Inc.            P. O. Box 524                 Dallas
Roger, Roger & Ray, Inc.      457 Happy Way                 Garland
```

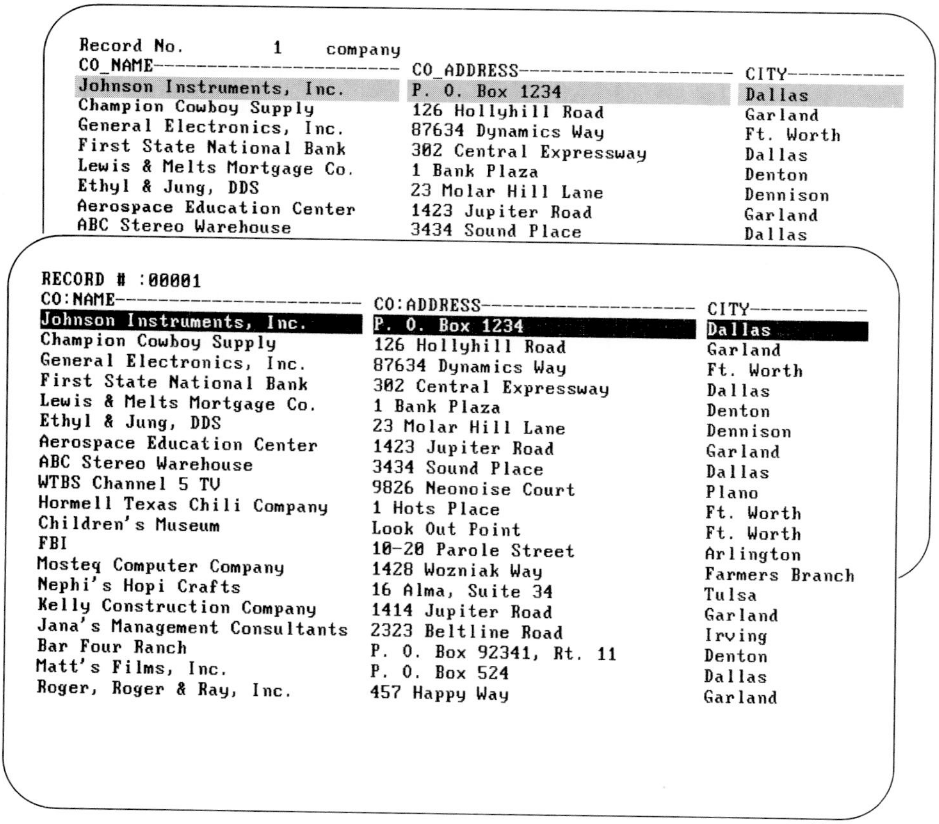

FIGURE 2.15
Changing the contents of a record—the BROWSE command

screen presentation will begin with the current record position (last record accessed) and will list that record and the records that follow. Thus, it might be necessary to use a command like GO TOP before executing the BROWSE command so that all the records in the database can be viewed. (GO TOP will always cause dBASE to reposition the current record marker to the first record in the database.)

Once records have been produced on the screen, the current record will be highlighted; the characters of the record will be in the normal display mode, whereas all others will be displayed in half-intensity. The record number of the current record will be displayed at the top of the screen, and this number will change as you move from one record to another. In addition, the field names (for example, "CO:NAME," "CO:ADDRESS," and "CITY") will be displayed above the data, followed by dashes to indicate the total width of the field. While you are in the BROWSE mode, if the field name is wider than the field width, characters of the field name are truncated (cut off). Finally, note that only those fields that fit across the 80-column screen will be initially produced for each record, and each record will occupy only one line of the screen. In addition, a maximum of 20 records will be displayed on the screen at one time.

To deal with the limitations imposed by the BROWSE command, dBASE supports a number of functions that permit movement through or examination of the records. For example, while in the BROWSE mode, you are permitted to "pan right" and "pan left." Not all fields of a record are visible (in the example), and you may wish to view the fields on the right of the last field shown. Thus, the BROWSE command permits the use of the control codes that are produced by simultaneously pressing the CTRL key and another key. A list of these control codes and the operations they perform is presented in Table 2.2.

If you are interested only in certain fields available in each record, you can use the FIELDS option to specify the fields of each record to be displayed. This approach reduces the necessity of panning, allows you to specify fields in any order, and permits fields to appear adjacent to one another even though they are several fields apart in the actual database structure.

What about actually changing the contents of a record? To do this, you will need to use several control codes. The control codes shown in Table 2.2 are not used only for the BROWSE mode. They apply to all modes (including EDIT) that permit you to modify the contents of a record or other structure. When it is necessary to change an entry, you can use these control codes. However, arrow keys are a bit easier to use than control codes, and you will probably prefer to use them.

When you reach the bottom of the screen, the current records disappear from view, and the next set of records become visible. This operation also works in reverse, should you be viewing records toward the bottom of the database and want to access records that are toward the top.

The functions indicated by data manipulation control codes have no substitute, and the actual changing of the contents of a field is accomplished

TABLE 2.2 Full-Screen Cursor Movement Codes

Control Code Sequence	Operation Performed
For Cursor Movement	
CTRL-B*	Moves BROWSE window right one field
CTRL-Z*	Moves BROWSE window left one field
CTRL-X, CTRL-F, or down-arrow key	Moves cursor down to the next field
CTRL-E, CTRL-A, or up-arrow key	Moves cursor up to the previous field
CTRL-D or right-arrow key	Moves cursor ahead one character
CTRL-E or left-arrow key	Moves cursor back one character
For Data Manipulation	
CTRL-G	Deletes a character under the cursor
DELete	Deletes a character to the left of the cursor
CTRL-Y	Erases current field to the right of the cursor
CTRL-V	Toggles between the ''overwrite'' and INSERT modes
CTRL-W	Saves changes and returns to the ''.'' prompt

* This function may be used only with the BROWSE command.

through this set. For example, if you wish to delete a character from the current field, use CTRL-G (if the cursor currently rests on that character) or the DELete key (if it is the next character). If you wish to delete several characters at once, you can repeat these functions. However, if you wish to delete a series of characters, you can use CTRL-Y. This function permits you to delete all characters in the field from the cursor position to the end of the field. To add characters to a field, use CTRL-V. To use this function, position the cursor at the location in the field where new characters are to be entered. This location may be any location in the field. Then press CTRL-V. All characters entered thereafter will appear at the point of the cursor (and to the right). Any characters following the cursor position will automatically be moved to the right. To terminate the operation, press CTRL-V again. This will return you to normal BROWSE mode. Finally, when you have made all the necessary changes and wish to save them, use CTRL-W to write the changes to the database and return to the "." prompt. CTRL-Q can be used to return to the "." prompt, but no changes are saved.

The EDIT command supports all the full-screen movements and editing commands permitted by the BROWSE command. The format of this command is EDIT [recordnumber]. However, there is a fundamental difference between the EDIT and the BROWSE commands. The EDIT command works on a single record at a time, whereas the BROWSE permits a visual examination of a group of records. To access a record for manipulation by the EDIT command, simply enter the command EDIT (or press the F10 key). In this event, dBASE will respond with the prompt ENTER RECORD # :, to which you should respond with the record number of the record to be edited. However, there is a shorter means of achieving the same result. As noted from the format of this command, you are permitted to enter a record number along with the command name. Therefore, you could enter EDIT 4. Once you have entered the EDIT mode, the content of that record will be displayed in the same form used when you originally entered the data, as shown in Figure 2.11. You are provided with the record number, the name of each field, the content of each field, and the length of each field (as indicated by the presence and placement of the colons). Movement from field to field is permitted by using either the control codes or the arrow keys. Furthermore, fundamental modifications can be done using the data manipulation control codes identified in Table 2.2.

There are a number of other control key combinations in the EDIT mode that enable certain functions. These control key sequences are presented in Table 2.3. The CTRL-U function provides the user with the capability of

TABLE 2.3 Control Codes Used for Database Manipulation

Control Code Sequence	Operation Performed
CTRL-U	Toggles the record delete marker "on" and "off"
CTRL-C	Writes the current record to disk and advances to the next record
CTRL-R	Writes the current record to disk and backs to the previous record
CTRL-Q	Ignores changes to the current record(s) and returns to the "." prompt
CTRL-W	Writes all changes to disk and returns to the "." prompt

marking a record for deletion (or removing the deletion marker). The deletion mark takes the form of an asterisk (*) adjacent to the record number. A record marked for deletion is physically retained in the database, but it is essentially eliminated from future "search" requests. If you wish to return a "deleted" record to active status, simply access that record and press CTRL-U. This will remove the deletion marker. More details about deleting records are provided later.

The remaining functions in the list of control codes are primarily for the purpose of accessing the next record by CTRL-C, accessing the previous record by CTRL-R, exiting the EDIT mode (without changes) and returning to dBASE mode by CTRL-Q, and writing the changes and returning to dBASE mode by CTRL-W.

There is a fundamental difference between changes made with the BROWSE command and those made with EDIT. EDIT assumes that all changes made to a record will be saved—that is, unless you choose to exit the EDIT mode by using CTRL-Q—and BROWSE does not. Thus, CTRL-C, CTRL-R, and CTRL-W all save changes. In addition, when you have performed the necessary modifications to the record in the EDIT mode, and you have reached the last field, an attempt to access the next (nonexistent) field will cause the current record to be saved and the prompt ENTER RECORD # : to appear on the screen. Thus, you will not only save the current record but will also be permitted to access any record in the database as the next record for editing.

As you will recall, the job hunting problem requires you to change the job status for several companies in the COMPANY database from "Ongoing" to "Rejected." To perform this operation, you must first access the correct database by entering the command USE B:COMPANY. Then you enter a command that permits you to modify one or more characteristics of the data within that database. Thus, you could select the command BROWSE FIELDS CO:NAME, STATUS. This command produces the screen shown in Figure 2.16. Note that the status of the job from WTBS Channel 5 TV (RECORD #9) has been changed from "Ongoing" to "Rejected." Your next requirement is to modify the job status of First State National Bank from "Ongoing" to "Offered" and add a job description in the JOBS database. While you are still working with the COMPANY database, all you have to do is access RECORD #4 and change the job status from "Ongoing" to "Offered."

Adding Records to a Database—The INSERT and APPEND Commands

dBASE contains two commands that permit the addition of new records to the database: INSERT and APPEND. The INSERT command is the more versatile of the two, because it allows you to insert a new record anywhere in the database. A record that is APPENDed is added to the end of the database. If it is important to maintain some particular order of records in the database, insertion will probably be your choice. The format of the INSERT command is

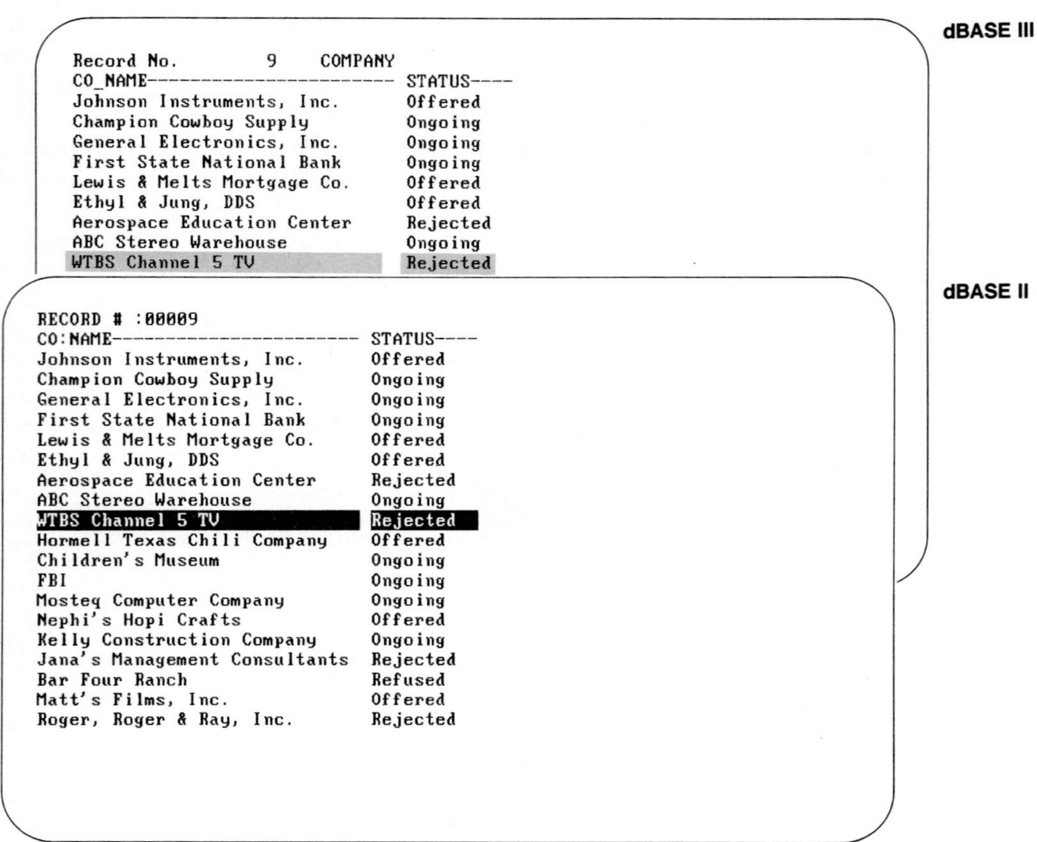

dBASE III

```
Record No.        9     COMPANY
CO_NAME----------------------- STATUS----
Johnson Instruments, Inc.      Offered
Champion Cowboy Supply         Ongoing
General Electronics, Inc.      Ongoing
First State National Bank      Ongoing
Lewis & Melts Mortgage Co.     Offered
Ethyl & Jung, DDS              Offered
Aerospace Education Center     Rejected
ABC Stereo Warehouse           Ongoing
WTBS Channel 5 TV              Rejected
```

dBASE II

```
RECORD # :00009
CO:NAME----------------------- STATUS----
Johnson Instruments, Inc.      Offered
Champion Cowboy Supply         Ongoing
General Electronics, Inc.      Ongoing
First State National Bank      Ongoing
Lewis & Melts Mortgage Co.     Offered
Ethyl & Jung, DDS              Offered
Aerospace Education Center     Rejected
ABC Stereo Warehouse           Ongoing
WTBS Channel 5 TV              Rejected
Hormell Texas Chili Company    Offered
Children's Museum              Ongoing
FBI                            Ongoing
Mosteq Computer Company        Ongoing
Nephi's Hopi Crafts            Offered
Kelly Construction Company     Ongoing
Jana's Management Consultants  Rejected
Bar Four Ranch                 Refused
Matt's Films, Inc.             Offered
Roger, Roger & Ray, Inc.       Rejected
```

FIGURE 2.16
Using the BROWSE command for selected fields

INSERT [[BEFORE] [BLANK]]. Because the insertion of a new record is based on the location (record #) of the last record accessed (the current record), the INSERT command permits you to perform the operation both BEFORE and after the current record. (Because the word "after" does not appear in the format of this command, "after" is the default insertion mode.) If BEFORE is specified, insertion occurs before the current record. If BLANK is also specified, a blank record (a record containing nothing but spaces) is inserted automatically without further user input.

When you think you are ready to INSERT a new record, it is always a good idea to DISPLAY the current record to check your location in the database. If you are not at the desired location, there are a number of commands you can use to adjust the current record position. Of course, GO TOP places you at the beginning of the database. Other formats of the GOTO command include GO BOTTOM — to reach the end of the database — and GO RECORD n, where "n" represents a specific record number. If you happen to be close to the location where a record is to be inserted, you can use the SKIP command. The format of this command is SKIP [-] [n], where "n" represents the number of records to be skipped while moving forward (down) in the database. The default for "n" is 1. If the "-" symbol is used, you move backward (up) in the database.

When the appropriate position for the insertion of a new record has been reached, you enter the command INSERT, and dBASE will indicate that you are in an input mode by supplying a screen format like that shown in Figure 2.11. Proceed by entering the values to be associated with the individual field names. After you have entered values for each field, you will automatically return to the "." prompt.

The APPEND command initiates a similar sequence of events. The syntax of the APPEND command is APPEND [BLANK]. As previously mentioned, when the APPEND command is used (or the F9 key is pressed), a new record is added to the end of the database. No prior positioning is required; dBASE knows the location of the last record in the database, so positioning to the last record is unnecessary. When the BLANK option is used, a blank record is added to the end of the database.

For the job hunting problem, you want to add a new record to the JOBS database. Because it makes no difference where you put this job description in the JOBS database, you could use the command sequence USE B:JOBS to gain access to the JOBS database and APPEND to add a record to the end of that database. dBASE will then respond with a screen format like the one in Figure 2.17. You can verify, by the RECORD #, how many job descriptions are included in the JOBS database.

Getting a Look at the Database — The LIST and DISPLAY Commands

Now that you have built the COMPANY and JOBS databases, perhaps you want to examine the records in one of them. One way to examine a database visually is to use the LIST command. (The LIST command was described earlier, but for different purposes.) The format of the LIST command is LIST [scope] [fieldlist] [FOR expression] [OFF]. As noted from the format, the short form of the command is LIST. This command can be either typed on the keyboard or entered by pressing the F3 key. Either choice produces a complete list of the database — all records and each record's fields. However, a full listing of a database is not particularly useful, especially if your records are longer than 80 characters (the LIST command will "wrap" fields from the end of one line to the beginning of the next line on the screen). Also, the list is produced rather rapidly; so, if the database is long, the top portion of the database will scroll off

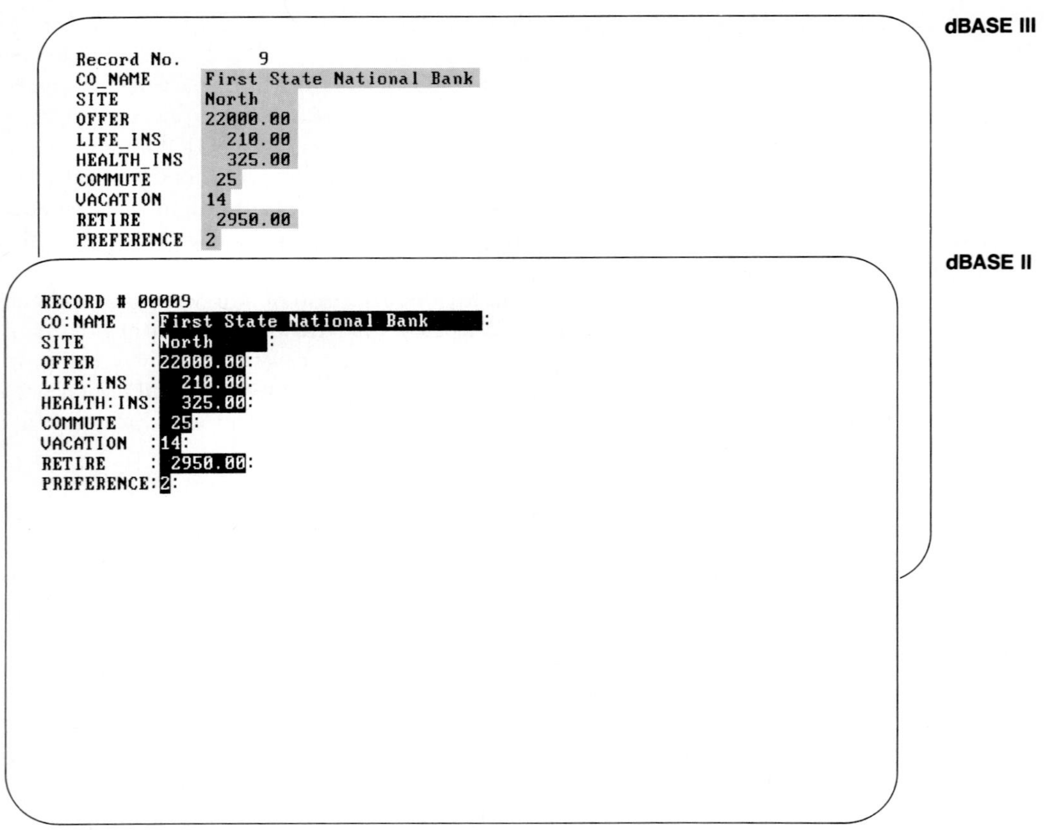

FIGURE 2.17
Using the APPEND command to add a record — a job description from the First State National Bank

the screen before you can read it. Note that all the records in the database are listed when only the word LIST is used. This means that the default scope for this command is for ALL the records in the database. If specified, "scope" indicates the number of records to be listed.

The complement of the LIST command is the DISPLAY command. The format of the DISPLAY command is DISPLAY [scope] [fieldlist] [FOR expression] [OFF]. As with the LIST command, there are multiple forms of the DISPLAY command. What happens when you simply enter the command DISPLAY (or press the F2 key)? With the simple DISPLAY command, only a single record is produced — the current record. Thus, the default scope for a DISPLAY command is 1 — the current record. Regardless of which command is used — LIST or DISPLAY — the format of the screen output is the same.

TABLE 2.4 Options for Indicating "Scope"

Scope Option	Meaning
ALL	Produces all of the records
NEXT n	Produces the next "n" records, where "n" is an integer number; count begins with the current record
RECORD n	Produces only the single record, located at the "nth" position in the database

As mentioned, the first option of both the LIST and the DISPLAY commands is "scope." This parameter identifies how many records of the database are to be produced. "Scope" provides three possibilities, as described in Table 2.4. Thus, the simple LIST command is equivalent to a DISPLAY ALL. A LIST RECORD n command is equivalent to a simple DISPLAY.

The field list option permits you to identify the fields within a database that you want to see as a result of using the LIST or the DISPLAY command. This option permits you to limit the number of fields produced and indicate the order in which the fields should appear. Obviously, when you need to specify field names, you should be familiar with the structure of the database currently in use. It might be wise to list the structure (LIST STRUCTURE) of the database before trying to identify which fields are to be shown.

Figure 2.18 shows that you have decided not to use all the fields of the COMPANY database—only a certain subset. The part of the command containing the field names "co:name" and "resume:ack" limits the number of fields produced. (However, the determination of which records are displayed is done through the FOR option, to be discussed shortly.)

Another part of the LIST or DISPLAY command that can be used to limit the length of output for a single record is the OFF option. The OFF option is used to suppress the presentation of record numbers. Use this option when you want to view only the contents of records and not their positions. Note that the OFF option is not used in Figure 2.18. As a result, the record numbers (7, 9, 16, and 19) are listed in the left margin. When the OFF option is used, the first database field produced occupies the first column on the screen.

Finally, note that dBASE II does not display the field names above the database values with a LIST or DISPLAY command. dBASE III shows the field names above the fields as the BROWSE command does.

The best has been saved for last: the FOR option. The LIST, DISPLAY, and other commands access each record; however, the FOR option permits you

dBASE III

```
. LIST CO_NAME, RESUME_ACK FOR STATUS = "Rejected"
Record#  CO_NAME                         RESUME_ACK
      7  Aerospace Education Center      11/16
      9  WTBS Channel 5 TV               12/03
     16  Jana's Management Consultants   01/06
     19  Roger, Roger & Ray, Inc.        12/15
.
```

dBASE II

```
. LIST CO:NAME, RESUME:ACK FOR STATUS = "Rejected"
00007  Aerospace Education Center     11/16
00009  WTBS Channel 5 TV              12/03
00016  Jana's Management Consultants  01/06
00019  Roger, Roger & Ray, Inc.       12/15
.
```

FIGURE 2.18
Looking at the COMPANY database— a simple use of the LIST command

to indicate whether the record is to be displayed on the screen. Therefore, with the FOR option, you are permitted to search a database selectively.

The FOR option follows the form for relational expressions. The permitted relational operators and their meanings are presented in Table 2.5.

In Figure 2.18, the FOR option is stated as "for status = 'Rejected'." This means that you want to search the COMPANY database and produce the "co:name" and "resume:ack" fields for all records that indicate that your job

TABLE 2.5 Relational Operators Used in a FOR Option

Relational Operator	Meaning
>	Greater than (for example, 500 > 300)
>=	Greater than or equal to (for example, 500 > 300; 500 = 500)
=	Equal to (for example, 500 = 500)
<> or #	Not equal to (for example, 500 <> 300)
<=	Less than or equal to (for example, 300 < 500; 300 = 300)
<	Less than (for example, 300 < 500)

TABLE 2.6 Logical Operators Used in a FOR Option

Logical Operator	Meaning
.OR.	Either relational expression may be true for the entire expression to be considered true.
.AND.	Both relational expressions must be true for the entire expression to be considered true.
.NOT.	The first relational expression must be true, but not the second, for the entire expression to be considered true; or the first relational expression must not be true for the expression to be considered true (unary .NOT. — .NOT. relational expression).

application has been "rejected." The FOR portion of the expression identifies a field name ("status") associated with the COMPANY database. The relational operator (=) is obvious — equal to. "Rejected" indicates a constant; in other words, you are looking for *all* records with a status of "rejected." Compare the list shown in Figure 2.18 with the known contents of the COMPANY database. Only those companies that have rejected your application are listed. (Note that WTBS Channel 5 TV is included in the list of company names, because its status was changed earlier.)

The logical operators used to combine relational expressions to create logical expressions in dBASE are shown in Table 2.6.

Eliminating Records from the Database — The DELETE, PACK, and RECALL Commands

The job hunting problem requires that you remove unwanted records from the COMPANY database. As previously mentioned in conjunction with the BROWSE and EDIT commands, it is possible to "mark" a record for deletion by using the CTRL-U key sequence. However, this isn't the only way to delete records within a database. You can also mark a record for deletion by using the DELETE command. The format of this command is DELETE [scope] [FOR expression] [WHILE expression]. When the DELETE command is entered, each record identified by the scope, FOR, or WHILE option is marked for deletion. The WHILE option indicates that all records are to be marked so long as the specified expression is true.

dBASE III

```
. LIST CO_NAME, RESUME_ACK FOR STATUS = "Rejected"
Record#  CO_NAME                          RESUME_ACK
      7 *Aerospace Education Center      11/16
      9 *WTBS Channel 5 TV               12/03
     16 *Jana's Management Consultants   01/06
     19 *Roger, Roger & Ray, Inc.        12/15
.
```

dBASE II

```
. LIST CO:NAME, RESUME:ACK FOR STATUS = "Rejected"
00007 *Aerospace Education Center     11/16
00009 *WTBS Channel 5 TV              12/03
00016 *Jana's Management Consultants  01/06
00019 *Roger, Roger & Ray, Inc.       12/15
.
```

FIGURE 2.19
List of "rejected" companies marked for deletion

There are a number of ways to delete unwanted records from the COMPANY database using the DELETE comand. One approach might be to locate the records to be deleted by using the LIST command, as illustrated in Figure 2.18. The Aerospace Education Center record is identified as record number 7. Thus, the command DELETE RECORD 7 marks this record for deletion. This operation is then performed for the other records in the list to mark them for deletion. (However, it would be easier to enter the command DELETE FOR STATUS = 'Rejected'.)

Now look at Figure 2.19. The list of the company names in the database indicates that all "rejected" records appear with an adjacent asterisk (*)—they have been marked for deletion but have not yet been removed. The PACK command can now be used to remove these records physically. After the PACK operation has been performed, the listing of company names shows that the "rejected" records have been removed from the database.

Finally, suppose you make a mistake and mark the wrong record for deletion. This problem is easily solved. If you want to return a marked record to a fully active status, all you have to do is enter the RECALL command. The format of this command is highly similar to the DELETE command: RECALL [scope] [FOR expression] [WHILE expression]. Thus, by using the RECALL command, records that have been marked for deletion can be "unmarked." *Note:* You must use the RECALL command *before* you use the PACK command. After the PACK command has been used and the records have been deleted, the RECALL command cannot restore them.

If you want to eliminate an entire database, enter the command: DELETE FILE filename. Obviously, you should use this command cautiously. Database files are not marked as are records; they are immediately eliminated. (Of course, you could always remove a file by using the operating system command for deletion.)

Building, Specifying, and Using Indexes — The INDEX, USE, and SET INDEX Commands

Recall that the data in the database has a particular order — the order in which records are entered into the database. However, there are times when it is desirable to access the records in a sequence other than their entry sequence. For dBASE to access the data in an order other than the entry order, an index must first be created and identified, otherwise the data must be actually sorted — that is, physically reordered. This section describes how the indexing process works.

Any number of indexes may be created for a single database and used either individually or jointly. To create an index for a currently active database, the INDEX command is used. INDEX creates a retrieval sequence by which data can be accessed, but, at the same time, the original physical order of the database is not altered. The format of this command is INDEX ON expression TO indexfile. The expression portion of this command identifies the characteristics by which the database is to be indexed. The expression can be as simple as a field name or more complicated (for example, multiple fields added together, such as OFFER + LIFE:INS + HEALTH:INS + RETIRE). For the job hunting problem, a single field will suffice.

The INDEX command produces an index file. An index file is a file name under which an index (a sequence of record numbers) is recorded. An index file may be any file name permitted by the operating system; however, the extension name ".NDX" will be automatically provided by dBASE. Thus, index files are distinguished by their extension name from other files used by dBASE. To illustrate the use of the INDEX command, suppose you entered the following: INDEX ON ZIP TO B:ZIP. Assuming that COMPANY is the currently active database, dBASE will examine the contents of the "ZIP" field and create a sequence of record addresses that will allow you to access records in an ascending order (from smallest to largest), based on the zip code value. These addresses will then be stored in the index file called ZIP.NDX on disk drive B. After the indexing operation has been completed, dBASE will respond with a message such as 00015 RECORDS INDEXED.

The INDEX command generates only an index file. It does not "activate" that file for use. To operate with an indexed database, use one of two commands: the USE command or the SET INDEX command. You will recall that the format of the USE command is USE [filename] [INDEX indexfile1 [,indexfile2] . . .]. Previously, this command was used to access a particular database. However, if you are using the INDEX option, you will access the database records in the order of the index file named. Thus, a command such as USE B:COMPANY INDEX B:ZIP would give you access to records in the COMPANY database in zip code order.

Suppose a database is already in use and you want to access the data in an index order. Reentering the USE command is redundant in this case. Instead, you could use the SET INDEX command. The format of this command is SET INDEX TO indexfile1 [indexfile2] . . . . All that is required to establish or change an index file for a currently active database is the SET INDEX command. Thus, a command such as SET INDEX TO B:ZIP could be used to specify an index file if the COMPANY database was currently active.

One final note about the index files that are listed by either the USE or the SET INDEX command: If more than one index file name is specified by the USE or SET INDEX command, only the first index file is used for accessing the records. The other index files are used only in the event reindexing is necessary. Reindexing is necessary after records are added to or deleted from a database. The command to perform this function is REINDEX. When this command is entered, all active indexes are automatically updated (into the current index file names) to reflect the presence of new records or the absence of deleted records.

Now that you can use an index file, how will this help you? Perhaps this question is best answered by examining the effect of an index on the LIST command. Look at Figure 2.20 (the INDEX and SET INDEX commands are included here only for purposes of clarity). Once an index has been declared, it remains active until another index is identified or the database is closed. Although you are presented with somewhat abbreviated contents of each record (by the FIELDS option), one fact is clear. The records are presented in order by the value of the "ZIP" field. Note that the record numbers are not in order. This is because the record numbers are associated with the entry order of the database, not the indexed order.

An Ordered Database from Old Data—The SORT Command

Perhaps after you have had the opportunity to use a database for a while, you find that the entry order is not to your liking. Or perhaps you entered data into the original database in a haphazard manner, and now that all the data has been entered, you want to create a new database (containing the same data) in a more useful order. For example, you can produce customer invoices in any order. However, in one case, you want the data for the invoices ordered by invoice number; in another situation, you want it in customer-number order. One way to change the order is to use the SORT command.

The SORT command is capable of accepting data contained in one database, ordering it, and placing the ordered data into another database. The format of this command is SORT ON fieldname TO filename [ASCENDING/

dBASE III

```
. INDEX ON ZIP TO B:ZIP
     15 records indexed
. LIST CO_NAME, CONTACT, CITY, STATE, ZIP FOR STATUS = 'Offered'
Record#  CO_NAME                        CONTACT                        CITY
       STATE   ZIP
      5  Lewis & Melts Mortgage Co.     Mrs. Roberta Accure            Denton
       TX    76202
      1  Johnson Instruments, Inc.      Personnel Department           Dallas
       TX    76234
      4  First State National Bank      Ms. Judith Welpit              Dallas
       TX    76243
     15  Matt's Films, Inc.             Personnel Office               Dallas
       TX    76341
      8  Hormell Texas Chili Company    Mr. Foster Brooks              Ft. Worth
       TX    76907
      6  Ethyl & Jung, DDS              Dr. Emil Franz Jung            Dennison
       OK    79034
     12  Nephi's Hopi Crafts            Mrs. Carletta Whitecloud       Tulsa
       OK    79345
. COUNT FOR STATUS = 'Offered'
      7 records
.
```

dBASE II

```
. INDEX ON ZIP TO B:ZIP
00015 RECORDS INDEXED
. LIST CO:NAME, CONTACT, CITY, STATE, ZIP FOR STATUS = "Offered"
00005  Lewis & Melts Mortgage Co.     Mrs. Roberta Accure            Denton
    TX  76202
00001  Johnson Instruments, Inc.      Personnel Department           Dallas
    TX  76234
00004  First State National Bank      Ms. Judith Welpit              Dallas
    TX  76243
00015  Matt's Films, Inc.             Personnel Office               Dallas
    TX  76341
00008  Hormell Texas Chili Company    Mr. Foster Brooks              Ft. Worth
    TX  76907
00006  Ethyl & Jung, DDS              Dr. Emil Franz Jung            Dennison
    OK  79034
00012  Nephi's Hopi Crafts            Mrs. Carletta Whitecloud       Tulsa
    OK  79345
. COUNT FOR STATUS = "Offered"
COUNT = 00007
.
```

FIGURE 2.20
Creating a database INDEX — using the "ZIP" field

descending]. When you use the SORT command, you must specify a field name from the currently active database that represents the sort key—the field by which the data is to be sorted. Next, you must identify the file (by name) into which the sorted data is to be placed. dBASE will create this file (with a ".DBF" extension) when the sorting operation has been completed. Finally, you may need to specify the sorting sequence. As indicated in the format of the command, the default sequence is ASCENDING—from smallest value to largest in the specified field. If you want the reverse order, you must specify DESCENDING—from largest to smallest. The field name can be any field that exists in the database structure, whether the field type is numeric or character.

If you want to produce a database ordered by the "ZIP" fields, the command would be SORT ON ZIP TO B:ZIP. dBASE immediately proceeds to sort the data, based on an ascending sequence of values in the "ZIP" field, in the current (COMPANY) database. When the sorting operation has been completed, a new DBF file, called ZIP, will be created on drive B and dBASE will display the message SORT COMPLETE. To access the new database, you must first indicate that ZIP should be the current database. Thus, enter the command USE B:ZIP. Otherwise, COMPANY will remain the current database.

Note that both a database file and an index file can exist on the same disk, using the same name (for example, ZIP). This is because a database file uses the extension ".DBF," whereas the index file uses the ".NDX" extension. One final note of caution. Several index files have been used in conjunction with the COMPANY database. These indexes are useful only with that database and should not be used in conjunction with the ZIP database. The record sequence of the new database is not the same as that for COMPANY. Therefore, any use of the previous indexes will result in logical sequence errors much the same as those produced after inserting a new record into an existing database but before reindexing.

dBASE II is limited to a single sort key; however, dBASE III has no such limitation. In addition, dBASE II must place all records in the current database into the new, sorted database; dBASE III, on the other hand, does not have this limitation. The format of the SORT command for dBASE III is SORT TO filename ON fieldname1 [/A] [/D] [fieldname2 [/A] [/D] . . . [scope] [FOR expression]. Note that in the dBASE III version, the filename has been moved toward the front of the command, followed by one or more sort keys. The first key identifies the major (most global) sort sequence, and other keys (if specified) identify minor keys. The minor key is important only if the major key data value for two or more records is the same. Then the data is ordered on the basis of the minor key for that subset of records. Following each field name is an indication of the direction of ordering—/A for ascending (the default order) and /D for descending. The newer version of the SORT command also provides you with the ability to limit the number of records placed into the sorted database by specifying either a scope or a FOR option (or both).

Note that in Figure 2.20 the data is ordered (using an index) only by the

"ZIP" field. The fact that the city names are grouped (Dallas) is only an accident—based on how zip codes are assigned. Even if you had chosen to create an index by city names and use it as a secondary index, the primary index is the only one that arranges the data. Furthermore, if a sort was used to order the data (using dBASE II), it would take two separate sorting operations, one on each key, or one sort operation followed by an index operation to achieve a zip code and city sequence absolutely. Only with the sort options provided by dBASE III can this operation be performed in a single step.

Building Readable Reports—The REPORT Command

To print reports, dBASE uses the REPORT command. The format of the dBASE II command is REPORT [FORM filename] [scope] [TO PRINT] [FOR expression] [PLAIN]. This command is used to recall a report file name and print the specified report.

Before using the REPORT command, you must build a report file name. If you enter the command REPORT, dBASE II assumes you wish to create a report file. dBASE will then provide a series of prompts (ask a series of questions) directing you toward the creation of a report file (see Figure 2.21). You will first be asked to provide a file name for the report FORM. Respond with any file name permitted by the operating system, and dBASE will add the extension ".FRM," which designates the file as a report FORM. In this example, the report FORM file name is OFFERS, and it will be stored on drive B.

The next prompt provides you with the opportunity to establish the characteristics of the printed page. If you want to identify the location of the left margin (M), number of printed lines per page (L), or page width (W), you may do so. (The default settings for the options are M=8, L=57, and W=80.) In the example, M=1 indicates that the report is to begin in the first column or at the left margin, and a maximum of 50 lines are to be printed per page (L=50). The default width of 80 characters is also used. (If you enter information for more than one option, you can separate the entries by either a comma or a space.)

The series of prompts continues with the characteristics controlling the appearance of the printed report. The next question asks if you want a heading at the top of each printed page. If you respond with "Y," the next prompt will ask you for the text of the heading. (If you respond with "N" to this or other questions, intermediate prompts are omitted.) In the example, the heading "Current Offers Received" was selected. This heading will be centered at the top of each printed page. If you want to have the report double-spaced, you should respond with "Y" to the next question (the default is for a single-spaced report). If you want totals of particular numeric data items, respond with "Y" to the next question.

The next series of prompts deal with the definition of the fields to be printed. Each field, referred to in the format as a print COLumn, is automatically assigned a number starting with 001, in a manner similar to the way the structure of a database is built. You must supply both the WIDTH of the field (in columns that are to appear in the report) and the CONTENTS associated with each position on the report. The WIDTH may be the same, greater, or smaller than the width of the data to be placed into the field. CONTENTS may be database field names or possibly other identifiers (to be illustrated later) that specify the data to be printed in the indicated position.

In the example, "30,CO:NAME" was supplied for the first field, indicating that you wish the field to be 30 columns wide and you want the data in the database field name "CO:NAME" to appear in this position. Recall from previous discussions of the structure of the COMPANY database that the field called "CO:NAME" can contain data up to 30 columns wide. If dBASE encounters a data value wider than 30 characters when producing the report, it will print the data on two (or more) lines. To make the printed report readable, you should closely examine the WIDTH of each field when designing a report form.

After you have indicated the width and the field name to be used for the first report field, dBASE will ask you for a HEADING. This heading is a column

dBASE III

```
. CREATE REPORT
Enter report file name:B:OFFERS
```

dBASE II

```
. REPORT
ENTER REPORT FORM NAME: B:OFFERS
ENTER OPTIONS, M=LEFT MARGIN, L=LINES/PAGE, W=PAGE WIDTH M=1,L=50
PAGE HEADING? (Y/N) Y
ENTER PAGE HEADING: Current Offers Received
DOUBLE SPACE REPORT? (Y/N) Y
ARE TOTALS REQUIRED? (Y/N) N
COL     WIDTH,CONTENTS
001     30,CO:NAME
ENTER HEADING: Company Name
002     20,CONTACT
ENTER HEADING: Contact Name
003     15,CITY
ENTER HEADING: City
004     2,STATE
ENTER HEADING: State
005     5,ZIP
ENTER HEADING: Zip Code
006
```

FIGURE 2.21
Creating a REPORT FORM file *(above and right)*

dBASE III

```
Structure of file B:COMPANY.dbf
CO_NAME     C  30 | ZIP        N   5 | INT_APP    C   8 |
CO_ADDRESS  C  30 | CONTACT    C  30 |                  |
CITY        C  15 | RESUME_ACK C   8 |                  |
STATE       C   2 | STATUS     C  10 |                  |

                                   Field  5         Columns left =   6
      Contact Name               City           State ------

XXXXXX XXXXXXXXXXXXXXXXXXXXXXXXXXXXXX XXXXXXXXXXXXXXX XX

Field        ZIP
```

```
Structure of file B:COMPANY.dbf
CO_NAME     C  30 | ZIP        N   5 | INT_APP    C   8 |
CO_ADDRESS  C  30 | CONTACT    C  30 |                  |
CITY        C  15 | RESUME_ACK C   8 |                  |
STATE       C   2 | STATUS     C  10 |                  |

                                   Field  1         Columns left =  90
------------------------------------------------------------------------

Field        CO_NAME
```

```
Structure of file B:COMPANY.dbf
CO_NAME     C  30 | ZIP        N   5 | INT_APP    C   8 |
```

```
Structure of file B:COMPANY.dbf
CO_NAME     C  30 | ZIP        N   5 | INT_APP    C   8 |
CO_ADDRESS  C  30 | CONTACT    C  30 |                  |
CITY        C  15 | RESUME_ACK C   8 |                  |
STATE       C   2 | STATUS     C  10 |                  |

                        Page heading:

     Current Offers Received

              Page width (# chars):          90
              Left margin (# chars):          0
              Right margin (# chars):         0
              # lines/page:                  50
              Double space report? (Y/N):     Y
```

heading to be printed above the associated column of data. For the first field, the appropriate column heading could be "Company Name." If you use a heading that is wider than the field, dBASE will automatically chop what you have provided into pieces so that it will fit above the column, even though it may have to be printed on more than one line. (For example, the heading for the last field is "Zip Code," which cannot possibly be printed in 5 columns on one line. Thus, it is broken into two parts and printed on two consecutive lines.) When you have finally completed your description of the report, you will be presented with yet another field number (006 in the example). To conclude building a report form, all you must do is press the RETURN key without entering information related to another field, and dBASE will assume you wish to terminate the report definition.

The dBASE III process of creating a report form is much different. dBASE III uses the CREATE REPORT command to build a report form and the REPORT command to print the form. As shown in Figure 2.21, once the report form name B:OFFERS has been entered, you are provided with a series of screens designed to assist you in building the report form. The first screen asks you to indicate the page heading and page size characteristics. You are provided with four lines into which the page heading can be entered.

After the page heading and size characteristics have been provided, you will be asked to supply group and subgroup total information. Totals are not required for the current report, and pressing the RETURN key will cause the next screen to appear. However, if totals are desired, you can specify the field names or other conditions on which a group (or subgroup) total is produced (a change in field name value causes the group to be printed). Then you can indicate if the complete report or only the totals are to be printed and if each group is to begin a new page. You can also enter the heading to be printed for each group (or subgroup).

The screen that follows the total information is repeated for each field to be printed in the report. You are provided with a complete list of field names and their characteristics at the top of the screen. The field information is followed by a status line, indicating which field you are to describe and the remaining length of the print line. The second part of the status line indicates where the field and its heading are to be printed. You begin your entries on this screen with the specification of the "Field contents." As with dBASE II, a field may be composed of a field name or an arithmetic expression that includes field names. Next, you should indicate if the field contains other than the default number of decimal places and if a total is required for this field. Then you should supply the "Field header" (column heading) for the field. Note that you may use up to four lines to describe the field header. Finally, the "Width" of the report field will default to the width of whichever is greater: the field name or the field header. Although you are permitted to modify the field width, any value smaller than the width of the field name or the field header—whichever is larger—will be ignored. Thus, unlike dBASE II, dBASE III must produce the complete field width—dBASE III does not wrap the data value or the column heading on multiple lines of the report. However, the report form created by dBASE III can be changed by using a MODIFY REPORT command (dBASE II does not provide this feature).

Immediately on completion of the REPORT prompting sequence, the report itself will be produced on the screen. This will permit you to make a visual inspection of the report form you have designed to decide if alterations are necessary.

Remember that this report form has been saved in a file called OFFERS.FRM on drive B. If you decide to use it again, you don't have to repeat the creation process. All you have to do is call for it. To produce the report shown in Figure 2.22, the command REPORT FORM B:OFFERS TO PRINT FOR STATUS = 'Offered' for dBASE II and REPORT FORM B:OFFERS FOR STATUS = 'Offered' TO PRINT for dBASE III was entered. Thus, you have recalled the OFFERS report form, indicated that it is to be sent to the printer rather than the screen, and only the record containing a "STATUS" of "Offered" should be printed.

The page number and the current date will automatically be produced at the top of each page— that is, unless you use the PLAIN option. Next, you can see that the report heading is centered, and each column of data has an appropriate column heading. Note that the column headings "State" and "Zip Code" could not be produced over the indicated field width, so they have been broken into parts. Also note the data placed under the "Contact Name" heading for the last record. The report definition of this field is 20 characters wide. The database definition of this field is 30 characters. Because the data within the "CONTACT" field wouldn't fit into the indicated print-field width, it was printed on two adjacent lines. Finally, note the order of the data in the report. Although you may not be able to establish exactly the order of the data on the basis of the fields that have been produced, the last time you accessed COMPANY you were using the ZIP index. A careful inspection of the zip codes should reveal that the report is ordered.

Now compare the output produced in Figure 2.20 with that shown in Figure 2.22. Which one would you want to use? Both contain exactly the same results, but the report presented in Figure 2.22 is much more readable.

Making One New Database from Two — The JOIN Command

What do you do when you want to manipulate the data in two (or more) databases at the same time? Depending on how difficult the manipulation is and how often you need the information, you might decide to create a new database based on data in two existing databases. This operation is performed by the JOIN command. The format of this command is JOIN TO filename FOR expression [FIELDS fieldlist]. The JOIN command creates a new database with the indicated file name based on the FOR expression. The new database will be

dBASE III

```
Page No.     1
01/01/87
                          Current Offers Received

Company Name               Contact Name               City          State  Zip
                                                                           Code

Lewis & Melts Mortgage Co.  Mrs. Roberta Accure       Denton        TX     76202
```

dBASE II

```
PAGE NO. 00001
01/01/87
                        Current Offers Received

     Company Name              Contact Name           City      St  Zip
                                                                at  Code
                                                                 e
Lewis & Melts Mortgage Co.  Mrs. Roberta Accure  Denton         TX 76202
Johnson Instruments, Inc.   Personnel Department Dallas         TX 76234
First State National Bank   Ms. Judith Welpit    Dallas         TX 76243
Matt's Films, Inc.          Personnel Office     Dallas         TX 76341
Hormell Texas Chili Company Mr. Foster Brooks    Ft. Worth      TX 76907
Ethyl & Jung, DDS           Dr. Emil Franz Jung  Dennison       OK 79034
Nephi's Hopi Crafts         Mrs. Carletta        Tulsa          OK 79345
                            Whitecloud
```

FIGURE 2.22
A printed report produced from a report form

composed of all the fields in the "most active" database, unless the FIELDS option is used to identify which fields should be placed into the new database.

The "most active" database designation depends on whether you are using dBASE II or dBASE III. In dBASE II, you are permitted to have only two databases active at one time. dBASE III allows up to ten active databases at once. A database is activated by employing the USE command. However, if you enter two USE commands in a row, you will have only one active database, because the USE command normally closes all previously opened databases. Thus, you must employ the SELECT command to indicate that you want more than one active database. The format of the SELECT command for dBASE II is SELECT [PRIMARY] [SECONDARY]; the same command for dBASE III is SELECT [number] [filename].

For an illustration of the use of the SELECT command, see Figure 2.23. The first command in the sequence is USE B:JOBS. Unless dBASE II is instructed to the contrary, B:JOBS is the PRIMARY database. Entering another USE command at this point would result in a new PRIMARY database. However, in the illustration, the command SELECT SECONDARY has been entered. As a result, the next USE command entered will cause the database to be designated as a SECONDARY database. Thus, in the illustration, COMPANY is the SECONDARY database. Based on this use of SELECT and USE commands, the "most active" database is the last one selected. At this point, the most active database is COMPANY. However, this is changed by the SELECT PRIMARY command, which indicates that JOBS is to become the most active database. The SELECT command can be used to switch the activity level between the two databases. If you were using dBASE III, a similar command sequence might be:

```
USE B:JOBS
SELECT 2
USE B:COMPANY
SELECT 1
```

dBASE III

```
. USE B:JOBS
. SELECT 2
. USE B:COMPANY
. SELECT 1
. JOIN WITH COMPANY TO B:GOOD FOR CO_NAME = COMPANY->CO_NAME .AND. ;
COMPANY->STATUS = 'Offered' .AND. OFFER > 19000 ;
FIELDS CO_NAME, OFFER, PREFERENCE, SITE, LIFE_INS, HEALTH_INS, RETIRE
```

dBASE II

```
. USE B:JOBS
. SELECT SECONDARY
. USE B:COMPANY
. SELECT PRIMARY
. JOIN TO B:GOOD FOR P.CO:NAME = S.CO:NAME .AND. S.STATUS = "Offered" .AND. ;
OFFER > 19000 FIELDS CO:NAME, OFFER, PREFERENCE, SITE, LIFE:INS, ;
HEALTH:INS, RETIRE
```

FIGURE 2.23
Using the JOIN and SELECT commands to create a new database

or, more simply,

```
SELECT B:COMPANY
SELECT B:JOBS
```

What happens if you have the same field name in two or more databases? In dBASE II, you may "qualify" or clarify a field name by indicating whether it comes from the PRIMARY (P) or SECONDARY (S) database. Again, look at Figure 2.23. Note that a portion of the FOR option is stated as P.CO:NAME = S.CO:NAME. This indicates that the field name "CO:NAME" appears in both databases. The prefix "P." indicates that you want to reference the field in the PRIMARY database, while "S." indicates a reference to the SECONDARY database field name. To qualify a field name in dBASE III, use the file name followed by the character sequence "->"—indicating that the field name should be referenced from that particular file name. Thus, if you were using dBASE III, this portion of the FOR expression might appear as JOBS->CO_NAME = COMPANY->CO_NAME. (Note that the dBASE III field names are slightly different in that they use an underline rather than a colon.)

What is the function of the particular JOIN command indicated? Because the FOR expression indicates that you want to retrieve records that have the same company names from both databases, only those records that match this condition will appear in the B:GOOD database. In addition, these records are to be placed into the new database only if the job "STATUS" is "offered" and the amount of the "OFFER" is greater than $19,000. Furthermore, note that the field names identified in the JOIN command come from both databases. Thus, by this method, one-to-one and one-to-many relationships can be established within dBASE. Finally, note that the FIELDS option indicates only some of the fields in the JOBS database are copied to the GOOD database.

The final requirement for the job hunting problem is to produce a report containing only "good" offers, ordered by "PREFERENCE" and "CO:NAME." The ordering is partially achieved by creating an index for the GOOD database on the "PREFERENCE" field. (The database could be first sorted on the "CO:NAME" field to guarantee the desired sequence.) Thereafter, a report form is created, as shown in Figure 2.24. The new report form is called GOOD. You are permitted to use the same database file name, index name, and report form name because each has a different file name extension. Within the report, a "Net Offer" field is created by summing the values of "OFFER," "LIFE:INS," "HEALTH:INS," and "RETIRE" for each record reported. Finally, the actual report containing these "good" offers is shown in Figure 2.25. Note that although there are several entries in the COMPANY and JOBS databases, only a few selected records meet all the established criteria. Furthermore, notice that both jobs from Johnson Instruments, Inc., are listed—verifying that a one-to-many check has been made between the COMPANY and the JOBS databases.

dBASE III

```
Structure of file B:GOOD.dbf

CO_NAME     C  30    LIFE_INS    N   8  2
OFFER       N   8  2 HEALTH_INS  N   8  2
PREFERENCE  N   1    RETIRE      N   8  2
SITE        C  10

                                         Field  4              Columns left =   27
>>>>>>>>>>Company Name                     Dollar   Pr ----------------------------
                                           Offer    ef

          XXXXXXXXXXXXXXXXXXXXXXXXXXXXXX 99999.99  9

Field          OFFER+LIFE_INS+HEALTH_INS+RETIRE
  contents
```

```
Structure of file B:GOOD.dbf

CO_NAME     C  30    LIFE_INS    N   8  2
```

```
Structure of file B:GOOD.dbf

CO_NAME     C  30    LIFE_INS    N   8  2
OFFER       N   8  2 HEALTH_INS  N   8  2
PREFERENCE  N   1    RETIRE      N   8  2
SITE        C  10

                        Page heading:

        Preferred Job Offers

                 Page width (# chars):             80
                 Left margin (# chars):            10
                 Right margin (# chars):            0
                 # lines/page:                     50
                 Double space report? (Y/N):        Y
```

dBASE II

```
. REPORT
ENTER REPORT FORM NAME: B:GOOD
ENTER OPTIONS, M=LEFT MARGIN, L=LINES/PAGE, W=PAGE WIDTH M=10,L=50
PAGE HEADING? (Y/N) Y
ENTER PAGE HEADING: Preferred Job Offers
DOUBLE SPACE REPORT? (Y/N) Y
ARE TOTALS REQUIRED? (Y/N) N
COL     WIDTH,CONTENTS
001     30,CO:NAME
ENTER HEADING: Company Name
002     9,OFFER
ENTER HEADING: Dollar Offer
003     2,PREFERENCE
ENTER HEADING: Pref.
004     9,OFFER+LIFE:INS+HEALTH:INS+RETIRE
ENTER HEADING: Net Offer
005
```

FIGURE 2.24
Creating REPORT FORM for "good" job offers

dBASE III

```
Page No.      1
01/01/87
                         Preferred Job Offers

Company Name                        Dollar Pr   Net Offer
                                     Offer ef


Lewis & Melts Mortgage Co.        22000.00  1    27500.00
```

dBASE II

```
PAGE NO. 00001
01/01/87

                         Preferred Job Offers


        Company Name                 Dollar    Pr Net Offer
                                      Offer    ef


Lewis & Melts Mortgage Co.          22000.00  1  27500.00

Ethyl & Jung, DDS                   20000.00  1  27275.00

Hormell Texas Chili Company         19300.00  1  21986.20

First State National Bank           22000.00  2  25485.00

Johnson Instruments, Inc.           19200.00  4  23022.00

Johnson Instruments, Inc.           19100.00  5  22922.00
```

FIGURE 2.25
Printing the "good" job offers report

Other Features of dBASE II and dBASE III

Perhaps while you were examining Figure 2.20 you noticed that the command COUNT FOR STATUS = 'Offered' was used, and the result of the operation was COUNT = 00007. This represents one of the additional features contained within dBASE. Obviously, the COUNT command counts the records within a database that match a particular set of conditions. The format of the COUNT command is COUNT [scope] [FOR expression] [TO variable], where scope and the FOR option are used in the same way as previously discussed. However, the TO option is new. When this option is added to the command, not only is a count performed but the results of that count are placed into a memory variable (see the following) and can later be recalled for viewing or used in other manipulations.

COUNT is not the only arithmetic command available within dBASE. You may also find the SUM command useful. The format of this command is SUM fieldname1 [fieldname2] . . . [scope] [FOR condition] [TO variable1 [variable2] . . .]. The command permits you to accumulate the values of a field (or list of fields). This total can also be saved as a memory variable.

What are *memory variables?* Memory variables are held in a "scratch pad" area and retained by dBASE, as they are created, for the duration of the dBASE session (or until a CLEAR or RELEASE command is entered). By using memory variables, you can keep track of particular statistics retrieved from a database or simply record "reminders" that you might want to refer to later. Memory variables can be created by the COUNT and SUM commands. However, they can also be created directly by the STORE command. The format of this command is STORE expression TO variable, where the expression may be the name of another variable, a character string, or an arithmetic expression. For example, suppose you entered the following commands while using the GOOD database:

```
COUNT ALL TO NO:OFFERS
SUM OFFER TO TOT:OFFERS
STORE 'Average Offer' TO TITLE
STORE TOT:OFFERS / NO:OFFERS TO AVJ:OFFER
```

This means that you would count the total number of records in the GOOD database, total "OFFER" for all records, store the character string "Average Offer," and calculate and store the average value of an offer.

If you want to recall any of the memory variables for later viewing, all you have to do is enter the "?" symbol, followed by the memory variable name. Thus you might enter ? AVJ:OFFER. In addition, you can use the ? command to perform arithmetic manipulations directly. For example, if you enter the command ? AVJ:OFFER / 12 you can determine an average monthly income. Finally, if you forget the names of memory variables or if you want to retrieve all memory variables and their values, simply enter DISPLAY MEMORY, and all memory variables and their values will be produced on the screen.

The last feature of dBASE to be mentioned here is its associated procedural language. dBASE will permit you to enter a series of commands (including many of those previously discussed plus many more) and save them as a procedure, or a program. This enables you to create procedures that will be frequently used, save them, and recall them for execution. Such procedures can eliminate the need for continually reentering the same commands time after time to retrieve frequently needed information. However, because programming is beyond the scope of this text, you should read a dBASE manual if you want more information about this procedural language. The manual also includes information about building screen formats (like report forms) for the data entry or the display of records in a database.

Special Features of dBase III

A special feature included only in dBASE III is the "Assistance" feature—also known as command ASSIST. The assistance feature converts many of the commands of dBASE III from a command-driven approach to a menu-driven approach. To use this feature, enter the command ASSIST when the "." prompt is the last character on the screen. You will be provided with some preliminary instructions and then a menu of general choices. The selection of a general choice results in a submenu, which usually provides a list of commands. Selections are made by moving the cursor and pressing the RETURN key, and all that is necessary thereafter is to answer prompting questions. To get an idea of how the assistance feature works, examine the report creation sequences shown in Figures 2.21 and 2.24.

In addition to providing assistance that makes using the package easier and increasing the size and number of relations that can be active at any one time, dBASE III has many added features that make it a more powerful package than dBASE II. The DATE data type, which is unique to dBASE III, also has a complete set of functions associated with it that allow you to display the day of the week (CDOW) and the month (CMONTH) and convert a date field to character form (DTOC) or a character field to date form (DTOC). The MEMO data type, also unique to dBASE III, is used to hold text/character data that contains more than 50 characters.

The SORT command has been improved in dBase III so that it can sort on more than one field in a single operation. To list the contents of your database you no longer have to SET PRINT ON. In dBASE III you can LIST or DISPLAY . . . TO PRINT. The TO PRINT option will automatically SET PRINT ON, perform the desired operation, and then SET PRINT OFF. The ZAP command is an addition that must be used carefully. Using this command has the same effect as issuing a DELETE ALL command followed by the PACK command. It will remove *all* the records contained in your database.

Uses of Databases

Now that you have been introduced to many of the characteristics of databases and database management systems, you're probably asking yourself: What good are they? Who can use them? Are they limited to those companies or organizations with large amounts of data to store and maintain? How can they be used in the world in which you live? The answer to all these questions is quite simple: Anyone can use a database package to store and manipulate data, whether data needs are great or small.

Brokerage firms use databases to keep records of stock activities. In some cases, the information obtained from these historical records is used to "predict" growth stocks and stocks that will be taking a turn for the worse.

Many organizations use databases to keep track of their inventory. For example, libraries frequently use databases to maintain inventories of books and other holdings. By using a database, the librarian can keep track of when books are checked out and returned, determine what types of books are frequently used (for example, mysteries, fiction, and nonfiction), determine usage patterns for particular types of books, establish which users frequent the library and which ones tend to be delinquent in returning books, perform searches for particular types of references, and so on.

Banks use databases to keep track of your checking accounts, savings account, IRAs, and loans. They also keep track of your credit history and the amount of money due the federal government because of the interest you earned on the money you invested.

Hospitals use databases to keep track of patients, bed utilization, drug distribution, physician performance, and billing. In some cases, hospitals are using databases to keep track of intensive care patients not only by monitoring their progress, but also by scheduling needed resources for their care. Resources like drug administration, physician visits, diet preparation, and physical therapy routines can also be monitored and scheduled.

Police units throughout the nation are using databases to track criminal patterns, types of crimes, and various violations, such as parking tickets. This data is stored and shared with law enforcement departments nationwide, including the FBI.

Museums use databases to keep track of their inventory. Some art galleries keep track of their artists, clients, holdings, and show schedules. Of course, like other organizations, museums and galleries also keep record of billing and accounts payable.

What about the individual? How can *you* use a database? How about keeping a log of all the checks you've written? You could keep track of your individual investments. Or how about a list of all the companies you have written to in search of a job? Or, perhaps, you could keep records on the books in your personal library—author, title, and person who has borrowed the book. Maybe you want to keep track of your classmates, maintain a list of credit cards and account numbers, have a mailing list for Christmas cards, and so on.

No matter what line of work you are in, no matter how large an organization you belong to, you will find that using databases will help you in keeping track of the data you will need to make decisions. Databases and database management systems are useful today; they are not coming into use, they are in use.

Guidelines for the Evaluation of Databases

Before you select a database package for your own use, familiarize yourself with the following questions you should ask about it:

- **Help facility** How extensive is the Help feature? Does it handle processes such as building, altering, and searching a database? Can it be accessed when needed?
- **Documentation** How complete is the documentation? Is it written in understandable terms? Is it organized in a useful manner? Does it provide tips or suggestions on how a database should be created, altered, and so on? Does the package come with a tutorial?
- **Package orientation** Is the package oriented toward commands or menus? Are the commands natural and meaningful to use? Is it obvious which parts of a command are required and which are optional? Under what conditions would they be used? Are menus easy to understand and well organized? Is it easy to get from one menu to another? Are the menus logically related to one another? Are the options easy to select?
- **Creating a database** What is the database creation process like? Do you have to know how the process works, or does the package lead you through the process? How many entities are permitted? How many attributes? What are the limitations on attribute names? What data types (alphabetic, numeric, logical, date) are permitted? What are the maximum lengths for each data type? Are default lengths available?
- **Data entry** What options are available? Can you create a data entry form into which data can be entered? Does the package automatically prompt you with the attribute name, data type, and length? Can entries be corrected while you are entering them? Are rules available that limit what types of values can be placed into an attribute? Does the package automatically advance to the next attribute once you have finished the one you are working on?
- **Data editing** Once data has been placed into a database, how difficult is it to change an attribute value? Is there more than one way to change an attribute value? Can entities be added? Can they be added at any location you choose? What is involved to delete an entity? Are the entities simply marked, or are they physically removed?
- **Creation and use of forms** Does the package support the use of forms for data entry and retrieval? Do you have the option of designing your own forms? Is the design process easy? Is it flexible? Is the form easy to edit? Is the form attached to a particular database, or can it be used on demand? How many forms are permitted? What are the limitations on forms design?
- **Retrieval operations** What retrieval commands and options are available? Is the format of the retrieval command logical and well laid out? Does it permit the selection of attributes to be listed? Does it permit the use of relational expressions? Logical expressions? Are the expressions easy to create? Are there hidden "tricks" to using the expressions? Does the re-

trieval operation have a print option? Can you search for partial field contents? Are wildcard operations permitted?

- **Error detection** Does the package tell you when you have entered a command incorrectly or when it doesn't understand your use of a command or a command sequence? Are error messages readable and useful? Are modifications and corrections obvious on the basis of error messages generated? Does the package warn you that you are attempting to do something that you probably don't want to do, such as accidentally erase a database or fail to save your work?
- **Sorting and indexing** Is sorting permitted? Do you create a new database through sorting, or is the newly ordered database placed over the old one? Can multiple keys be used in sorting? Can mathematical combination of fields be used as a sort key? Can the order be descending as well as ascending? Is indexing permitted? Can you index on multiple attributes? Can you index on a mathematical combination of attributes? Can an index be in ascending or descending order?
- **Printing reports** Are report forms available? How easy are they to create and modify? What are the limitations on the size of the report (for example, page length and width)? Are page headings available? Column headings? Page footings? Group breaks? Totals on numeric attribute values? Both horizontally and vertically? What other mathematical operations can be performed during the reporting process? Can working variables be created? Can you view the report on the screen as well as have it printed? Are numeric attribute value editing functions (for example, dollar and cent and date formats) available? Are there any other special features of the reporting process?
- **Database manipulations** Once a database has been established, can its structure be modified? Can a new database be extracted from an existing database? Can the extraction be conditional? Can a limited number of attributes be extracted? Can an existing database be joined with another? Can this joining operation be conditional? With a limited number of attributes?
- **Extended functions** Does the package provide a means of security such as passwords? Is the package accompanied by additional capabilities, such as a procedural language? Natural language? Extended processors?
- **Performance characteristics** How fast can you set up a database? How fast can you enter data? How fast does it sort? How fast does it perform an indexing operation? How fast does it search? As the database gets larger (for example, 200 records), does sorting and searching take considerably longer? How much memory is required? How many disks and how much disk space are required? As entities are added, is extra space required

above what is normal for an entity that was originally placed into the database? As entities are deleted, is the size of the database reduced?

Summary

dBASE II and dBASE III are very powerful database packages; although dBASE III is more powerful than dBASE II, both are highly flexible packages that can be tailored to meet your individual needs. The use of the HELP command and the ASSIST command in dBASE III makes the package easy to learn and use. Table 2.7 gives a summary of the commands available in both dBASE II and dBASE III, and Table 2.8 shows the functions that are available in dBASE III.

TABLE 2.7 dBASE II and dBASE III Commands (The commands and options below are available on both dBASE II and dBASE III unless otherwise indicated. Commands and options available only in dBASE II are in boldface. Commands and options available only in dBASE III are underlined.)

Command Name		Meaning and Format
?		Evaluates and displays the value of an expression. In command files (and elsewhere) can be used without expression to space down a line at output.
??		Same as ?, but displays results on the same line as the entry.
!		See the RUN command.
@	★	Displays user formatted data on screen or printer at specified x,y coordinates (x = row or line and y = character position or column).
-Format-		**@ <row>, <col> [SAY <expression> [USING '<picture>']] [GET <variable> [PICTURE '<picture>']]** @ <row>, <col> [CLEAR] @ <row>, <col> [SAY <expression> [PICTURE '<picture>']] [GET <variable> [PICTURE '<picture>'] [RANGE <lower bound>, <upper bound>]]

TABLE 2.7 *(continued)*

Command Name		Meaning and Format
ACCEPT	★	Prompts user to enter character string information into a designated memory variable.
-Format-		ACCEPT ['prompt character string>'] TO <memory variable>
APPEND		Allows the user to add new records to a database in use from another database, SDF (System Data Format) or from a keyboard.
-Format-		**APPEND FROM <file> [SDF] [DELIMITED] [FOR <condition>]** APPEND FROM <file> [FOR/WHILE <condition>] [SDF/DELIMITED [WITH BLANK/<delimiter>] APPEND [BLANK]
AVERAGE		Computes the arithmetic mean of the expressions involving numeric fields.
-Format-		AVERAGE [<numeric expression list>] [<scope>] [FOR/WHILE <condition>] [TO <memory variable list>]
BROWSE		Permits full screen viewing and editing of the database in use.
-Format-		BROWSE [FIELDS <field list>]
CANCEL	★	Stops command file execution and returns the user to the dBASE "." prompt.
CHANGE		Permits non-full-screen editing of database in use, by field. Press ESCape to terminate.
-Format-		CHANGE [<scope>] FIELD <list> [FOR/WHILE <condition>]
CLEAR		Closes all database in use, releases all memory variables, and selects Primary work area. CLEAR MEMORY only releases all memory variables.
-Format-		CLEAR **[ALL] [MEMORY]**
CLEAR GETS	★	Instructs dBASE to eliminate all active GET statements without erasing the screen.
CLOSE		Closes all alternate, database, format, index, or procedure files.
-Format-		CLOSE [ALTERNATE] [DATABASES] [FORMAT] [INDEX] [PROCEDURE]
CONTINUE		Causes dBASE to continue the searching action of a LOCATE command. (See IF command.)
COPY		Copies a database in use or only its structure to another file.
-Format-		**COPY TO <file> [SDF] [DELIMITED [WITH <delimiter>]]** **[FOR <condition>]** **COPY TO <file> STRUCTURE [FIELD <list>]** **COPY TO <file> STRUCTURE EXTENDED** COPY TO <file> [<scope>] [FIELDS <list>] [FOR/WHILE <condition> [SDF/DELIMITED [WITH BLANK/<delimiter>] COPY STRUCTURE TO <file> [FIELD <list>] COPY STRUCTURE EXTENDED TO <file>
COPY FILE		Copies the contents of any file to another file name.
-Format-		COPY FILE <oldfile> TO <newfile>

TABLE 2.7 *(continued)*

Command Name	Meaning and Format
COUNT	Counts the number of records in the database in use that satisfy the specified criteria. (Default scope value is "ALL.")
-Format-	COUNT [<scope>] [FOR/WHILE <condition>] [TO <memory variable>]
CREATE	Creates a new database, possibly from a previously existing database.
-Format-	CREATE [<filename>] CREATE <newfile> FROM <oldfile> **EXTENDED**
DELETE	Deletes a file or marks records for deletion
-Format-	DELETE FILE <file> DELETE [<scope>] [FOR/WHILE <condition>] DELETE RECORD <numeric expression>
DIR	Displays all or part of a disk directory. The files listed by default are database files.
-Format-	DIR [<drive>:] [<path>\] [<skeleton>]
DISPLAY	Displays files, database records or structure, memory variables, or status. (See LIST Command.)
-Format-	DISPLAY [<scope>] [FIELDS <field list>] [FOR/WHILE <condition>] [OFF] [TO PRINT] **DISPLAY FILES [ON <disk drive>] [LIKE <skeleton>]** DISPLAY FILE [LIKE <skeleton>] [TO PRINT] DISPLAY MEMORY [TO PRINT] DISPLAY STATUS [TO PRINT] DISPLAY STRUCTURE [TO PRINT]
DO ★	Executes a command or procedure file.
-Format-	DO <program/procedure file> [WITH <parameter list>]
DO CASE ★	Executes a structured loop within a command file
-Format-	DO CASE CASE <condition> commands CASE <condition> commands [OTHERWISE commands] ENDCASE
DO WHILE ★	Executes a structured loop within a command file
-Format-	DO WHILE <condition> commands [LOOP] ENDDO
EDIT	Enables the selective editing of records in the database currently in use.
-Format-	EDIT [<record number>]

Command Name		Meaning and Format
EJECT		Causes the printer to do a form feed when the printer is set ON and zeros row and column counters for @ SAY commands.
ELSE	★	Provides an alternate command path execution for the IF command. (See IF command.)
ENDCASE	★	Terminates a DO CASE command. (See DO command.)
ENDDO	★	Terminates a DO WHILE command. (See DO command.)
ENDIF	★	Terminates an IF command. (See IF command.)
ENDTEXT	★	Terminates a TEXT command. (See TEXT command.)
ERASE		Clears the screen. In interactive mode, a "." prompt will appear at top left corner of screen. Deletes the indicated file from a disk drive.
-Format-		ERASE <filename>
EXIT	★	Escapes from a DO loop without terminating the command file's execution.
FIND		When using an indexed file, dBASE positions to the first record indexed by the indicated character string.
-Format-		FIND <character string>
GO or GOTO		positions to specific record or location in the database in use.
-Format-		GO or GOTO [RECORD <n>] [<n>] [TOP] [BOTTOM] [<memory variable>]
HELP		Causes an access to the help file for general or specific information.
-Format-		**HELP [<topic>]**
IF	★	Allows conditional execution of commands in a command file.
-Format-		IF <expression> <any statements> [ELSE <any statements>] ENDIF
INDEX		Creates an index file for the database in use based the contents of fields indicated as a key through the expression.
-Format-		INDEX ON <expression> TO <index file>
INPUT	★	Prompts the user to enter numeric or logical data into the indicated memory variable.
-Format-		INPUT ["<character string>"] TO <memory variable>
INSERT		Inserts a new record into the database at the location of the current record.
-Format-		INSERT [[BEFORE] [BLANK]]
JOIN		Creates a new database by combining the records of a Primary and Secondary databases.

TABLE 2.7 *(continued)*

Command Name	Meaning and Format
-Format-	JOIN WITH <alias> TO <file> FOR <condition> [FIELDS <field list>]
LABEL	Displays labels using a label file created by a CREATE LABEL OR MODIFY LABEL command
-Format-	LABEL FORM <label file> [<scope>] [SAMPLE] [TO PRINT] [FOR/WHILE <condition>] [TO FILE <file>]
LIST	Lists files, database records or structure, memory variables, and status. (See DISPLAY command.)
-Format-	LIST [<scope>] [FIELDS <field list>] [FOR/WHILE <conditions>] [OFF] [TO PRINT] **LIST FILES [ON <disk drive>] [LIKE <skeleton>]** LIST FILE [LIKE <skeleton>] [TO PRINT] LIST MEMORY [TO PRINT] LIST STATUS [TO PRINT] LIST STRUCTURE [TO PRINT]
LOCATE	Find a record that fits a condition.
LOOP ★	Causes the command file to return to processing at location of the DO WHILE command. (See DO Command.)
MODIFY	Creates or edits command files, database structures, label files, and report files.
-Format-	MODIFY COMMAND <file> MODIFY STRUCTURE MODIFY LABEL <file> MODIFY REPORT <file>
NOTE OR ★	Permits the insertion of comments into a command file.
PACK	Erases records marked for deletion for the database in use.
PARAMETERS ★	Provides the means to pass variables and expressions from a calling command file to the command file being called.
-Format-	PARAMETERS <parameter list>
PRIVATE ★	Hides the higher-level definitions of the specified variables from the current subroutine and all lower-level command files.
-Format-	PRIVATE [ALL [LIKE/EXCEPT <skeleton]]
PROCEDURE ★	Identifies the beginning of a utility program in a command file.
-Format-	PROCEDURE <name>
PUBLIC ★	Declares memory variables as global. Identified memory variables may be used by any command file at any level.
-Format-	PUBLIC <memory variable list>
QUIT	Terminates dBASE and returns control to the operating system or executes an operating systems level program.

Command Name		Meaning and Format
-Format-		QUIT [TO <command file list>]
READ	★	Initiates the full-screen mode for entry or editing of variables accepted as input by a GET command.
RECALL		Erases deletion marks for current database records.
-Format-		RECALL [<scope>] [FOR/WHILE <condition>]
REINDEX		Performs the updating of index files not automatically "reindexed" after record alterations.
RELEASE		Eliminates unwanted memory variables and releases memory space.
-Format-		RELEASE ALL RELEASE ALL EXCEPT <skeleton> RELEASE ALL LIKE <skeleton> RELEASE [<memory variable list>]
REMARK	★	Permits display of any characters either directly or within a command file.
RENAME		Permits the renaming of a file in an operating system directory.
-Format-		RENAME <file> TO <new filename>
REPLACE		Allows the user to change the contents of specified fields in the database in use.
-Format-		REPLACE [<scope>] <field> WITH <expression> [,<field2> WITH <expression2>] . . . [FOR/WHILE <condition>]
REPORT		Used to create a report form file (FRM) or produce a report on the screen or printer.
-Format-		**REPORT [FORM <form file>] [<scope>] [TO PRINT]** **[FOR <condition>] [PLAIN]** REPORT [FORM <form file>] [<scope>] [FOR <condition>] [PLAIN] [HEADING <character string>] [NOEJECT] [TO PRINT] [TO FILE <file>]
RESET		Used to indicate to the operating system that a new diskette is now in the indicated drive.
-Format-		RESET [<drive>]
RESTORE		Retrieves and stores a set of memory variables previously saved in a MEM file. Also allows the addition of saved memory values to those already in memory.
-Format-		RESTORE FROM <file> [ADDITIVE]
RETURN	★	Used in a command file to return executing control to dBASE or the command file which called it. MASTER returns to the original calling file.
-Format-		RETURN [TO MASTER]
RUN		Executes the specified command from the operating system while within dBASE. (! may be used as a substitute for the word RUN.)
-Format-		RUN <command>
SAVE		Copies all memory variables in use or specified memory variables to an indicated MEM disk file.

TABLE 2.7 *(continued)*

Command Name		Meaning and Format
-Format-		SAVE TO <file> [ALL LIKE/EXCEPT <skeleton>]
SEEK		Searches an indexed file for the first record containing the specified expression in the leading character(s) of the index key.
-Format-		SEEK <expression>
SELECT		Allows the user to switch between two (dBASE II) or up to ten (dBASE III) databases, thus permitting two (up to 10) active databases at the same time. (See, for example, JOIN command.)
-Format-		**SELECT [PRIMARY] [SECONDARY]** SELECT <work> area/alias>
SET		A full-screen command that displays the current processing parameters and provides the means to select and change them. (This format available only in dBASE III.)
-Format-		SET
SET		Sets dBASE control parameters (See below.)
-Format-	★	SET ALTERNATE ON/OFF ON sends all screen output (except full-screen) to a disk file. (Must be preceded by SET ALTERNATE TO <file> command). OFF shuts off output.
		SET BELL ON/OFF ON rings when invalid data is entered or data field boundary is passed. OFF suspends ringing.
		SET CARRY ON/OFF ON repeats data in current record from previous record when using APPEND in Full-screen mode. OFF leaves field blank.
		SET COLON ON/OFF ON displays colons to bound input variables when using Full-screen display. OFF suspends display of colons.
		SET CONFIRM ON/OFF ON disables automatic skipping to next field when current field is filled while in Full-screen mode. OFF requires a wait for <return> before going to next field.
	★	SET CONSOLE ON/OFF ON sends all output to screen. OFF suspends all output to screen. System will appear dead.
	★	SET DEBUG ON/OFF ON sends output created by ECHO and STEP options to printer. OFF sends this output to the screen.
		SET DELETED ON/OFF ON disables dBASE from FINDing or processing records marked for deletion with any command allowing a <scope>, e.g., LIST, DISPLAY, COUNT. OFF enables dBASE to see all records.

Command Name	Meaning and Format
★	SET ECHO ON/OFF ON enables monitoring of command file execution by echoing all commands to screen. OFF sends no report on execution.
	SET EJECT ON/OFF ON causes REPORT command to perform a form-feed (page eject) before sending report output to printer. OFF disables the page eject.
★	SET ESCAPE ON/OFF ON allows user to abort execution of command file by hitting ESCape key. OFF disables ESC key interrupt.
	SET EXACT ON/OFF ON requires exact matches in any comparison of character strings (in FOR <condition>, FIND commands, etc.). OFF allows matches between character strings of different lengths (in this order): 'ABCDEF' = 'ABC'.
	SET FIXED ON/OFF Determines whether a fixed number of decimal places will be displayed on all numeric output, as indicated by a SET DECIMAL command.
	SET HEADING ON/OFF Determines whether field headings are displayed above each field when DISPLAY and LIST commands are used.
	SET HELP ON/OFF Determines whether the message "Do you want some Help? (Y/N)" is displayed when an error occurs.
	SET INTENSITY ON/OFF ON enables inverse video or dual intensity in Full-screen operations (if allowed by hardware). OFF disables these features.
	SET LINKAGE ON/OFF ON enables movement of record pointers in both PRIMARY and SECONDARY areas, by commands which allow a <scope>, i.e., downward movement only. OFF suspends pointer linkage.
	SET MENUS ON/OFF Determines whether a menu containing cursor movements will be presented on the screen when full-screen commands are in use.
	SET PRINT ON/OFF ON sends output to printer. OFF stops printer output.
	SET RAW ON/OFF ON DISPLAYs and LISTs records without inserting spaces between fields; OFF inserts an extra space between fields.
	SET SAFETY ON/OFF Determines whether dBASE will warn you when attempting to overwrite or otherwise destroy an existing file.

TABLE 2.7 *(continued)*

Command Name	Meaning and Format
	SET SCREEN ON/OFF ON enables Full-screen operation for APPEND, EDIT, INSERT, READ, and CREATE commands.
★	SET STEP ON/OFF ON aids debugging of command file by halting execution after dBASE performs each command. OFF does not halt execution.
★	SET TALK ON/OFF ON sends results of command execution to screen. OFF suppresses additional screen output.
	SET UNIQUE ON/OFF Determines whether records with the same value for the key (index) field are included in an index file.
	SET ALTERNATE TO [<file>] Creates a disk file with .TXT extension for saving screen output. SET ALTERNATE TO closes the .TXT file.
	SET COLOR TO <n1,n2> SET COLOR TO <n2>[,<n1>][,<n3>] Sets color or CRT attribute of terminal output. <n1> indicates desired color or attribute of dim or reverse video, <n2> the desired color or attribute of normal display, n3 specifies the desired color of the border.
	SET DATE TO <xx/xx/xx> Stores a string to system date, but does not perform date validation.
	SET DECIMALS TO <numeric expression> Selects the minimum number of decimal places that will be displayed in the result of certain functions and calculations.
	SET DEFAULT TO <drive> Makes specified drive the drive where dBASE will look for files when instructed.
	SET DELIMITER TO ['<character>'] [DEFAULT] SET DELIMITER ON/OFF Determines how field widths are marked in full-screen mode. OFF indicates reverse video and ON marks fields with colons.
★	SET DEVICE TO SCREEN/PRINT Sends the results of executed @ . . . SAY commands to the screen or the printer.
	SET FILTER TO [<condition>] Causes a database file in use to appear as if it contains only records that meet the specified condition.
★	**SET FORMAT TO <SCREEN/PRINT>** SCREEN sends output from @ SAY commands to screen. PRINT sends formatted output to printer.

Command Name	Meaning and Format
	SET FORMAT TO [<format file>] Opens .FMT file, which dBASE will use to format screen for READ, APPEND, EDIT, INSERT, CREATE, @ SAY commands. SET FORMAT TO closes any open .FMT file.
	SET FUNCTION <key number> TO <'character string'>[;] Stores 'character string' in the buffer of the identified function.
	SET HEADING TO <character string> Saves the <character string> internally and prints it as the Report header line.
	SET INDEX TO <index file list> Sets up index files for use with corresponding database. First .NDX file in list will be engaged as the active index; all other index files will be automatically updated to reflect any changes to the database.
	SET MARGIN TO <n> Sets left-hand margin of printer to <n> columns.
	SET PATH TO [<path list>] Specifies additional file searching paths.
	SET PROCEDURE [<file>] Opens the specified command file. Only one such file can be open.
	SET RELATION [TO <key expression/numeric expression> INTO <alias> Links a database file in use to an opened database according to a key expression (or a numeric expression) that is common to both files. The opened database is identified by means of its alias.
SKIP -Format-	Moves the record pointer forward or backward in the database. SKIP [-] [<n>]
SORT -Format-	Creates a new copy of the current database with the record arranged in order based on the specified field. **SORT ON <field> TO <file> [ASCENDING] [DESCENDING]** SORT TO <file> [ASCENDING/DESCENDING] ON <field> [/A] [/D] [,<field2> [/A] [/D]] . . . [<scope>] [FOR <condition>]
STORE -Format-	Creates a memory variable and assigns it the value of an expression. STORE <expression> TO <memory variable>[,<memory variable list>] <memory variable> = <expression>
SUM -Format-	Computes and displays the sum of numeric database field(s). The default scope is ALL. **SUM <field> [,<field2>] [<scope>] [TO <memory variable list>] [FOR <condition>]** SUM <scope> [<expression list>] [TO <memory variable list>] [FOR/WHILE <condition>]

TABLE 2.7 *(continued)*

Command Name	Meaning and Format
TEXT ★	In a command file, it allows the output of character strings without the use of @ or ? commands. Text block is terminated with an ENDTEXT command.
TOTAL	Creates a summary version of an indexed or presorted database by copying only records with unique keys. Records with the same key value can have their numeric fields totaled by using the FIELDS option.
-Format-	**TOTAL TO <file> ON <key> [FIELDS <field list>]** TOTAL ON <key> TO <file> [<scope>] [FIELDS <field list>] [FOR/WHILE <condition>]
TYPE	Views the contents of any text file that may be manipulated by a word processor.
-Format-	TYPE <file> [TO PRINT]
UPDATE	Allows batch updating of presorted or indexed databases by matching records on the basis of a specified key in the USE and FROM databases.
-Format-	**UPDATE FROM <file> ON <key> [ADD <field list>]** **[REPLACE <field list> WITH <field list> [RANDOM]** **UPDATE FROM <file> ON <key> [ADD <field list>]** **[REPLACE <field> WITH <field list>] [RANDOM]** UPDATE [RANDOM] ON <key> FROM <alias> REPLACE <field> WITH <expression> [,<field2> WITH <expression2>] . . .
USE	Specifies the database to be used for subsequent operations. It automatically closes databases previously in use. Index indicates ordering sequence.
-Format-	USE <file> [INDEX <index file list>] [ALIAS <alias>]
WAIT ★	Temporarily halts the execution of a command file until a single character input is received from the keyboard.
-Format-	WAIT ['<prompt>'] [TO <memory variable>]
ZAP	Deletes all records from the file in use. ZAP is equivalent to DELETE ALL followed by PACK.

TABLE 2.8 dBASE III Functions

Function Name and Format	Description
ASC (<character expression>)	Returns the ASCII value of the leftmost character of the specified character expression.
AT (<character expression1>, <character expression2>)	Returns a number indicating the starting position of the first character string within the second character string. If the second character string is not contained within the first character string, AT( ) returns a zero.
BOF( )	Returns a logical TRUE (.T.) if the record pointer is positioned before the first record.
CDOW (<date variable>)	Returns a character string indicating the day of the week of the specified data variable.
CHR (<numeric expression>)	Returns the ASCII equivalent of the specified numeric expression.
CMONTH (<date variable>)	Returns a character string indicating the month of the specified date variable.
COL ( )	Returns a number indicating the next available column.
CTOD (<character expression>)	Returns a date-type value indicating the date specified in character-type format. The format of the character expression is 'mm/dd/yy'.
DATE( )	Returns the system date in date-type format.
DAY (<date variable>)	Returns a number indicating the day of the month specified by the date variable.
DELETED( )	Returns a logical TRUE (.T.) if the current record is marked for deletion.
DOW (<date variable>)	Returns a number indicating the day of the week. Number 1 indicates Sunday.
DTOC (<date variable>)	Converts a date-type variable to a character-type string of the format mm/dd/yy.

TABLE 2.8 *(continued)*

Function Name and Format	Description
EOF( )	Returns a logical TRUE (.T.) if the record pointer is positioned after the last record.
EXP (<numeric expression>)	Returns the natural exponent of a numeric expression.
FILE('[<path>/]<file>')	Returns a logical TRUE (.T.) if the specified file name exists.
INT (<numeric expression>)	Returns the truncated integer value of a numeric expression.
LEN (<character expression>)	Returns a number indicating the length of the named character string.
LOG (<numeric expression>)	Returns the natural logarithm of a numeric expression.
LOWER (<character expression>)	Converts a character expression to lower case.
&<character memory variable>	Substitutes the contents of the memory variable for the memory variable name. & can be used only for character variables.
MONTH (<date variable>)	Returns a number indicating the month specified by the date variable.
PCOL( )	Returns a number indicating the next available printer column.
PROW( )	Returns a number indicating the next available row on the printer.
RECNO( )	Returns the current record number.
ROUND (<numeric expression>, <decimal>)	Rounds the value of a numeric expression to the specified decimal place.
ROW( )	Returns a number indicating the next available row on the screen.
SPACE (<numeric expression>)	Creates a character string with a specified number of blank spaces.
SQRT (<numeric expression>)	Returns the square root of a numeric expression.

Function Name and Format	Description
STR (<numeric expression>[, <length>[, <decimal places>]])	Converts a numeric expression to a character string.
SUBSTR (<character expression>, <starting position> [, length>])	Extracts the specified part of a character string from a character expression.
TIME( )	Returns the system time in the character format hh:mm:ss.
TRIM (<character expression>)	Removes trailing blanks from a character string.
TYPE ('<expression>')	Returns the expression type--C (character), D (date), L (logical), N (numeric), or U (undefined).
UPPER (<character expression>)	Converts a character expression to upper case.
VAL (<character expression>)	Converts a character expression consisting of numbers to a to a numeric expression. VAL returns zero for all non-numeric characters.
YEAR (<date variable>)	Returns a number indicating the year specified by the date variable.

Module Three Spreadsheet, Database, and Graphics: Lotus 1-2-3

3

Introduction to Lotus 1-2-3

Lotus 1-2-3 is a software package that can be a very powerful tool. It is based on three major types of software that use numeric data: spreadsheets, database, and graphics. This module starts with a general discussion of spreadsheets, followed by a description of the use of the Lotus spreadsheet feature to solve a problem using the job hunting data found in Appendix A. Next, this module covers Lotus's database features; this discussion includes the use of Lotus macros. (For a general discussion of database usage on a microcomputer, read the beginning of Module 2.) Finally, the module ends with a discussion of business graphics and a problem that will require you to use the Lotus graphics features.

Introduction to Spreadsheets

Suppose you are planning a ski trip during the next break in classes; you know that some of your friends will go with you, but you don't know how many. You need to calculate the total shared expenses for the trip, as well as each person's cost. To do this, you have gathered the following information:

1. **Getting there**
   You have available a van that can carry 8 people and gets 14 miles per gallon and a car that can carry 4 people and gets 26 miles per gallon. The travel distance is 821 miles one way, and you can expect to add another 200 miles while you are there.
2. **Staying there**
   Even if you drive straight through by rotating drivers, you will need a place to stay while skiing. You can rent a condominium that will hold 6 people for \$60.00 a night double occupancy plus \$20.00 a night for each additional person. You will need the condominium for 6 nights. Food for the 6 days that you will be there will cost about \$50.00 per person for breakfast and dinner. Lunch, if not a bag lunch, will be about \$8.00 per day.

3. **Equipment**
   Lift tickets will be $17.00 per day, and ski rental will cost $15.00 per day, if you rent skies for all 6 days.

Clearly, as people decide to go, you could calculate the cost per person with a pencil and paper. Doing the calculations in this manner would require a lot of arithmetic and time, whereas using one of the spreadsheet packages would quickly and easily give you the results shown in Figure 3.1.

Obviously, using the computer to do these calculations is easier and faster than doing them by hand. If you were presented with a complex problem—for example, developing monthly budgets for a company or an organization—the ability to use electronic spreadsheets would be even more valuable. This chapter will cover the basics of electronic spreadsheets and examine some of their uses in business.

Definition of Spreadsheets

Electronic spreadsheets have been called many names; the most common of these are **worksheets** and **scratchpads.** Conceptually, a spreadsheet is nothing more than a large sheet of paper divided into rows and columns. With an electronic spreadsheet, the "paper" is the memory of the computer, with part of the spreadsheet shown on the computer screen.

SKI TRIP	NUMBER OF PEOPLE				
	2	3	4	5	6
Transportation	83.53	83.53	83.53	155.12	155.12
Lodging	60.00	80.00	100.00	120.00	140.00
Food	100.00	150.00	200.00	250.00	300.00
Total	243.53	313.53	383.53	525.12	595.12
Cost per peson	121.76	104.51	95.88	105.02	99.19
Ski cost	320.00	320.00	320.00	320.00	320.00
Total per person	441.76	424.51	415.88	425.02	419.19

SKI TRIP	NUMBER OF PEOPLE					
	7	8	9	10	11	12
Transportation	155.12	155.12	238.65	238.65	238.65	238.65
Lodging	200.00	200.00	220.00	240.00	260.00	280.00
Food	350.00	400.00	450.00	500.00	550.00	600.00
Total	705.12	755.12	908.65	978.65	1048.65	1118.65
Cost per peson	100.73	94.39	100.96	97.87	95.33	93.22
Ski cost	320.00	320.00	320.00	320.00	320.00	320.00
Total per person	420.73	414.39	420.96	417.87	415.33	413.22

FIGURE 3.1
The cost calculations for the ski trip

Matrix Terminology

A **work space** (the part of a spreadsheet where data is displayed) that is divided into rows and columns, as shown in Figure 3.2, is usually thought of as a **matrix.** In a matrix, an individual cell (a specific row and column position in the work space capable of retaining a series of characters or a value) containing data is referenced by indicating the row and column identifiers for the desired cell; that is, rows are usually identified by numbers (1, 2, 3, and so on), and columns may be identified by numbers (1, 2, 3, and so on) or letters (A, B, C, and so forth). By pressing the arrow keys on your keyboard, you can move the cursor around within the work space and look at different cells. When the cursor accesses portions of the spreadsheet that are not yet visible on the screen, this movement is called **scrolling.**

The type of cell-referencing system previously described is fairly common. If you look at a city map, you will find numbers down both sides indicating the rows and letters across the top and bottom of the map indicating the columns. These row and column indicators are used to show the location of streets and public buildings on the map. Your seat in a concert hall is also indicated by a row number or letter and a seat number in that row—a column indicator.

Although the term *matrix* may be new to you, the use of row and column identifiers to indicate a position or cell is not. When using row and column identifiers to indicate a position in a matrix, there are a couple of rules that must be followed. First, when identifying a particular cell—for example, the cell in the third row of column D, as shown in Figure 3.2—you normally indicate the column first and the row second.

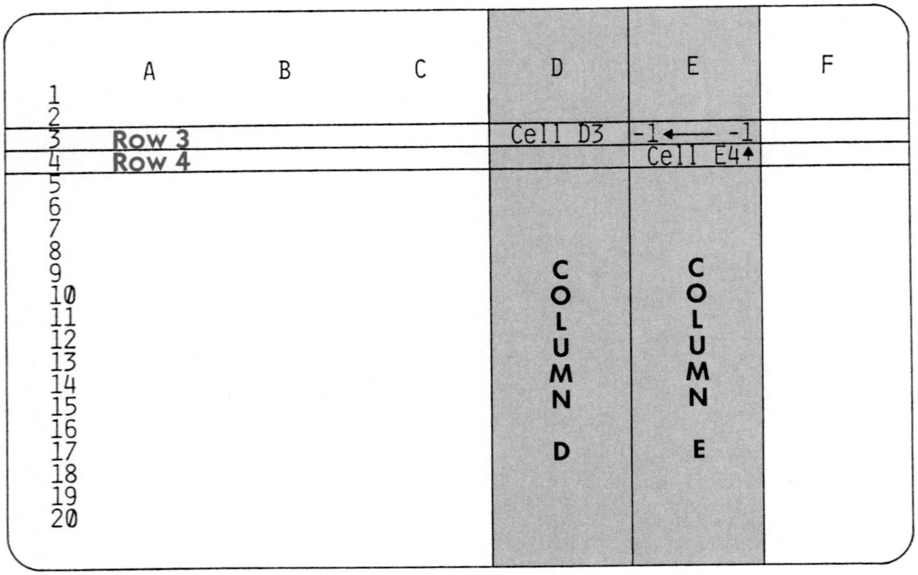

FIGURE 3.2
Rows and columns of a spreadsheet on a screen

If you don't provide the row indicator, then you have identified the entire column as a cell; conversely, eliminating the column indicator identifies the entire row as a cell.

Second, a cell can be identified by its **absolute address** — that is, row 3 column D — or by its **relative address** — that is, its position relative to another cell. For example, if the current cursor location is on row 4 column E, then row 3 column D would be row −1 column −1 (see Figure 3.2). This relative position is indicated by the number of rows and columns and the directions you would have to move the cursor to arrive at the indicated cell (usually "+" for down or right and "−" for up or left).

Arithmetic Operations

Although the spreadsheet is structured as a matrix, it does not use advanced **matrix arithmetic** operations, such as matrix multiplication, inversion, or the calculation of determinants. Instead, it uses **scalar arithmetic** — the set of operations that you learned in elementary school. These arithmetic operations are addition, subtraction, multiplication, and division, plus some special functions that have proven useful, such as squares, square roots, averages, and logarithms.

Although specific arithmetic operations are discussed later, it is important to mention how an arithmetic operation is entered in a spreadsheet. To do arithmetic, move the cursor to the location in which you want the answer to appear. The equation or arithmetic operation is then entered, indicating the address of cells, if any, to be used in the operation. For example, suppose you had entered the values 97, 85, and 88 in cells row 1 column A, row 2 column A, and row 3 column A, as shown in Figure 3.3. To add these three numbers together and place the result in row 4 column A, place the cursor in the cell row 4 column A and type either +97+85+88 or +A1+A2+A3, and the number 270 will appear in row 4 column A. The advantage of using cell references rather than the actual values can be seen when one or more of the actual values change. If the value 97 is changed to 87, the arithmetic operations based on the values would have to be changed to be correct. However, if cell references are used to indicate the locations of the actual values, the resulting sum based on this operation would automatically be changed by the software to reflect the new value in cell A1.

There are, of course, many other arithmetic operations that can be done with these numbers. However, before you learn about the functions of spreadsheets, you need to know a little about the characteristics of the data you can use in spreadsheets.

There Are Different Kinds of Data — Data Types

In general, **data types** are forms of data representation inside the computer. Although there are many different ways to represent data in spreadsheets, you are concerned with only two types: **character data** and **numeric data.**

Character Data

Typically, when you think of character data, you think of the letters of the alphabet — A through Z. However, when a computer uses character data, it can be the letters of the alphabet — A through Z — special characters — such as −, +, $, @, and # — and the "characters" 0 through 9.

```
A4: 97+85+88

          A           B           C           D           E           F
1           97
2           85
3           88
4          270
5
6
7
8
9
10
11
12
13
14
15
16
17
18
19
20
```

a

```
A4: +A1+A2+A3

          A           B           C           D           E           F
1           97
2           85
3           88
4          270
5
6
7
8
9
10
11
12
13
14
15
16
17
18
19
20
```

b

FIGURE 3.3
Using a speadsheet to add three numbers

Because character data, often referred to as **alphanumeric data,** is represented differently than numeric data, you cannot perform arithmetic operations on it. In fact, the only operations you can do directly with character data is sorting it into alphabetical order.

Numeric Data

Numeric data is any combination of the digits 0 through 9 used to represent a numeric value. Numeric data can also contain a minus symbol and a decimal point. For example, a quantity such as 50 or a price such as 1.95 is usually considered numeric data. Cells containing numeric data can be used in arithmetic operations. In fact, in most spreadsheets, formulas and mathematical functions are treated as numeric data. Although this may seem a little confusing now, because mathematical functions are considered numeric data, you can perform arithmetic operations on cells containing other arithmetic operations. For example, in Figure 3.1, the "Total per person" is the sum of the "Cost per person" and the "Ski cost." The "Cost per person" is the "Total" divided by the number of people, and the "Total" is the sum of "Transportation," "Lodging," and "Food." To calculate the "Total per person," you will perform three levels of arithmetic operations, some of which depend on arithmetic operations in other cells.

Lotus 1-2-3 Spreadsheet

Learning to Use Lotus 1-2-3

Lotus 1-2-3 is one of the more recently developed spreadsheet packages. It is designed to overcome some of the shortcomings of earlier spreadsheet packages by providing additional capabilities. In fact, Lotus 1-2-3 may be considered an integrated package, because it possesses capabilities far beyond those of a simple spreadsheet package. 1-2-3 represents the spreadsheet portion of the Lotus package and thus is used to identify the spreadsheet function. It is one of the easiest packages to learn and use. Furthermore, it is currently one of the most popular software packages ever produced.

When you begin to use 1-2-3, start by booting the operating system. If you are using a computer with two disk drives, place a disk that has been prepared to hold your data in drive B. Once the operating system has been loaded, all that is required is to place the Lotus system disk in drive A and type LOTUS. Press the RETURN key, and you will be greeted by the Lotus log-on menu, as shown in Figure 3.4. Note that the version number is shown on this screen(V.1A)—if you have any questions about which version of Lotus you are using, you can check the log-on screen.

In the Access System menu, Lotus identifies the other functions the package is capable of performing. The discussion presented in this module addresses only the spreadsheet functions of Lotus. As noted at the bottom of the screen, you may select other functions by using the arrow keys to identify the function. In any case, after you have made your selection, press the RETURN key. Before the first 1-2-3 screen appears, you will see a screen that identifies which release number of 1-2-3 you are using. As indicated toward the bottom of the screen, you may press any key on the keyboard to enter the spreadsheet function.

The Arrangement—What a 1-2-3 Spreadsheet Looks Like

After the log-on screens disappear, you will be presented with an empty spreadsheet, as shown in Figure 3.5. Whether you have previously built and

```
Lotus Access System  V.1A  (C)1983 Lotus Development Corp.                MENU
--------------------------------------------------------------------------------
1-2-3  File-Manager  Disk-Manager  PrintGraph  Translate  Exit
Enter 1-2-3 -- Lotus Spreadsheet/Graphics/Database program
================================================================================

                              Thu  01-Jan-87
                                 8:28:02am

      Use the arrow keys to highlight command choice and press [Enter]
 Press [Esc] to cancel a choice; Press [F1] for information on command choices
```

FIGURE 3.4
The Lotus Access System command menu (log-on menu)

saved other spreadsheets or not, this is always the starting point. The initial screen is divided into two basic areas. The bottom of the screen represents the spreadsheet work space, and the top is the command menu area.

A 1-2-3 spreadsheet is capable of handling a spreadsheet of up to 2048 rows and 256 columns, depending on the internal memory capability of your computer (some later versions support a much larger work space). The initial (default) width of each cell is 9 characters, but a cell can be modified to be as few as 1 character or as many as 72 characters. However, do not confuse the column width (which determines the cell size) with the data length. The width of a column may be narrower or wider than the data shown in that column. The width of each column can be expanded or contracted independently of the others to provide the clearest picture of what is in the spreadsheet.

The highlighted portion of the screen at the upper-right corner, the status indicator, will contain the word READY, which indicates that 1-2-3 is ready to proceed and that you are in data-entry mode. As you perform different types of operations, the status indicator changes to reflect your current state of operation. For example, when you enter the command selection mode, the status changes to MENU (as in Figure 3.5). When you place a number into a cell, the status is VALUE. When you enter text into a cell, the status is LABEL. When you are in a cell-addressing mode, the status will be POINT. When 1-2-3 is in

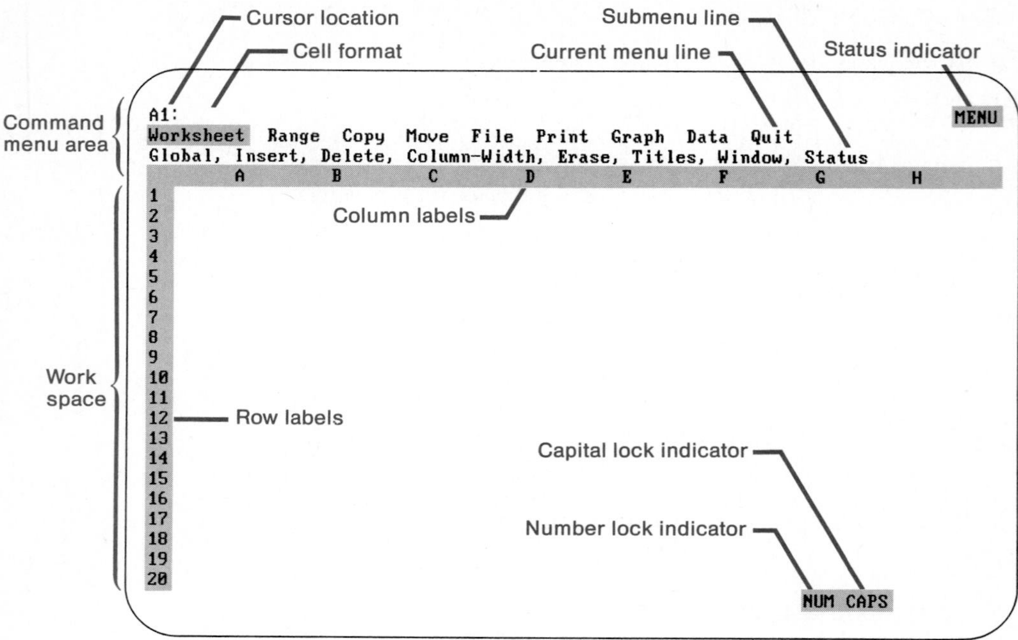

FIGURE 3.5
The 1-2-3 screen layout—work space

the process of completing an activity, the status will temporarily be WAIT. (In the automatic recalculate mode, you must WAIT until the function has been performed before you proceed.)

The status in Figure 3.5 is MENU. To move from the log-on screen to this screen, press the slash (/) key. This causes the initial command menu to appear. In the MENU mode, the first line under the current cell marker identifies the types of functions that can be performed. The second line provides an additional explanation of the functions (or directions on how to complete a selected function, as will be shown later). A brief description of each of these functions is presented in Table 3.1. The function to be used will be highlighted, as shown in Figure 3.5. Many of the functions, when selected, will provide additional menus that more fully describe the operation to be performed. A function can be selected either by pressing the first letter of the function (for example, "R" for the Range function) or by pressing the right- or left-arrow key, which causes the highlighted area to move from one function to the next. If you continue to press the right-arrow key when Quit is reached, the highlighted area will return to the Worksheet function, and you may restart the selection process. As you select command functions (which may in turn have subfunctions), you could

TABLE 3.1 General Lotus 1-2-3 Commands

Function	Operation
Worksheet	Performs operations that affect the entire spreadsheet, including: Global—modification of all cells Insert—add new rows or columns Delete—remove new rows or columns Column-Width—change the default size of cells Erase—delete the entire spreadsheet Titles—establish a "title" window Window—establish a "general" window Status—provide current operational information
Range	Performs operations that affect a cell or a specified range of cells, including (many available under Worksheet/Global as well): Format—modify the presentation mode Label-Prefix—modify cell alignment Erase—remove the contents of a cell or range of cells Name—provide an identifying name for a cell or range of cells Justify—adjust width of text paragraph Protect—turn cell "locking" on Unprotect—turn cell "locking" off Input—turn on/off entry access to protected cell
Copy	Reproduces the contents of one or more cells into another area of the spreadsheet
Move	Reproduces the contents of one or more cells into another area of the spreadsheet while erasing the contents of the original cells
File	Performs disk file manipulations, including: Retrieve—get a spreadsheet file from disk Save—retain the current spreadsheet on disk Xtract—save a portion of the current spreadsheet on disk Erase—remove a file from disk List—show the names of disk files and available disk space Import—get a spreadsheet "print" file from disk Directory—set the default disk drive
Print	Produces a printed copy of the spreadsheet, including: Print—produce output on the printer File—produce output to a disk file Page—advance to the top of the next page Options—establish headers, footers, margins, and so on Setup—send special print codes to the printer Page-Length—establish the number of lines per page Other—indicate the cell characteristics desired

TABLE 3.1 *(continued)*

Function	Operation
	Clear—erase previously established print options Align—reposition the top of page Go—produce the indicated output Quit—terminate the print function
Graph	Creates a graphic presentation of the material contained in the spreadsheet
Data	Performs general functions on existing data, including: Fill—fill the cells of the spreadsheet with a set of predetermined-determined values Table—perform table manipulations Sort—arrange the specified cells in the designated order Query—perform database retrieval functions Distribution—calculate frequency distribution
Quit	Terminates the 1-2-3 session and returns to the Lotus menu of general functions

make a mistake and enter the wrong function or supply an incorrect response. However, 1-2-3 performs a "return to previous step" operation when you press the ESCape key. Thus, if you have entered the Worksheet function and you decide you should have selected another function, press the ESCape key, and the menu (as shown in Figure 3.5) will return to the screen. If you are currently looking at the command screen and you want to return to the data-entry mode, press the ESCape key again and you will be back to the original appearance of the command area.

Learning About Your Keyboard— Cursor Movement and Function Keys

When you enter an "empty" spreadsheet, your cell reference will be "A1"—row 1 and column A. However, as you build your spreadsheet, you will want to reference other cells. As you move from place to place in the spreadsheet, the highlighted area also moves, and the current cell marker in the command area of the screen is updated.

The simplest way of moving from one cell to another is by using the

TABLE 3.2 Function Key Designations for 1-2-3

Function Key	Operation Performed
F1	Enter the Help mode
F2	Enter the Edit mode for current cell contents
F3	List the currently specified range names
F4	Identify the current cell as an absolute address
F5	Go To a specified cell position
F6	Move to the next available window
F7	Repeat most recently specified data query
F8	Repeat most recently specified table operation
F9	Perform recalculation
F10	Create the most recently specified graph
F11*	Change meaning of arrow keys from cell-addressing to window-addressing
F12*	Move to the end of a block of cells, an entry, or a menu

* Not available on all versions of Lotus or certain keyboards.

cursor-movement or arrow keys. If using the arrow keys is not quick enough for you, you can traverse the spreadsheet more rapidly if you press the ALTernate key and a cursor-movement key at the same time. If you press the ALTernate key and the right-arrow key together, the entire screen scrolls to reveal the next full set of columns to the right of the current screen. If the last column identified in the current screen is column H, the first column in the next screen presentation will be column I. Of course, similar operations may be achieved by using the left-, up-, and down-arrow keys.

Suppose you are at the bottom-right corner of a spreadsheet and you want to get back to cell A1. All that is necessary is to press the HOME key. Regardless of where you are in the spreadsheet, you will go to cell A1. However, if you want to reference a cell other than A1, you may want to use the Go To function. This function requires the use of one of the function keys, as identified in Table 3.2. When you press the F5 key, you will be asked to supply a cell reference. On completing this entry, 1-2-3 will move directly to that cell regardless of its direction from the previous location. Alternately, you are permitted to access a "named" portion of the spreadsheet by selecting the Name option of the Range function. If you don't know which cells have a designated name, you can find out by pressing the F3 key. On those keyboards equipped with "extra" function keys, you can press the F12 and HOME keys together to address the last cell of the active spreadsheet—the lower-right corner.

Trying to Remember—The Help Function

The Help function is selected by pressing the F1 function key. If you are currently working in the READY mode and you press F1, you will be provided with general information in the first help screen. From this point, you may select the highlighted topic or use the arrow keys to move through the list to select any of the other topics. When you make a selection, the list of topics changes so that you can reach other Help information. When you are ready to return to what you were doing, simply press the ESCape key. When you return, your spreadsheet is at exactly the position you left it.

If you are using one of the many command menus and you press the F1 function key, you will receive information related to the previously highlighted command selection. At any time, whether you are currently using the command menu or some lower-level menu, you can press the F1 key and retrieve information about that specific topic or operation.

Solving the Job Hunting Problem

The remaining sections of this module are devoted to solving the job hunting problem. Find the data for the job hunting problem in Appendix A. You will use this data and the problem stated as an example of how spreadsheets can be used to manipulate data and produce interesting results.

When ready to seek employment, everyone is interested in evaluating job offers in as many ways as possible. What is the salary offered? Does it include certain benefits (life insurance, health insurance, paid vacation days, and retirement contributions paid by the company)? Will I have to commute? How far? Do I really want to work for that company?

Once you have an idea of what you want, you can build a spreadsheet and use it to compare companies and job offers. The following list represents the types of manipulations and comparisons you might want to make once the spreadsheet has been built.

1. Across the top of your spreadsheet, set up the following titles:

```
Company Name
Salary Offer
Life Benefits
```

```
Health Benefits
Retirement
Commuting Distance
Vacation Days
Job Preference
```

2. After setting up the column headings (you will probably need more than one row for the headings) and making them TITLES so that they will always appear at the top of your spreadsheet, format the cell sizes in each of your columns so that your spreadsheet will be readable and will hold the data you are going to enter.
3. Now enter the data for all the companies listed in Table A.2, **Offers from Companies,** found in Appendix A. Form two windows by splitting the spreadsheet between the columns labeled Company Name and Salary Offer. Be sure these windows are synchronized.
4. Before you start manipulating the data, insert a new column after the column labeled Vacation Days and label it Vacation Value. To fill in the values for Vacation Value, use the formula Vacation Days times Salary Offer divided by 250.
5. Add a new column to your spreadsheet. This column should be labeled Actual Offer and is the sum of Salary Offer, Health Benefits, Life Benefits, and Retirement.
6. Set up a row for an Average Company and calculate averages for each of the columns.
7. You have received a letter of acceptance from First State National Bank. You need to enter this information in your spreadsheet. Enclosed with the letter of acceptance was a description of the job containing the following details:

```
Salary Offer: $22,000.00
Life: $210.00
Health: $325.00
Vacation Days: 14
Retirement: $2950.00
```

   You have established that the commuting distance is 25 miles, and your preference for the job is 2. After inserting a new row with this information, recalculate the totals and averages.
8. Now sort the companies in your spreadsheet by your preference ranking. Remember, when you perform the SORT, do not include Average Company in the sort area.
9. Lewis & Melts Mortgage Company has told you that at the end of the first year you will receive a pay raise of 10% plus a cost-of-living adjustment (as a percentage of your salary). Set up a table to calculate your Actual Salary and the Vacation Value for a cost-of-living adjustment of 1% through 10%.

What's in a Name?—Entering Headings and Labels

Now you are ready to put the job offer data into the spreadsheet. Examine Figure 3.6. The contents of cell A2 are entered by first pressing the down-arrow key so that cell A2 is the currently active cell. Since no command menu is currently on the screen, as you enter the letter "C" of "Company Name," the status mode changes to LABEL. Thus, the label "Company Name" is to be placed in cell A2. Initially, the complete text ("Company Name") of cell A2 is visible. As you enter the contents of adjacent cells, the original text will be truncated to the width of the cell ("Company"), as in Figure 3.6. However, 1-2-3 retains the complete length of the text even though you may not be able to see all of it in the spreadsheet. When numeric values are too long for the cell, the cell is filled with the * symbol.

After you enter the text "Company Name," you can press the RETURN key. However, you will then have to use the arrow keys to move to the next cell into which a value is to be placed. Entering text in this manner will take a while to complete. As an alternative, 1-2-3 permits you to move the cursor without pressing the RETURN key—that is, by using the cursor-movement keys. 1-2-3 assumes that as soon as you move from the current cell, you want what you have

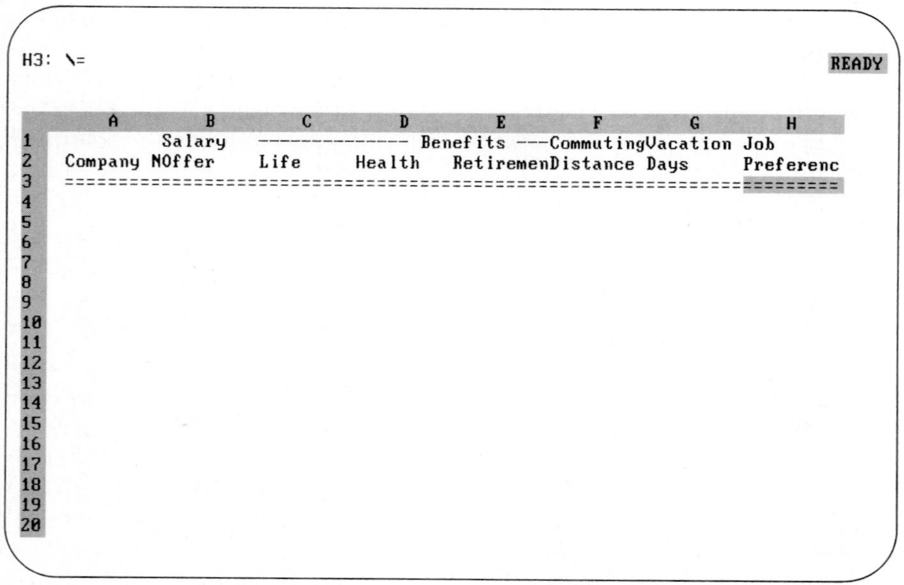

FIGURE 3.6
Column headings for the job offers problem

entered for that cell to be stored in that cell. Thus, by pressing a cursor-movement key, you store the contents of the previous cell and move to another cell. This requires fewer keystrokes than pressing RETURN for each entry.

While you are in the data entry mode, if the first character you enter for a cell is a digit or an arithmetic operation, 1-2-3 assumes you want to enter a numeric value, formula, or function in that cell. An examination of Figure 6b.3 reveals that some of the cells begin with what would normally be considered a numeric value or an arithmetic operation (for example, - in cell C1 or = in cell A3). If you want to enter digits or arithmetic operation symbols but want to have them treated as text, begin the entry with an apostrophe ('), which indicates that the characters are to be treated as text. If you want to fill a cell completely with a character or symbol, press the Backslash (\) key and the symbol you want to use. This option was used for the cells in row 3.

Too Large or Too Small?—Changing Column Widths

Now that you have entered the column headings for the job offers problem, it's time to tidy up a bit. You ought at least to increase the size of the "Company Name" column. After all, the company names that will be entered later will all be longer than 9 characters. You should plan to make a column as wide as the longest piece of data you want to see in the spreadsheet in that column, although you may change the column width at any time without losing any of the data.

Look at the top of Figure 3.7. Note that the command menu now reflects that you have selected the Worksheet function and you are currently referencing the column containing the "Company Name" heading. By selecting the Column-Width option, the command screen will change, and you will be asked if you want to Set (create a new width) or Reset (return to the default setting) the column. If the Set option is selected, you will be asked to supply the number of character positions for cells in the current column. Note that as you change the default width from 9 to 25 characters, the status mode changes to EDIT, indicating that you are changing the current value.

Although many of the other columns in the spreadsheet might be wide enough to contain the data you plan to place in them, you may decide to make them wider so that visible breaks exist between the columns after the data has been entered. Move the cursor to cell B1 and re-enter the Worksheet function. This time, select the Global option. You may still select a Column-Width option within the Global operation. Now increase the column width to 12 characters per column. Since this is a global operation, all of the columns from the current column position to the right are modified to a width of 12 characters. Figure 3.8 shows that each of the column headings is now at the desired width. Thus, you may change the column width of a single column or a range of columns, depending on the options selected from the Worksheet function.

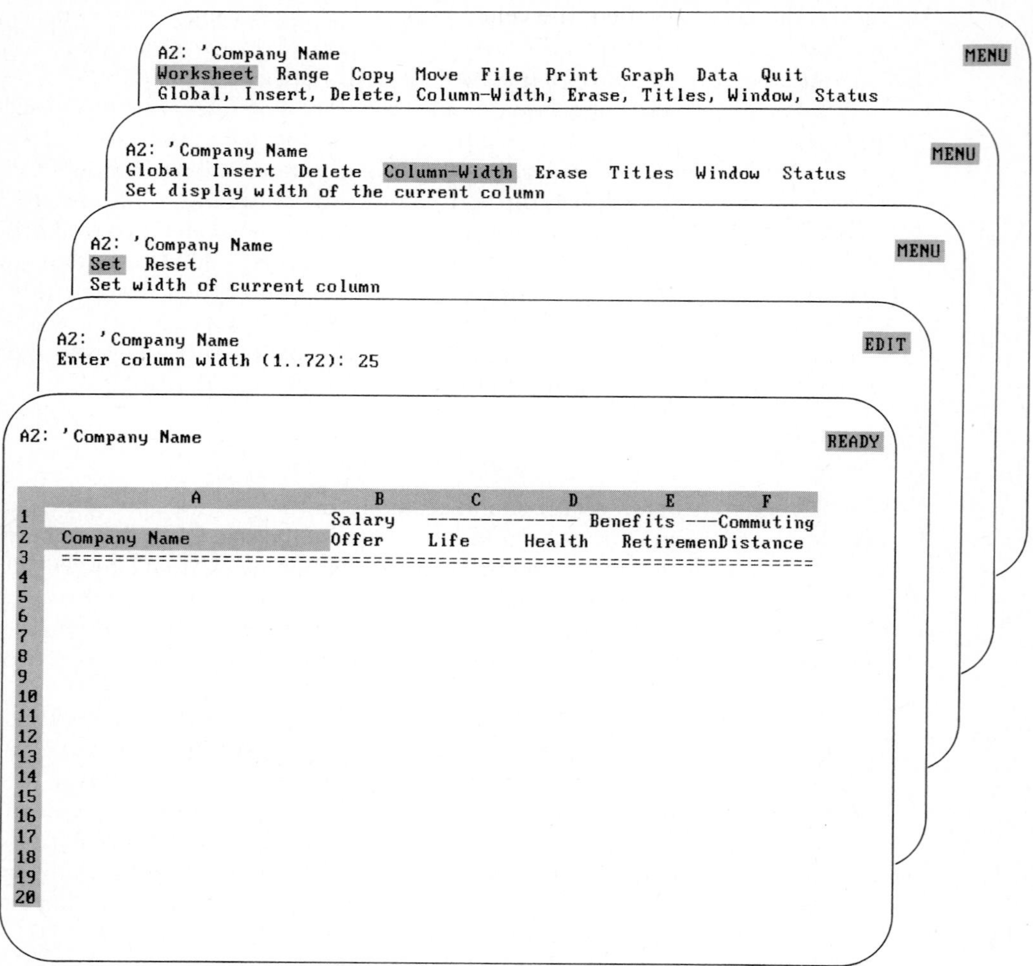

FIGURE 3.7
Changing the width of one column

Creating a New Look! — Formatting Cells for Text

When looking at Figure 3.8, you might have noticed that all of the text you have supplied occupies the left-most portion of each of the cells — that is, it is left-justified. This is acceptable, but it might be more visually appealing if you adjusted these headings so they are centered within the character positions of the columns. This time, you should select the Range function. Within the Range function, select the Label-Prefix option. As a result of this selection, you will be asked for the desired alignment of the cell contents — Left, Right, or

Center. If Left is specified, the cell contents will be left-justified. If Right is selected, the contents of the cell will be right-justified—will occupy the rightmost columns. If Center is chosen, the contents will be centered within the available character positions. For the job offers problem, you might want to center all the column headings, beginning with the "Salary Offer" heading, within the 12-character width of these columns. After you have selected the Center option, 1-2-3 will ask you to "Enter range of labels." This entry is followed by the cell range "B1..B1." This means that unless you indicate other-

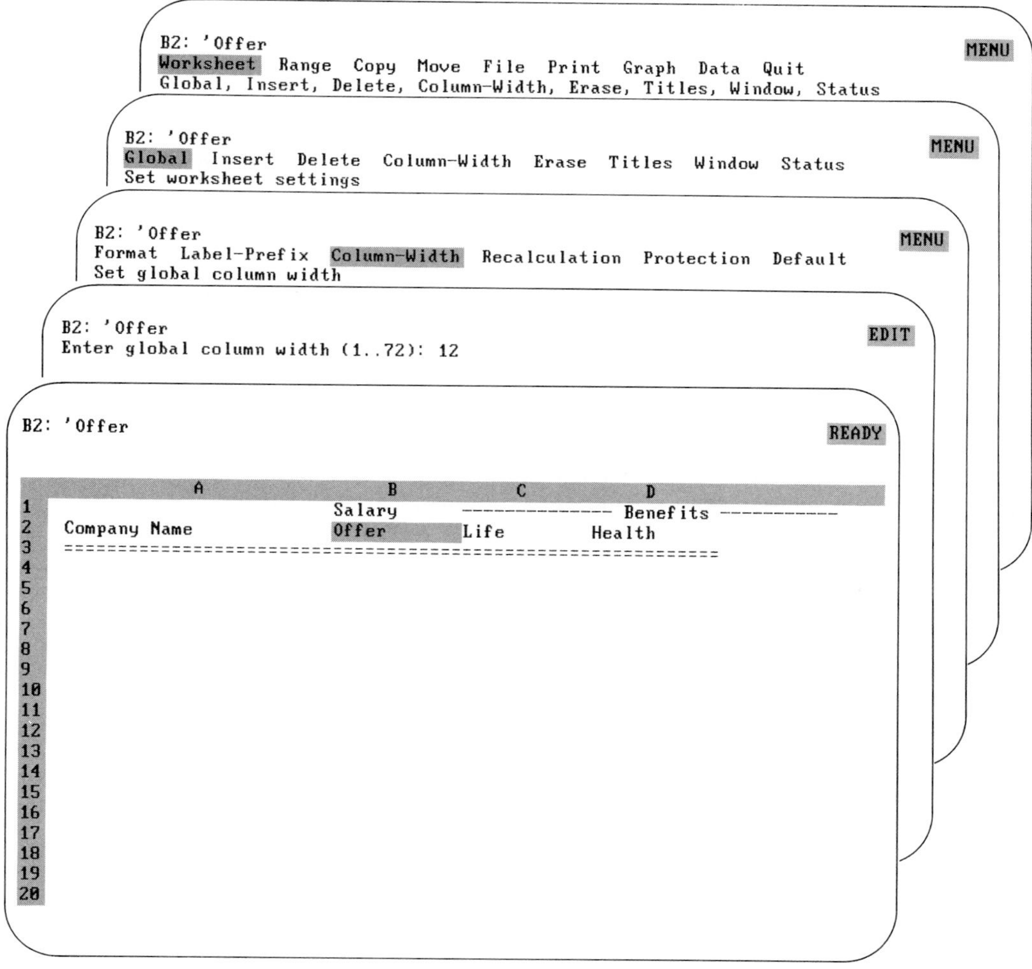

FIGURE 3.8
Changing the width of all the columns

wise, the only cell to be affected by the operation is cell B1. However, note that the status mode has changed to POINT. This means that you can modify this reference at this time.

Before you proceed with a modification, however, one important question needs to be answered. If a range is to be indicated, where does the range begin? If the range begins at B1, simply press the period (.) key. (Actually, two periods will appear in the command line.) This provides an "anchor" for the beginning cell reference. If you would like an anchor at a position other than the current cell, simply enter the beginning cell reference or use the arrow keys to move to the desired cell. Once the initial position has been identified, you may enter the ending point of the range or use the arrow key to address the ending cell. If you use the arrow key for this addressing operation, the entire area to be affected by the operation is highlighted. Anytime the status mode is POINT, cell addressing (or identifying a range of cells) can be performed in this manner. The range for this particular operation is from B1 to H2, including all cells bounded by B1 in the "northwest" and H2 in the "southeast." The results of this operation and of adjusting the group headings are shown in Figure 3.9.

A View with Numbers — Formatting Cells for Numeric Values

Now that you have had a chance to see how cells can be manipulated when they contain text, it is time to examine the type of presentations you might want to see under each of the column headings. Look at Figure 3.10. Note that the data to be recorded under the "Company Name" heading could easily be entered in the default mode — the company names are text and would be satisfactory in appearance if they were left-justified. However, many of the other columns need some special treatment. For example, you would expect the values placed under the "Salary Offer" heading to represent dollars and cents. Thus, you might begin your definition of the values to be presented in this column by changing the format. The command screen portion of this figure indicates that cell B4 is currently being referenced — the location of the first salary amount. The default alignment (right-justified for numeric values) is satisfactory, but you might want to change the format style. Figure 3.10 indicates that the Range function has been selected, along with the Format option. Once in the Format option, you can choose from a rather wide range of format styles. For your problem, the Currency presentation is desirable, an illustration of which is shown in the command message area when you move the cursor to the Currency option. The default number of decimal positions for the Currency mode is 2, but it can be modified. Finally, a range of cells is specified. (B4 to E11 is the area of the spreadsheet expected to contain dollar values from your job offers). After the operation has been completed, note that the cell format (at the top of the screen, adjacent to the cell location) now shows C2 — Currency format with two decimal places.

```
B1: 'Salary                                                      MENU
Worksheet  Range  Copy  Move  File  Print  Graph  Data  Quit
Format, Label-Prefix, Erase, Name, Justify, Protect, Unprotect, Input
```

```
B1: 'Salary                                                      MENU
Format  Label-Prefix  Erase  Name  Justify  Protect  Unprotect  Input
Align a label or range of labels (Left, Right, or Center)
```

```
B1: 'Salary                                                      MENU
Left  Right  Center
Center labels in cells
```

```
B1: 'Salary                                                      POINT
Enter range of labels: B1..B1
```

```
H2: 'Preference                                                  POINT
Enter range of labels: B1..H2
```

```
B1: ^Salary                                                      READY

            A                 B          C           D
1                           Salary  ------------- Benefits -----------
2    Company Name           Offer       Life        Health
3    ==========================================================
4
5
6
7
8
9
10
11
12
13
14
15
16
17
18
19
20
```

FIGURE 3.9
Centering the column headings

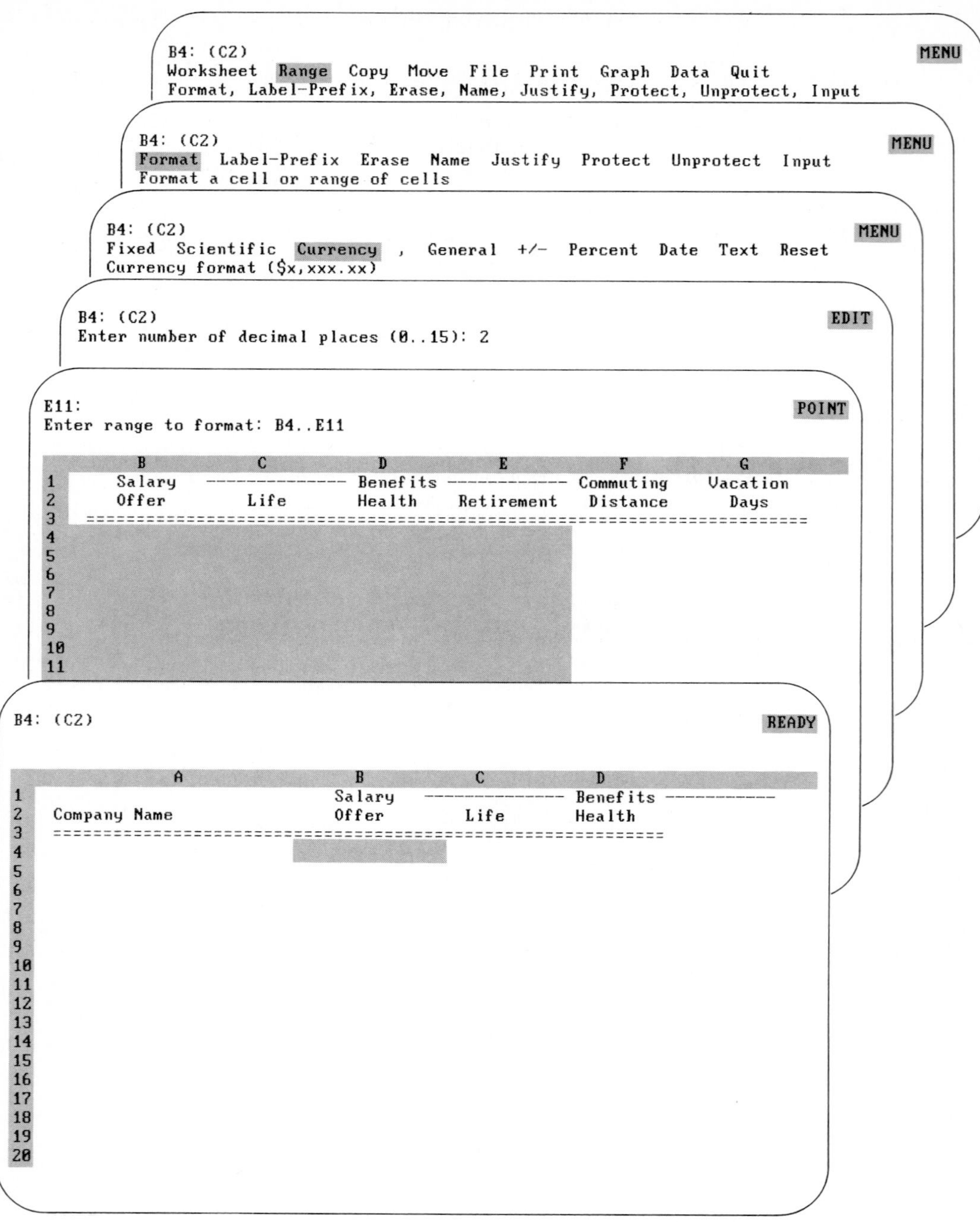

FIGURE 3.10
Selecting the currency presentation format—it makes cents

Entering the Company Names—Another Example of Entering Text

Now that all the column headings have been established and all the numeric cells are in an appropriate format, it is time to begin to enter the data associated with each of the companies in the job offers spreadsheet. The first company is "Johnson Instruments, Inc.," which should appear in row 4 column A. All that is necessary to enter the company name, or other character data, is to place the cursor in the appropriate cell and type the needed text. After the first company name has been entered, you may decide it is easier to enter all company names first and later enter the numeric values associated with each company. If this is the case, simply press the down-arrow key and continue typing individual company names in column A of each new row. The result of this activity is shown in Figure 3.11.

Two Views of the Spreadsheet—Using the Window Function

Now that you have entered all the company names, it is time to enter the numeric values associated with them. However, before you proceed, stop for a moment and think about how you might enter these numbers. If you decide to enter the values a row at a time, the spreadsheet will scroll to the left when you reach the right edge of the screen. When this happens, the company name will

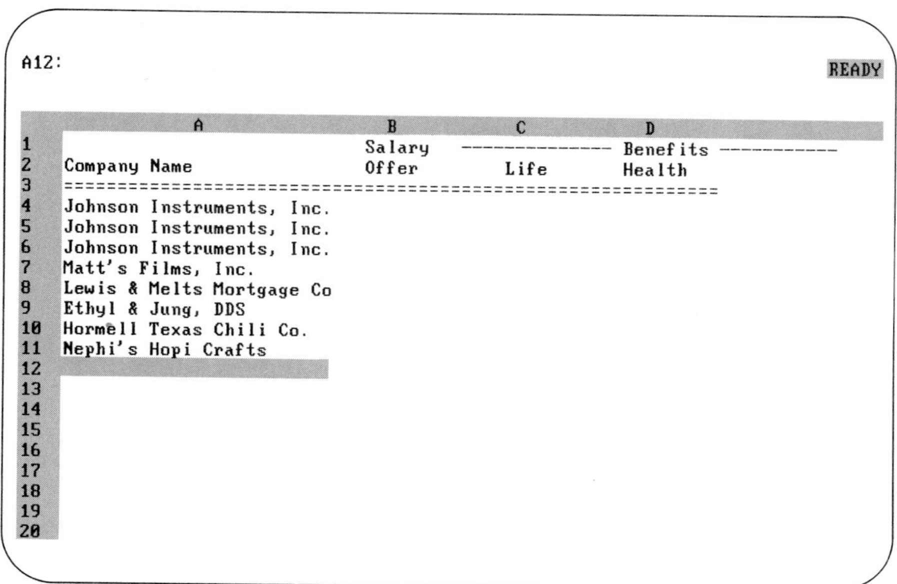

FIGURE 3.11
Entering the company names

no longer be visible. To avoid confusion and possible incorrect placement of numbers in the spreadsheet (associating a numeric value with the wrong company name), it would be desirable to have the company name always on the screen. This is exactly what spreadsheet windows are designed to support.

In Figure 3.12, the Worksheet function and the Window option have been selected, producing the third command menu. As you begin the screen-splitting operation, note that the current cell indicates a position in column B. As you examine the current menu, you will be asked to select a Horizontal (left-to-right) or Vertical (up-and-down) split. For the job offers problem, you want to

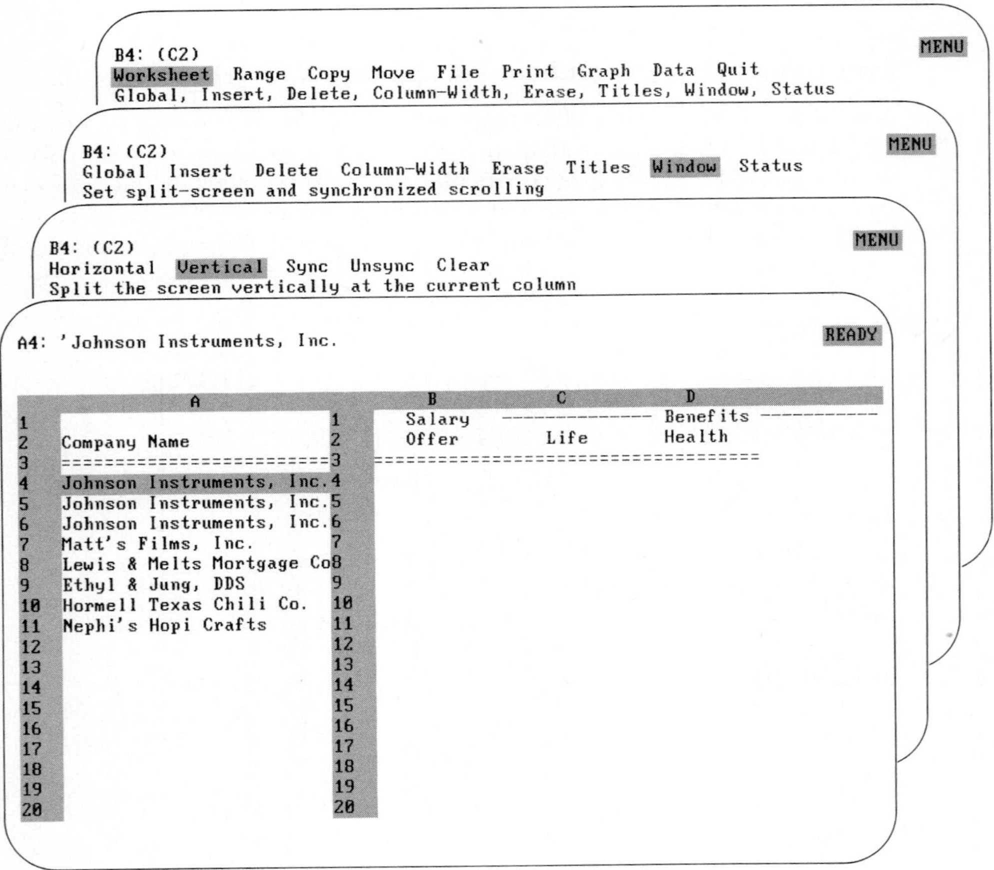

FIGURE 3.12
Creating a vertical window

split the screen vertically at column B. This means that all columns to the left of column B, the company names, will be in one window, and the columns to the right will be in another window. Horizontal and vertical windows are normally synchronized—linked so that they move together. However, after a window has been established, you may later decide that the window should be unsynchronized (Unsync), resynchronized (Sync), or removed (Clear) to make viewing the spreadsheet easier.

The results of establishing a new window are shown in Figure 3.12. Note that a break now exists between the "Company Name" and the "Salary Offer" headings and a new set of row numbers appears on the screen. The currently active window is based on the current cell reference. In this figure, cell A4 is identified as the current cell. If you find that you need to move between windows, arrow keys won't help you. However, remember that the function key F6 will allow you to move between (among) windows. Based on the current screen, if you pressed F6, you would be in the area identified as columns B through D. By pressing F6 again, you return to the window containing column A.

What Is Your Offer?—Placing Numeric Values in the Spreadsheet

Now it is time to place numeric values in the spreadsheet. The process is basically the same as entering text. So long as you begin the contents of a cell with a digit, an arithmetic operator (for example, + or −), or an "@" symbol (which identifies functions), 1-2-3 will interpret the data as a numeric value and the status mode changes to VALUE. Thus, in Figure 3.13, as soon as the 1 in 19200 was pressed on the keyboard, the status indicator changed to VALUE.

As you proceed down the length of row 4, entering the values under each column heading, the value 19200 is automatically converted to $19,200.00. (Remember that you are using the Currency format for each of these cells.) Then, as you enter the value under the "Retirement" heading and proceed to the right, the screen scrolls to the left, but the company names still appear in the first window. Finally, note that the values under "Commuting Distance," "Vacation Days," and "Job Preference" are single digits rather than in a dollars and cents format. (Remember, you stopped formatting columns of values with the "Retirement" column—column E.) Thus, these columns remain in the default format. Note also that the company names are still visible on the screen even though you are far to the right of column A.

After entering the first row, all that remains is to repeat this activity (entering numeric values) until all the job offer data has been placed in the spreadsheet. However, since you are now far away from column A, you may decide to return rapidly to the beginning columns by using the HOME key or ALTernate and left-arrow keys rather than return one cell at a time.

```
B12:                                                                      READY

                 A                          B             C          D
1                                  1     Salary    -------------- Benefits -----------
2   Company Name                   2     Offer         Life        Health
3   ===========================3   ===================================
4   Johnson Instruments, Inc.4      $19,000.00    $135.00     $354.00
5   Johnson Instruments, Inc.5      $19,200.00    $135.00     $354.00
6   Johnson Instruments, Inc.6      $19,100.00    $135.00     $354.00
7   Matt's Films, Inc.         7    $18,950.00    $155.00     $456.00
8   Lewis & Melts Mortgage Co8      $22,000.00    $500.00     $600.00
9   Ethyl & Jung, DDS          9    $20,000.00    $325.00     $950.00
10  Hormell Texas Chili Co.    10   $19,300.00    $164.00     $320.00
11  Nephi's Hopi Crafts        11   $15,670.00    $250.00     $425.00
12                             12
13                             13
14                             14
15                             15
16                             16
17                             17
18                             18
19                             19
20                             20
```

FIGURE 3.13
Entering the job offer data

Holding On to What You've Got—Saving the Spreadsheet

Although you will want to perform other operations in this spreadsheet, you may decide to save the work you have done up to now. To save a spreadsheet, enter the File function. As shown in Figure 3.14, the File function permits you to Retrieve (load) a saved spreadsheet, Save a spreadsheet (record the current spreadsheet on a disk), Xtract (save) a portion of a spreadsheet, Erase (delete) an existing spreadsheet on a disk, List (view) the spreadsheet names on a disk, Import (retrieve) a nonspreadsheet file, and produce a Directory of a disk.

Because you want to save or record the current spreadsheet, select the Save option. 1-2-3 will then ask for a file name by which the spreadsheet will be saved on the disk. If you want the spreadsheet saved on your data disk, you will have to supply the disk drive designation. The file name must be a "legal" file name for the operating system in use. However, 1-2-3 provides its own extension (WKS for WorKSheet). Hereafter, your spreadsheet will be called "JOBS," and it will be on drive B. When the spreadsheet is saved, not only are the individual cells saved, but your current cell position and windows are saved as well. Thus, if you were to exit 1-2-3 at this point and later retrieve the jobs spreadsheet, when the first screen appeared, B11 would be the current cell, and it would appear in the second window. This process allows you to begin again at some later time at exactly the position in which you last saved the spreadsheet.

A Spreadsheet with Room to Grow — The Insert Function

It is often difficult, if not impossible, to predict the exact layout that will be needed in a spreadsheet when you begin. Such is the case with the jobs spreadsheet. Now you need a new column between "Vacation Days" and "Job Preference" in which to place an estimate of the value of your vacation time. You begin by moving the current cell pointer to the location in the spreadsheet where the new column is to appear. Then you select the Insert option of the Worksheet function. Note that the Insert option allows you to insert either a column or a row. You currently need a column, so you can select this option by pressing the RETURN key, since "Column" is already highlighted. Then you

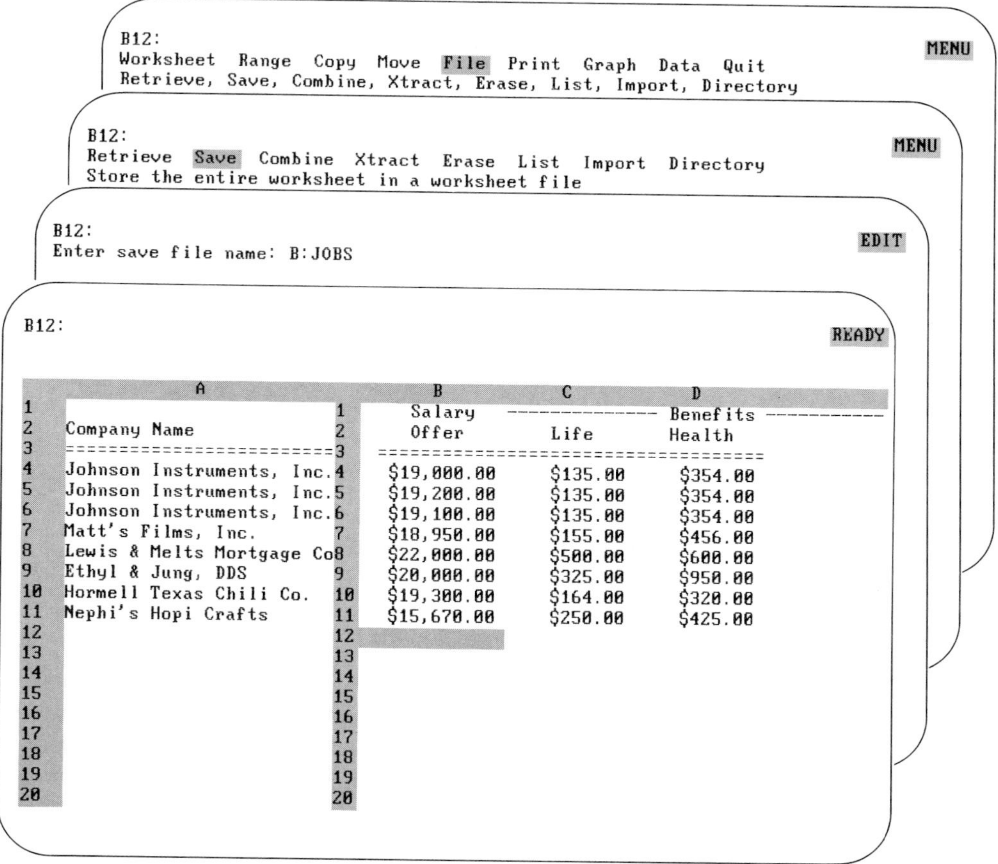

FIGURE 3.14
Saving the spreadsheet

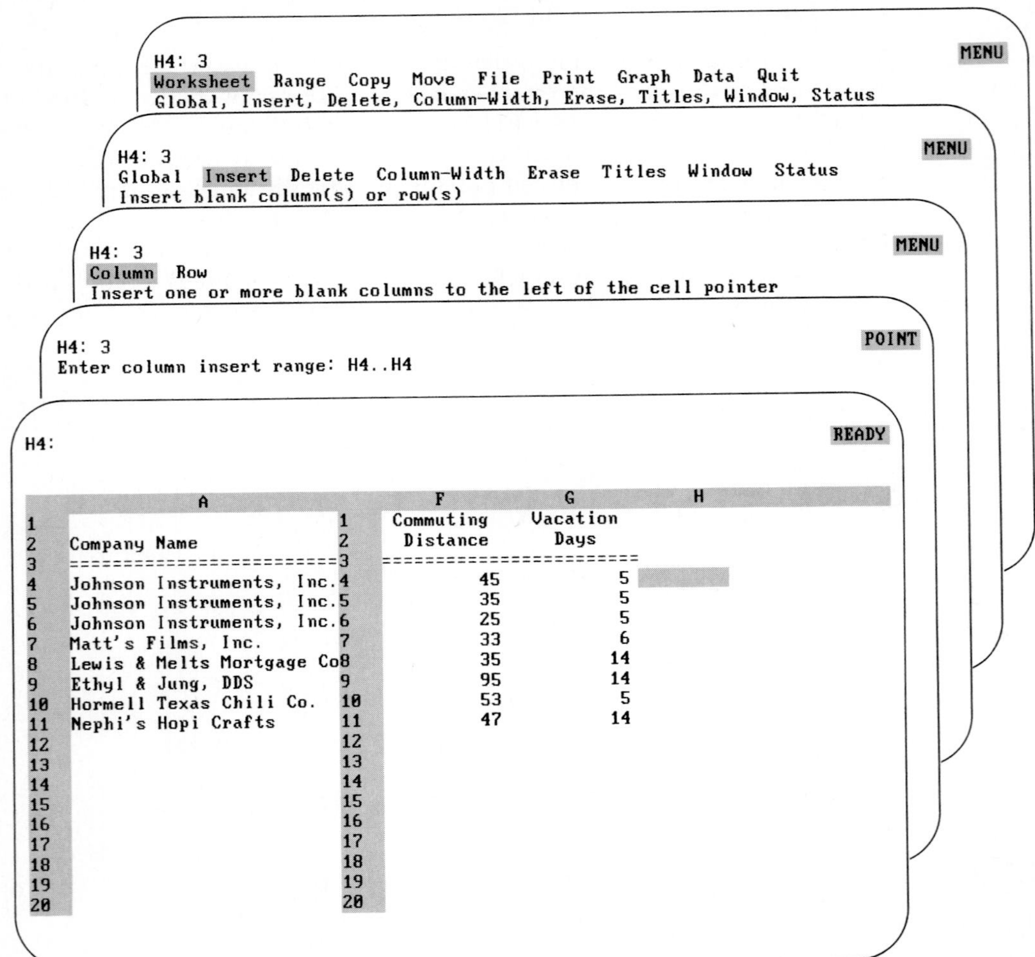

FIGURE 3.15
Inserting a new column

will be presented with other menus that control the insertion process. First, you are requested to indicate where the insertion process is to begin. As shown in Figure 3.15, when cell H4 is identified, the new column is to appear before column H. Next you are asked to specify the range of columns to be inserted. If more than one column is to be added, the number of columns represented by the range corresponds to the number of columns to be added. The columns that follow this position will be shifted to the right. Column H is now empty, and the other columns to the right of this position now have new column identifiers (for example, "Job Preference" is now in column I).

Figure It This Way—Using Formulas

You intend column H to hold approximate values of vacation time. You have determined that on the average you would work approximately 250 days in a calendar year (365 days less weekends and holidays). Thus, the "Salary Offer" of each company can be established on a per-day basis (salary divided by 250). Since vacation time is stated in terms of number of days, you could then determine the "Vacation Value" for each company. You can see this is a perfect place to use a formula. To enter a formula into a cell, begin with a digit or an arithmetic operator. (A formula will ultimately result in a numeric value.) Thus, + is entered first, to which 1-2-3 responds with the VALUE status. (1-2-3 will try to designate the formula as text if it begins with B—a column reference.) The formula is +B4/250*G4. The cell reference B4 addresses the cell in this row containing the salary offered. Salary offered is divided by 250 ("/" means to divide). The result is then multiplied ("*" means to multiply) by the contents of cell G4—the value of vacation days.

Note that spaces are not permitted in formulas. When the RETURN key is pressed, rather than the formula being placed in the cell, its value is placed there, as shown in Figure 3.16. However, if you look at the command area, you will see that the formula, not the value, is the actual contents of cell H4. Since

```
H4: (C2) +B4/250*G4                                                          READY

                  A                            F           G           H
1                                        1  Commuting    Vacation    Vacation
2  Company Name                          2  Distance       Days        Value
3  ==========================3  ===================================
4  Johnson Instruments, Inc.4             45           5      $380.00
5  Johnson Instruments, Inc.5             35           5
6  Johnson Instruments, Inc.6             25           5
7  Matt's Films, Inc.        7             33           6
8  Lewis & Melts Mortgage Co8             35          14
9  Ethyl & Jung, DDS         9             95          14
10 Hormell Texas Chili Co.   10            53           5
11 Nephi's Hopi Crafts       11            47          14
12                           12
13                           13
14                           14
15                           15
16                           16
17                           17
18                           18
19                           19
20                           20
```

FIGURE 3.16
Entering the formula for "Vacation Value"

column H is now associated with column G, any change in the value of "Vacation Days" will result in an automatic change in "Vacation Value."

Note that cell H4 is formatted in dollars and cents. Several functions have been performed between Figures 3.15 and 3.16. Some of these functions include entering the column heading, increasing the width of the column, centering the heading, and changing the format of cell H4 to a Currency format.

Duplicating — The Copy Function

Now that cell H4 has an established format, you might want to replicate (copy) the contents of that cell and its format to other cells. For the screen setup in Figure 3.16, the Copy function is used to copy the contents and format of H4 to other cells in the same column of the spreadsheet. The first command menu of the Copy function asks you to provide the anchor position. Cell H4 is the point from which you wish to copy. Since you are not copying a range of cells to another range of cells, "H4" is the only entry necessary. When you press the

```
H4: (C2) +B4/250*G4                                                   MENU
Worksheet  Range  Copy  Move  File  Print  Graph  Data  Quit
Copy a cell or range of cells
                A                    F          G           H
1                              1  Commuting   Vacation    Vacation
2  Company Name                2  Distance      Days        Value
3  ==========================3  ================================
4  Johnson Instruments, Inc.4        45           5      $380.00
5  Johnson Instruments, Inc.5        35           5
```

```
H4: (C2) +B4/250*G4                                                   POINT
Enter range to copy FROM: H4..H4
                A                    F          G           H
1                              1  Commuting   Vacation    Vacation
2  Company Name                2  Distance      Days        Value
3  ==========================3  ================================
4  Johnson Instruments, Inc.4        45           5      $380.00
5  Johnson Instruments, Inc.5        35           5
```

```
H5: (C2)                                                              POINT
Enter range to copy FROM: H4..H4        Enter range to copy TO: H5
                A                    F          G           H
1                              1  Commuting   Vacation    Vacation
2  Company Name                2  Distance      Days        Value
3  ==========================3  ================================
4  Johnson Instruments, Inc.4        45           5      $380.00
5  Johnson Instruments, Inc.5        35           5
```

FIGURE 3.17
Copying a formula to other cells in the same column

```
H11: (C2)                                                              POINT
Enter range to copy FROM: H4..H4        Enter range to copy TO: H5..H11

               A                           F          G           H
1                                  1  Commuting   Vacation    Vacation
2   Company Name                   2   Distance     Days        Value
3   ===========================    3  ====================================
4   Johnson Instruments, Inc.      4         45          5      $380.00
5   Johnson Instruments, Inc.      5         35          5
6   Johnson Instruments, Inc.      6         25          5
7   Matt's Films, Inc.             7         33          6
8   Lewis & Melts Mortgage Co      8         35         14
9   Ethyl & Jung, DDS              9         95         14
10  Hormell Texas Chili Co.        10        53          5
11  Nephi's Hopi Crafts            11        47         14
```

```
H4: (C2) +B4/250*G4                                                    READY

               A                           F          G           H
1                                  1  Commuting   Vacation    Vacation
2   Company Name                   2   Distance     Days        Value
3   ===========================    3  ====================================
4   Johnson Instruments, Inc.      4         45          5      $380.00
5   Johnson Instruments, Inc.      5         35          5      $384.00
6   Johnson Instruments, Inc.      6         25          5      $382.00
7   Matt's Films, Inc.             7         33          6      $454.80
8   Lewis & Melts Mortgage Co      8         35         14    $1,232.00
9   Ethyl & Jung, DDS              9         95         14    $1,120.00
10  Hormell Texas Chili Co.        10        53          5      $386.00
11  Nephi's Hopi Crafts            11        47         14      $877.52
12                                 12
13                                 13
14                                 14
15                                 15
16                                 16
17                                 17
18                                 18
19                                 19
20                                 20
```

FIGURE 3.17
(continued)

RETURN key, you can then enter the "range of cells to copy TO." The receiving range is established in exactly the same way as when you were centering the heading. After you have established the range to copy "FROM" and the range to copy "TO," as soon as the Copy function is completed, you will see the results, as indicated in Figure 3.17. When a formula is copied in this manner, the cell reference H4 is changed to H5 for row 5, H6 for row 6, and so on.

Figure 3.18 illustrates the process of adding another column, further to the left than before, which is essentially the same as entering "Vacation Value." In fact, when the "Actual Offer" column is added, the previously used relative addresses (used in the "Vacation Value" column) are adjusted so that the

```
C11: (C2) +B11+D11+E11+F11                                          READY

                  A                      B          C           D
1                         1        Salary      Actual     ------------- Benefits
2  Company Name           2        Offer       Offer          Life
3  ========================3  =================================
4  Johnson Instruments, Inc.4  $19,000.00  $22,822.00     $135.00
5  Johnson Instruments, Inc.5  $19,200.00  $23,022.00     $135.00
6  Johnson Instruments, Inc.6  $19,100.00  $22,922.00     $135.00
7  Matt's Films, Inc.      7  $18,950.00  $24,561.00     $155.00
8  Lewis & Melts Mortgage Co8  $22,000.00  $27,500.00     $500.00
9  Ethyl & Jung, DDS       9  $20,000.00  $27,275.00     $325.00
10 Hormell Texas Chili Co. 10  $19,300.00  $21,986.20     $164.00
11 Nephi's Hopi Crafts     11  $15,670.00  $17,678.00     $250.00
12                         12
13                         13
14                         14
15                         15
16                         16
17                         17
18                         18
19                         19
20                         20
```

FIGURE 3.18
Another formula—computing the value of the "Actual Offer"

operation is still accurate. The formula to be used in the "Actual Offer" column is relatively the same as the one used before. The formula is +B4+D4+E4+F4, where B4 indicates the salary offer cell, D4 the life insurance cell, E4 the health insurance cell, and F4 the retirement contribution cell. Thus, cell references that appear in formulas can indicate cells that are either left or right (up or down) from the current column, or both. The result of this formula is placed in cell C4, formatted to the Currency presentation mode, and copied to the remaining cells in the same column, as shown in Figure 3.18.

Providing a Visual Break—The Copy Function Again

Now that all the values have been entered for all the companies, it is time to start thinking about what else you want to do. First, you might decide to place a visual break across the bottom of the list of companies similar to the one immediately under the column headings. To do this, you could duplicate the contents of cell A11 (see Figure 3.19). Select the Copy function and indicate that you want to copy the contents FROM that cell TO another cell or, as shown in Figure 3.19, a range of cells.

Letting 1-2-3 "Compute"—Using Functions

Most spreadsheet packages provide a number of very useful functions. Although the result of many of the functions could be achieved by using formulas, often it is much easier to use a function than to create just the right formula or set of formulas. The functions that are available with 1-2-3 are presented in Table 3.3.

For the job offers problem, you might want to establish averages (for comparison purposes) for many of the columns that contain numeric values. As shown in Figure 3.20, you can begin by entering the title "Average Company" in A12. Then move to B12 and indicate the function you want to enter. You then enter @AVG(list), where "list" is a range of cell references including all of the salary offers. Of course, you could simply type in a range reference, but many of the 1-2-3 functions permit you to address the cells by using the arrow keys. For example, if you entered AVG(and began to move the cursor, you would see that a cell reference is added after the left parenthesis. As you move, the cell reference is updated until you enter .. (two periods), indicating that the first part of the range has been established. Then you proceed downward (using

B12: \- READY

	A		B	C	D	
1		1	Salary	Actual	--------------	Benefits
2	Company Name	2	Offer	Offer	Life	
3	=========================	3	============	============	============	
4	Johnson Instruments, Inc.	4	$19,000.00	$22,822.00	$135.00	
5	Johnson Instruments, Inc.	5	$19,200.00	$23,022.00	$135.00	
6	Johnson Instruments, Inc.	6	$19,100.00	$22,922.00	$135.00	
7	Matt's Films, Inc.	7	$18,950.00	$24,561.00	$155.00	
8	Lewis & Melts Mortgage Co	8	$22,000.00	$27,500.00	$500.00	
9	Ethyl & Jung, DDS	9	$20,000.00	$27,275.00	$325.00	
10	Hormell Texas Chili Co.	10	$19,300.00	$21,986.20	$164.00	
11	Nephi's Hopi Crafts	11	$15,670.00	$17,678.00	$250.00	
12	-------------------------	12	------------	------------	------------	
13		13				
14		14				
15		15				
16		16				
17		17				
18		18				
19		19				
20		20				

FIGURE 3.19
Creating a visual break with the Copy function

TABLE 3.3 Lotus 1-2-3 Functions

Function Name	Meaning and Operation
@ABS(n)	Absolute value, where "n" is a numeric value, a cell reference, or a formula
@ACOS(n)	Arc cosine "n," where "n" is a numeric value, a cell reference, or a formula
@ASIN(n)	Arc sine "n," where "n" is a numeric value, a cell reference, or a formula
@ATAN(n)	Arc tangent "n," where "n" is a numeric value, a cell reference, or a formula (2-quadrant)
@ATAN2(n)	Arc tangent "n," where "n" is a numeric value, a cell reference, or a formula (4-quadrant)
@AVG(list)	Average, where "list" is a series of numeric values, a series of cell references, or a range of cell references
@CHOOSE(n,list)	Selects the "nth" value from a "list" of values, where "n" is a numeric value, a cell reference, or a formula and "list" is a series of numeric values, cell references, or formulas
@COS(n)	Cosine "n," where "n" is a numeric value, a cell reference, or a formula
@COUNT(list)	Counts the number of values in a designated list, where "list" is a series of numeric values, a series of cell references, or a range of cell references
@DATE(value1,value2,value3)	Determines the number of days elapsed since the turn of the century, where "value1" is a year, "value2" is a month, and "value3" is a day
@DAY(value)	Determines day number (1 to 31) based on a "value" representing the number of days elapsed since January 1, A.D. 1
@ERR	Returns the special value "ERR"—error
@EXP(n)	Calculates "e to the nth," where "n" is a power and may be a numeric value, a cell reference, or a formula
@FALSE	Returns the value 0, if "false"
@FV(value1,value2,value3)	Determines the Future Value of an investment, where "value1" represents the payment amount, "value2" represents the interest rate, and "value3" represents the investment period
@HLOOKUP(value,area,number)	Searches a designated "area" composed of rows, columns, or both for the indicated "value," where "value" is a numeric

Function Name	Meaning and Operation
	value, a cell reference, or a formula and "number" is the initial row value
@IF(logical,value1,value2)	Determines if the "logical" expression is true. If true, "value1" is assigned to the cell. If false, "value2" is assigned to the cell.
@INT(n)	Integer value of "n," where "n" is a numeric value, a cell reference, or a formula
@ISERR(value)	Indicates if indicated value is an error and returns the value 1 if true
@ISNA(value)	Indicates if indicated value is not available and returns the value 1 if true
@IRR(value,list)	Internal Rate of Return for an initial estimated "value" of the rate for the specified "list" of cells, where "list" is a range of cells
@LN(n)	Natural logarithm of "n," where "n" is a numeric value, a cell reference, or a formula
@LOG(n)	Logarithm (base 10) of "n," where "n" is a numeric value, a cell reference, or a formula
@MAX(list)	Maximum value in a "list," where "list" is a series of numeric values or a range of cells
@MIN(list)	Minimum value in a "list," where "list" is a series of numeric values or a range of cells
@MOD(value1,value2)	Returns the remainder when "value1" is divided by "value2," where "value1" and "value2" are numeric values, cell references, or functions
@MONTH(value)	Determines month number (1 to 12) based on a "value" representing the number of days elapsed since January 1, A.D. 1
@NA	Returns the special value "NA"—not available
@NPV(value,list)	Net Present Value of a "list," where "value" is the interest rate and "list" is a series of numeric values, a series of cell references, or a range of cell references
Function Name	Meaning and Operation
@PI	Returns the mathematical value of "pi"
@PMT(value1,value2,value3)	Determines the amount of a loan Payment, where "value1" represents the principal amount, "value2" represents the interest rate, and "value3" represents the loan period

TABLE 3.3 *(continued)*

Function Name	Meaning and Operation
@PV(value1,value2,value3)	Determines the Present Value of an annuity, where "value1" represents the payment amount, "value2" represents the interest rate, and "value3" represents the investment period
@RAND	Generates a random number between 0 and 1
@ROUND(n,digits)	Rounds "n" to a value indicated by "digits," where "n" is a numeric value, a cell reference, or a formula and "digits" is the number of decimal points in the desired result (if positive) or position to the left of the decimal point (if negative)
@SIN(n)	Sine of "n," where "n" is a numeric value, a cell reference, or a formula
@SQRT(n)	Square root of "n," where "n" is a numeric value, a cell reference, or a formula
@STD(list)	Standard Deviation of a "list," where "list" is a series of numeric values, a series of cell references, or a range of cell references
@SUM(list)	Sum (total) of a "list," where "list" is a series of numeric values, a series of cell references, or a range of cell references
@TAN(n)	Tangent of "n," where "n" is a numeric value, a cell reference, or a formula
@TODAY	Determines the number of days elapsed since January 1, A.D. 1
@TRUE	Returns the value 1, if "true"
@VAR(list)	Variance (differences) of a "list," where "list" is a series of numeric values, a series of cell references, or a range of cell references
@VLOOKUP(value,area,number)	Searches a designated "area" composed of rows, columns, or both for the indicated "value," where "value" is a numeric value, a cell reference, or a formula and "number" is the initial column value
@YEAR(value)	Determines year number (0 to 99) based on a "value" representing the number of days elapsed since January 1, A.D. 1

```
B13: (F2) @AVG(B4..B11)                                                        READY

                  A                          B            C            D
1                                    1    Salary       Actual      -------------- Benefits
2   Company Name                     2    Offer        Offer          Life
3   ========================3    ====================================
4   Johnson Instruments, Inc.4    $19,000.00  $22,822.00     $135.00
5   Johnson Instruments, Inc.5    $19,200.00  $23,022.00     $135.00
6   Johnson Instruments, Inc.6    $19,100.00  $22,922.00     $135.00
7   Matt's Films, Inc.       7    $18,950.00  $24,561.00     $155.00
8   Lewis & Melts Mortgage Co8    $22,000.00  $27,500.00     $500.00
9   Ethyl & Jung, DDS        9    $20,000.00  $27,275.00     $325.00
10  Hormell Texas Chili Co.  10   $19,300.00  $21,986.20     $164.00
11  Nephi's Hopi Crafts      11   $15,670.00  $17,678.00     $250.00
12  ------------------------12   ------------------------------------
13  Average Company          13     19152.50
14                           14
15                           15
16                           16
17                           17
18                           18
19                           19
20                           20
```

FIGURE 3.20
Creating an "Average Company"—using the AVG function

the arrow keys) to establish the ending position of the range—B11 for your problem. When you have reached the ending position, conclude the cell function by entering the closing parenthesis. When the RETURN key is pressed, the function is stored in cell B12, and 1-2-3 determines the value of the function and places it in the cell. The result of using the average function is shown in Figure 3.20. Be careful when specifying the range (for a function in this case and for other commands that use ranges): Make sure the first cell reference is above the last cell reference, if you are copying down a column. If you are copying a row, the beginning position must be to the left of the ending position.

Look at Figure 3.21. Note that the presentation format of cell B13 has been altered to the Currency form, and the contents of B13 have been copied to the remaining cells in this row. However, this causes a bit of a problem. The averages for "Commuting Distance," "Vacation Days," and "Job Preference" are shown in the Currency format, but they are not dollars and cents. Thus, for these cells, it is necessary to re-enter the Format function and change their presentation format code back to the Fixed mode.

New Information on a Job Offer—Adding a New Row

Next, you need to add the new job offer from First State National Bank. Insert a new row at row 11 of your spreadsheet for the new job information. Figure

```
B13: (C2) @AVG(B4..B11)                                              READY

               A                  B           C            D
1                              1   Salary      Actual     ------------- Benefits
2  Company Name                2   Offer       Offer          Life
3  ============================3 ==================================
4  Johnson Instruments, Inc.   4 $19,000.00  $22,822.00      $135.00
5  Johnson Instruments, Inc.   5 $19,200.00  $23,022.00      $135.00
6  Johnson Instruments, Inc.   6 $19,100.00  $22,922.00      $135.00
7  Matt's Films, Inc.          7 $18,950.00  $24,561.00      $155.00
8  Lewis & Melts Mortgage Co   8 $22,000.00  $27,500.00      $500.00
9  Ethyl & Jung, DDS           9 $20,000.00  $27,275.00      $325.00
10 Hormell Texas Chili Co.    10 $19,300.00  $21,986.20      $164.00
11 Nephi's Hopi Crafts        11 $15,670.00  $17,678.00      $250.00
12 --------------------------12 ----------------------------------
13 Average Company            13 $19,152.50  $23,470.78      $224.88
14                            14
15                            15
16                            16
17                            17
18                            18
19                            19
20                            20
```

FIGURE 3.21
Averages after formatting and copying

```
B12: (C2) 22000                                                      READY

               A                  B           C            D
1                              1   Salary      Actual     ------------- Benefits
2  Company Name                2   Offer       Offer          Life
3  ============================3 ==================================
4  Johnson Instruments, Inc.   4 $19,000.00  $22,822.00      $135.00
5  Johnson Instruments, Inc.   5 $19,200.00  $23,022.00      $135.00
6  Johnson Instruments, Inc.   6 $19,100.00  $22,922.00      $135.00
7  Matt's Films, Inc.          7 $18,950.00  $24,561.00      $155.00
8  Lewis & Melts Mortgage Co   8 $22,000.00  $27,500.00      $500.00
9  Ethyl & Jung, DDS           9 $20,000.00  $27,275.00      $325.00
10 Hormell Texas Chili Co.    10 $19,300.00  $21,986.20      $164.00
11 Nephi's Hopi Crafts        11 $15,670.00  $17,678.00      $250.00
12 First State National Bank  12 $22,000.00  $25,485.00      $210.00
13 --------------------------13 ----------------------------------
14 Average Company            14 $19,152.50  $23,470.78      $224.88
15                            15
16                            16
17                            17
18                            18
19                            19
20                            20
```

FIGURE 3.22
Entering a new row—the values for First State National Bank

```
B14: (C2) @AVG(B4..B12)                                              READY

                  A                          B            C             D
1                             1        Salary       Actual      -------------- Benefits
2   Company Name              2        Offer        Offer            Life
3   ========================= 3   ===================================
4   Johnson Instruments, Inc. 4    $19,000.00   $22,822.00        $135.00
5   Johnson Instruments, Inc. 5    $19,200.00   $23,022.00        $135.00
6   Johnson Instruments, Inc. 6    $19,100.00   $22,922.00        $135.00
7   Matt's Films, Inc.        7    $18,950.00   $24,561.00        $155.00
8   Lewis & Melts Mortgage Co 8    $22,000.00   $27,500.00        $500.00
9   Ethyl & Jung, DDS         9    $20,000.00   $27,275.00        $325.00
10  Hormell Texas Chili Co.   10   $19,300.00   $21,986.20        $164.00
11  Nephi's Hopi Crafts       11   $15,670.00   $17,678.00        $250.00
12  First State National Bank 12   $22,000.00   $25,485.00        $210.00
13  ------------------------- 13  -----------------------------------
14  Average Company           14   $19,468.89   $23,694.58        $223.22
15                            15
16                            16
17                            17
18                            18
19                            19
20                            20
```

FIGURE 3.23
Correcting the "Average Company" row

3.22 shows the data entered in row 12 for First State National Bank. Note that the formula for "Actual Offer" (and "Vacation Value") has been copied into this row from row 11 and that the format has been set to Currency. Also note that none of the averages have changed and that no message currently exists in the error line area.

Since the new row is outside the range of cells used to calculate the average company values, the numbers you have entered had no effect on the values in row 14. To get the new averages for row 14 that include First State National Bank, you must re-enter the average function and copy it across the entire row, and again change the formats for "Commuting Distance," "Vacation Days," and "Job Preference." When you have finished, your screen should be the same as the one in Figure 3.23.

Putting Rows in Order — The Sort Function

The next requirement of this problem is to order the job offers by your job preference. The list of companies is adequate, but you will probably want the jobs you prefer (the smaller numbers) at the top of the list. To accomplish this, you can use the Move function to specify the cells you wish to move and then specify the location to which you wish to move them. One word of caution: When you move cells that are used in a mathematical function — in this case,

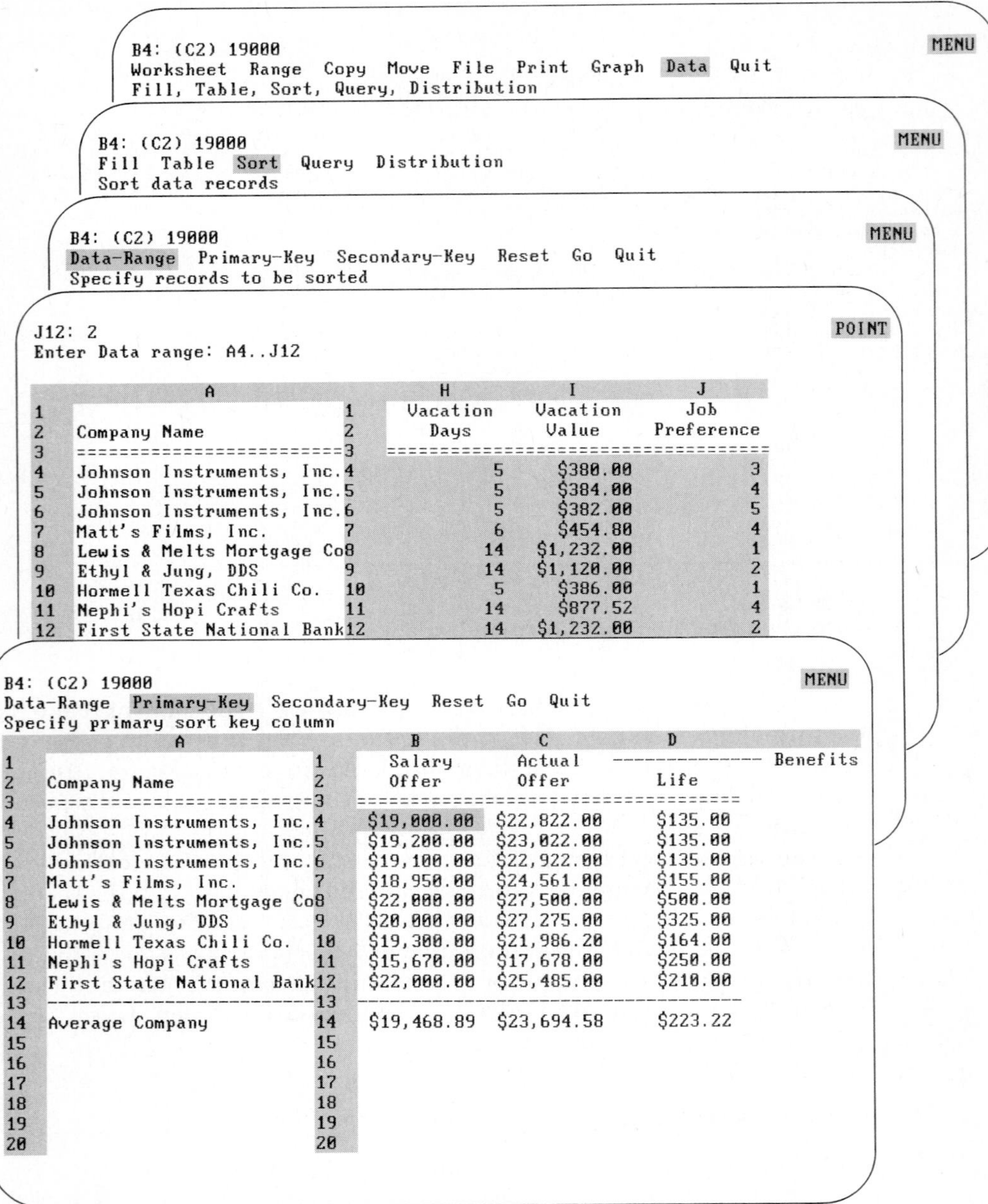

FIGURE 3.24
Getting the job preferences in sorted order

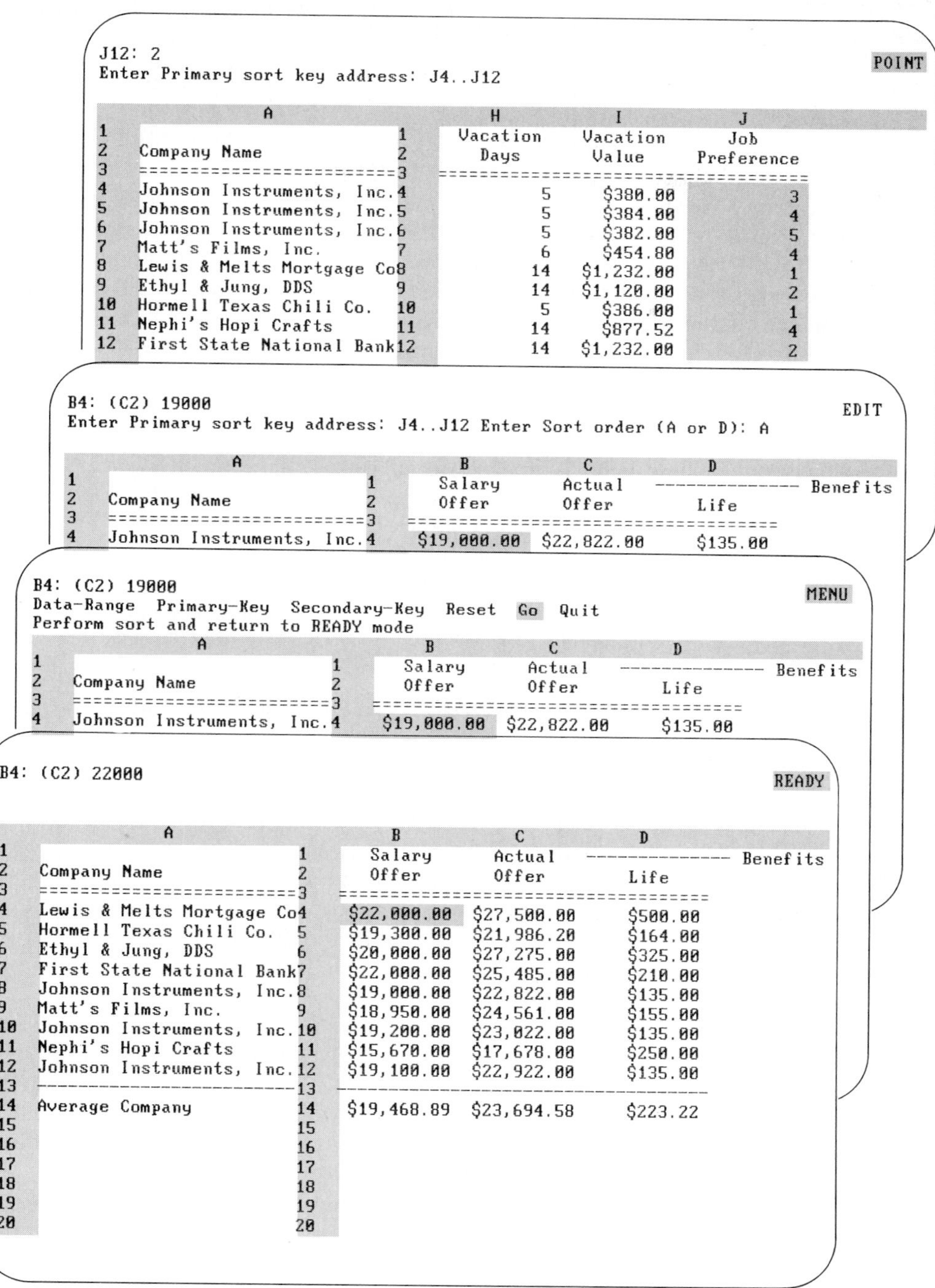

J12: 2
Enter Primary sort key address: J4..J12
POINT

	A	H	I	J
1		Vacation	Vacation	Job
2	Company Name	Days	Value	Preference
3	=========================	===========	===========	===========
4	Johnson Instruments, Inc.	5	$380.00	3
5	Johnson Instruments, Inc.	5	$384.00	4
6	Johnson Instruments, Inc.	5	$382.00	5
7	Matt's Films, Inc.	6	$454.80	4
8	Lewis & Melts Mortgage Co	14	$1,232.00	1
9	Ethyl & Jung, DDS	14	$1,120.00	2
10	Hormell Texas Chili Co.	5	$386.00	1
11	Nephi's Hopi Crafts	14	$877.52	4
12	First State National Bank	14	$1,232.00	2

B4: (C2) 19000
Enter Primary sort key address: J4..J12 Enter Sort order (A or D): A
EDIT

	A	B	C	D	
1		Salary	Actual	--------------	Benefits
2	Company Name	Offer	Offer	Life	
3	=========================	===========	===========	===========	
4	Johnson Instruments, Inc.	$19,000.00	$22,822.00	$135.00	

B4: (C2) 19000
Data-Range Primary-Key Secondary-Key Reset Go Quit
Perform sort and return to READY mode
MENU

	A	B	C	D	
1		Salary	Actual	--------------	Benefits
2	Company Name	Offer	Offer	Life	
3	=========================	===========	===========	===========	
4	Johnson Instruments, Inc.	$19,000.00	$22,822.00	$135.00	

B4: (C2) 22000
READY

	A	B	C	D	
1		Salary	Actual	--------------	Benefits
2	Company Name	Offer	Offer	Life	
3	=========================	===========	===========	===========	
4	Lewis & Melts Mortgage Co	$22,000.00	$27,500.00	$500.00	
5	Hormell Texas Chili Co.	$19,300.00	$21,986.20	$164.00	
6	Ethyl & Jung, DDS	$20,000.00	$27,275.00	$325.00	
7	First State National Bank	$22,000.00	$25,485.00	$210.00	
8	Johnson Instruments, Inc.	$19,000.00	$22,822.00	$135.00	
9	Matt's Films, Inc.	$18,950.00	$24,561.00	$155.00	
10	Johnson Instruments, Inc.	$19,200.00	$23,022.00	$135.00	
11	Nephi's Hopi Crafts	$15,670.00	$17,678.00	$250.00	
12	Johnson Instruments, Inc.	$19,100.00	$22,922.00	$135.00	
13	-------------------------	-----------	-----------	-----------	
14	Average Company	$19,468.89	$23,694.58	$223.22	
15					
16					
17					
18					
19					
20					

FIGURE 3.24
(continued)

the "Average" function—the cells involved in the calculations may change, giving you incorrect results.

There is an alternative to the Move function, as indicated in Figure 3.24 (preceding pages), you can select the Data function and from this function select the Sort option. When the next menu appears, you should specify both a Data-Range and a Primary-Key before executing the sorting operation. First, the Data-Range is selected, and the range of cells representing the computational area (A4 through J12) is identified. Since you must specify a Data-Range, you can sort only a portion of the spreadsheet; that is, columns can be sorted independently. Second, you must identify the Primary-Key. The Primary-Key consists of the cell values in Column J—the values representing job preference. After the key has been identified, you will be asked to indicate whether you want the order of sorting to be ascending (A). [Select descending (D) for a largest to smallest order.] Finally, after all of the characteristics of the sorting operation have been specified, the Go option is selected and the operation is executed. The sorted spreadsheet is shown in Figure 3.24.

Note that the company names are now ordered by job preference. At this point it is probably a good idea to save your work again. However, this time the spreadsheet file JOBS already exists, and you will be asked if you want the new spreadsheet to Replace the old one.

Calculations Without Changing the Spreadsheet—The Table Function

The last requirement of this problem is to calculate your salary at the end of the first year if you accept the offer from Lewis & Melts Mortgage Company. To accomplish this you can use the Table function to perform the calculations without changing your spreadsheet.

A table is a defined area of a spreadsheet that records the results of different values being placed in the spreadsheet without changing the spreadsheet. A table works by allowing you to change the value in an Input Cell and see how formulas in various Output Cells change in value. Lotus supports two types of tables that work in slightly different ways.

Table type 1 allows you to enter a set of values for one Input variable and see the changes in one or more Output Cells. To set up this type of table, place the different values for the Input variable in the first column of the table. Place the Output Cells to be investigated in the first (top) row of the table. The cell to use as the Input variable is then specified, and the table's Output Cells are filled with the resulting values.

Table type 2 allows you to enter a set of values for two Input variables and see the changes in one Output Cell. To set up this type of table, place the different values for the first Input variable in the first column, and place the different values for the second Input variable in the first (top) row of the table. The Output formula (or cell) is placed in the upper-left cell of the table. When you specify which cell to use for the first Input and which cell to use for the second Input, the table is filled with the resulting values in the Output cell for all possible combinations of the two Input Cells.

To set up a table that will calculate your salary next year for different cost-of-living increases, move the cursor to cell B17 and enter the value 2200 as illustrated in Figure 3.25. You will use this value as the "base value" for your input values. Next move to cell C17 and enter the formula +B4+D4+E4+F4. This is the output variable for your Actual Salary in your table. Now, move the cursor to cell D17 and enter the formula +B4/250*H4. This is the

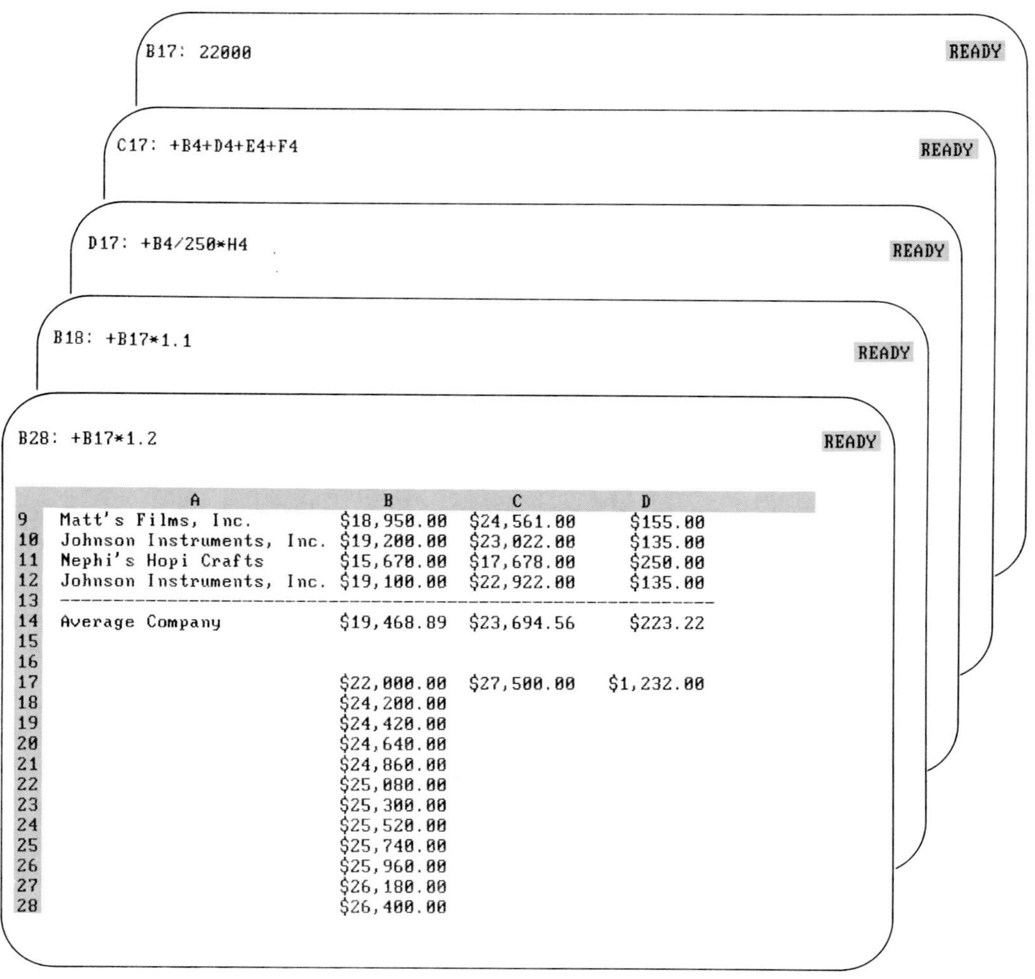

	A	B	C	D
9	Matt's Films, Inc.	$18,950.00	$24,561.00	$155.00
10	Johnson Instruments, Inc.	$19,200.00	$23,022.00	$135.00
11	Nephi's Hopi Crafts	$15,670.00	$17,678.00	$250.00
12	Johnson Instruments, Inc.	$19,100.00	$22,922.00	$135.00
13	----------------------------	----------	----------	----------
14	Average Company	$19,468.89	$23,694.56	$223.22
15				
16				
17		$22,000.00	$27,500.00	$1,232.00
18		$24,200.00		
19		$24,420.00		
20		$24,640.00		
21		$24,860.00		
22		$25,080.00		
23		$25,300.00		
24		$25,520.00		
25		$25,740.00		
26		$25,960.00		
27		$26,180.00		
28		$26,400.00		

FIGURE 3.25
Setting Up the Values for a Table

output variable for your Vacation Value. Finally, enter the formulas +B17*1.10 . . . +B17*1.20 in cell B18 through B28 so that your spreadsheet looks like the final screen in Figure 3.25.

You are now ready to enter the Table commands shown in Figure 3.26. Select the Data function from the main menu, and from this menu select the

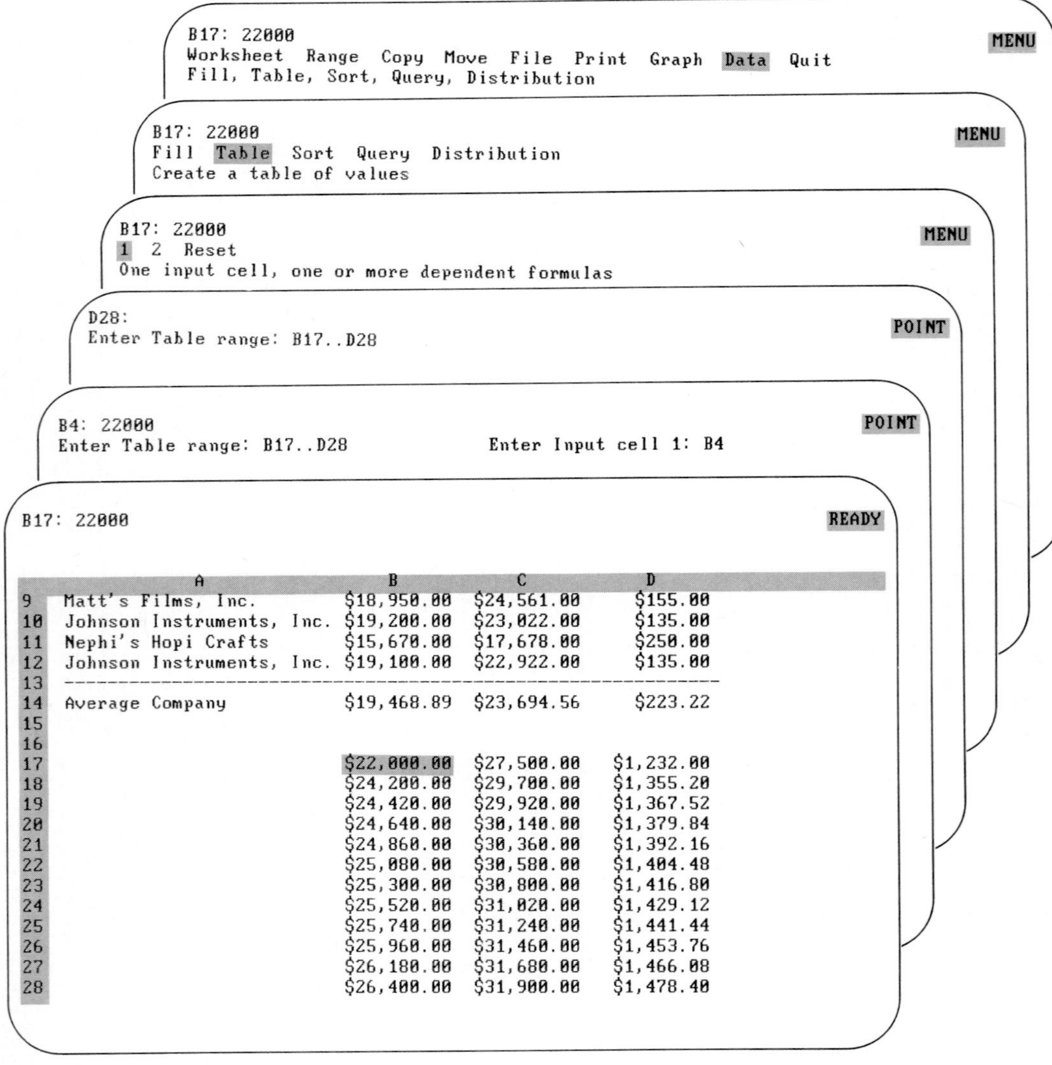

FIGURE 3.26
Entering the Table Commands

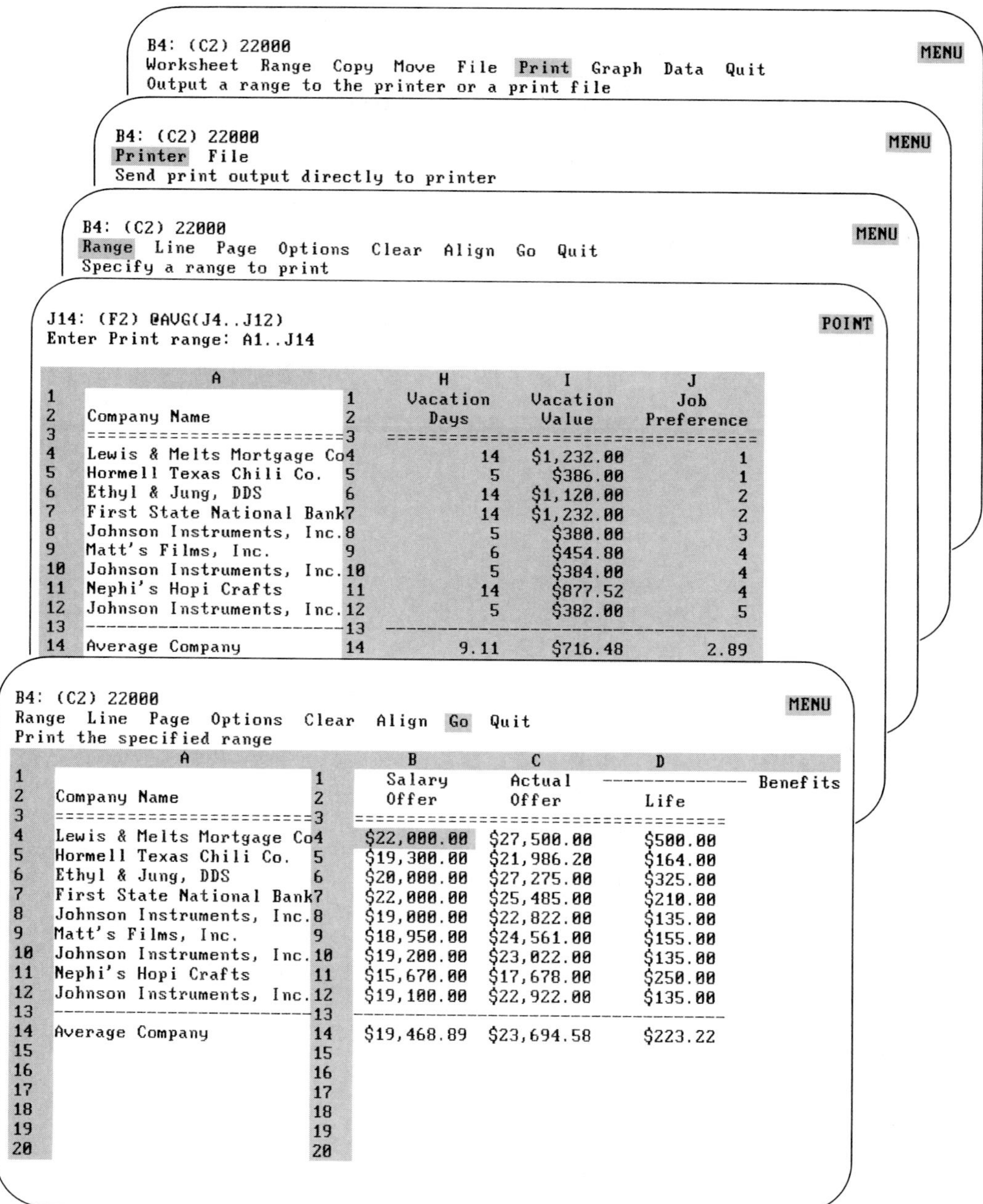

FIGURE 3.27
Controlling the printed output

Table option. When the next menu appears, specify 1 and enter the table range, as shown in Figure 3.26. After you specify the input cell as B4, the table will be calculated automatically, giving the results shown. If you make any changes in the spreadsheet or in the input or output variables of the table, simply press the F8 key and the table will be recalculated.

Showing Off Your Spreadsheet — The Print Function

Your spreadsheet is now complete. Perhaps you would like to see the entire spreadsheet in printed form. To print the spreadsheet, select the Print function. This function then produces the Print menu, as shown in Figure 3.27, on the preceding page. Your choices are to send the spreadsheet to the Printer or send the spreadsheet to a print File. The next menu provides output controls.

			Benefits							
Company Name	Salary Offer	Actual Offer	Life	Health	Retirement	Commuting Distance	Vacation Days	Vacation Value	Job Preference
Lewis & Melts Mortgage Co	$22,000.00	$27,500.00	$500.00	$600.00	$4,400.00	35	14	$1,232.00	1
Hormell Texas Chili Co.	$19,300.00	$21,986.20	$164.00	$320.00	$2,202.20	53	5	$386.00	1
Ethyl & Jung, DDS	$20,000.00	$27,275.00	$325.00	$950.00	$6,000.00	95	14	$1,120.00	2
First State National Bank	$22,000.00	$25,485.00	$210.00	$325.00	$2,950.00	25	14	$1,232.00	2
Johnson Instruments, Inc.	$19,000.00	$22,822.00	$135.00	$354.00	$3,333.00	45	5	$380.00	3
Matt's Films, Inc.	$18,950.00	$24,561.00	$155.00	$456.00	$5,000.00	33	6	$454.80	4
Johnson Instruments, Inc.	$19,200.00	$23,022.00	$135.00	$354.00	$3,333.00	35	5	$384.00	4
Nephi's Hopi Crafts	$15,670.00	$17,678.00	$250.00	$425.00	$1,333.00	47	14	$877.52	4
Johnson Instruments, Inc.	$19,100.00	$22,922.00	$135.00	$354.00	$3,333.00	25	5	$382.00	5
Average Company	$19,468.89	$23,694.58	$223.22	$459.78	$3,542.69	43.67	9.11	$716.48	2.89

FIGURE 3.28
A printed report from the job offers spreadsheet

First, specify the portion of the spreadsheet to be printed by using the Range option and indicating the range of cells. Next, select the Options from the menu. As a result of entering the Go mode, the contents of the spreadsheet are printed, as illustrated by Figure 3.28.

Getting Out of Lotus — The Quit Function

When your spreadsheet work has been completed, terminate 1-2-3 by using the Quit function and return to the Lotus Access System menu. From there, you may decide to select another Lotus function or return to the operating system. When you select the Quit function, you will be asked if you are sure that you want to exit 1-2-3. Remember to save your spreadsheet now if you plan to use it later—this is your last chance before you leave 1-2-3. Once you exit from 1-2-3, you will again see the initial menu, and you will be able to select the Exit function. Finally, you will be asked to confirm an exit to the operating system. If you indicate "Yes" to this question, the next set of symbols to appear on the screen will be produced by the operating system. You are now successfully out of Lotus.

Other Features of Lotus Spreadsheet

Lotus is an integrated package and so includes a number of features that are not covered here. However, there are some features of 1-2-3 that do need to be mentioned here. The first of these is selected through the Status option, Worksheet function. This option permits you to examine some default characteristics that help control the way 1-2-3 operates. One of the features shown through the Status option is the Recalculation mode. When you begin working on a large spreadsheet, it is often desirable to have the Recalculation mode turned "off" so that individual cell entries can be made more quickly. You can change the Recalculation mode through the Global option of the Worksheet function. You can, of course, have the Recalculation performed anytime by pressing the F9 key. The default Recalculation sequence is "Natural" (it first evaluates cells that contain formulas and functions from which other cells derive their values), although this may be changed to sequences (such as Columnwise, Rowwise, or Manual).

Other character default characteristics of the worksheet that are presented through the Status menu are values of General cell format, label entries prefixed by an apostrophe ('), cell width of 9 characters, and Protection mode "off." These features may be changed to new values, most by using the Global option of the Worksheet function. Finally, the Status menu indicates the amount of available memory for your spreadsheet. This is one way to determine how much work space you have left.

Another handy feature of 1-2-3 is available through the Name option of the

Range function. Suppose you have a series of cells that are frequently used as a group. This could be a row, a column, several rows, or several columns. If you select the Name option, you are permitted to refer to this group of cells by a *range name*. For example, the Name function can be used to name the column of values representing the "Salary Offer" as "Salary." "Salary" could now be used to reference this group of cells for the purposes of computation. To establish the average salary offered, it would be possible to use the function @AVG(Salary). The range name itself must be a continuous string of characters, without blanks or hyphens. However, the underline character may be used in place of blanks or hyphens. Also remember that the F3 key can be used to provide a list of the range names for your spreadsheet.

These are but a few of the additional capabilities of the Lotus spreadsheet. As you explore this package more fully, you will become familiar with still other features that you can develop and use to assist you in solving particular types of problems or reducing the time it takes to create a spreadsheet. As you encounter unfamiliar features of the package, remember that the Help function (F1) provides explanations of how they work.

Lotus 1-2-3 Database

Learning to Use Lotus 1-2-3 Database

The previous section introduced you to the spreadsheet capabilities of Lotus. This section will investigate how Lotus can be used to perform database functions. Because many of the operations performed by Lotus database derive from the spreadsheet package, you should be familiar with the material presented in the previous section. For a short discussion of general database functions, read the material in the beginning of Module 2.

To use the database capabilities of Lotus, place your Lotus system disk in drive A and enter LOTUS. After the Lotus Access System screen appears, select the 1-2-3 option. Thus, the same procedure used to access a Lotus spreadsheet is also used to access a Lotus database.

Solving the Job Hunting Problem

The remaining sections of this module are devoted to solving the job hunting problem. This problem will require you to build a database and maintain the contents of the database by adding new records, modifying attribute values, and deleting unwanted records. In addition, you will be required to query the database and produce reports based on the contents of the database.

As a job seeker, you are interested in keeping track of interviews and offers (or rejection letters) as they come in. Items to keep track of include company name and address, contact person within the company, date the company responded to the application, and the scheduled interview date or notice of "no openings." Once you get an interview, you want to be able to keep track of the salary offered, the amount of certain benefits (life insurance, health insurance, vacation days, and retirement contributions). You may also want to know the commuting distance to the job site and to order the job offers according to your personal job preferences.

Once you know what information you want to keep track of, you can build a database and use it to produce reports and comparisons. The data needed for this problem is presented in Appendix A. The following list represents the types of activities you will perform on the database once it has been built. (Note that some database packages permit the use of only one database at a time. Thus, steps 1 and 2 below may be combined because of this limitation.)

1. Build the structure of the COMPANY part of the database and enter the data.
2. Build the structure of the JOBS part of the database and enter the data.
3. You have just received a letter of rejection from WTBS Channel 5 TV. You need to enter the COMPANY part of the database and change the status of the offer from that company from "Ongoing" to "Rejected."
4. You have received a letter of acceptance from First State National Bank. You need to enter the COMPANY part of the database and change the status of the offer from that company from "Ongoing" to "Offered." Enclosed with the letter of acceptance was a description of the job containing the following details:

   Site: North
   Amount of Offer: $22,000.00
   Life Insurance: $210.00
   Health Insurance: $325.00
   Vacation: 14 Days
   Retirement contribution: $2950.00

   You have established that the commuting distance is 25 miles, and your preference for the job is 2. This information needs to be added to the JOBS database.
5. Find all companies that have rejected your employment application. You want to delete any job details that appear in the database for these companies.
6. Find all the jobs in the COMPANY part of the database for which offers have been extended. The report is to contain the company name, contact person, city, state, and zip code. You want the companies listed in order by zip code. You also want a count of the number of job offers.
7. Find all companies in the COMPANY part of the database for which you have an offer and for which the amount of the offer (from the JOBS database) is greater than $19,000. You want to produce a report containing the company name, the amount of the offer, your preference for the job, and the "net" offer (the amount of the offer plus life, health, and retirement contributions). You want these jobs listed by preference (and also by company name if the preferences happen to be the same for two or more jobs).
8. Since you will be sending letters to all the companies listed in your database, use the Lotus macro capabilities to produce mailing labels for them.

Loading Data into a Lotus Database

Once the spreadsheet skeleton appears on the screen, you may begin to enter data, using the same techniques demonstrated for Lotus spreadsheets. However, if you compare the data presented in Figure 3.29 with previous Lotus spreadsheets, you will notice that only a single-line heading appears above each column. Each column heading becomes a field name that can be used to identify the data within that column. The difference between "normal" headings and database headings will be explained in the *search criteria* discussion.

Although only a portion of the spreadsheet is shown in Figure 3.29, all of the job hunting data has been entered—one row per company. (Note that Johnson Instruments was entered three times because you have received three different offers from them.) This format represents one of the weaknesses of Lotus database when compared to other database packages. For example, dBASE and R:base have the capability of loading data into two or more databases and joining elements of those databases to create other relationships. Lotus database has no such feature.

To correct an entry in the Lotus database, follow the same procedure used for the Lotus spreadsheet. Thus, to change the "Status" of the job offer for

```
A1: ^Company Name                                                    READY

                 A                          B                   C
1          Company Name                  Address              City
2   ----------------------------------------------------------------------
3   Johnson Instruments, Inc.    P. O. Box 1234          Dallas
4   Johnson Instruments, Inc.    P. O. Box 1234          Dallas
5   Johnson Instruments, Inc.    P. O. Box 1234          Dallas
6   Champion Cowboy Supply       126 Hollyhill Road      Garland
7   General Electronics, Inc.    87634 Dynamics Way      Ft. Worth
8   First State National Bank    302 Central Expressway  Dallas
9   Lewis & Melts Mortgage Co.   1 Bank Plaza            Denton
10  Ethyl & Jung, DDS            23 Molar Hill Lane      Dennison
11  Aerospace Education Center   1423 Jupiter Road       Garland
12  ABC Stereo Warehouse         3434 Sound Place        Dallas
13  WTBS Channel 5 TV            9826 Neonoise Court     Plano
14  Hormell Texas Chili Company  1 Hots Place            Ft. Worth
15  Children's Museum            Look Out Point          Ft. Worth
16  FBI                          10-20 Parole Street     Arlington
17  Mosteq Computer Company      1428 Wozniak Way        Farmers Branch
18  Nephi's Hopi Crafts          16 Alma, Suite 34       Tulsa
19  Kelly Construction Company   1414 Jupiter Road       Garland
20  Jana's Management Consultants 2323 Beltline Road     Irving
```

FIGURE 3.29
Creating the original database

```
I13: 'Ongoing                                                        LABEL
Rejected

                     A                           I       J         K        L
1           Company Name              1    Status   Worksite  Distance Vacation
2  -----------------------------------2    ----------------------------------------
3  Johnson Instruments, Inc.          3   Offered  South            45        5
4  Johnson Instruments, Inc.          4   Offered  Mid-cities       35        5
5  Johnson Instruments, Inc.          5   Offered  North            25        5
6  Champion Cowboy Supply             6   Ongoing
7  General Electronics, Inc.          7   Ongoing
8  First State National Bank          8   Ongoing
9  Lewis & Melts Mortgage Co.         9   Offered  Mid-cities       35       14
10 Ethyl & Jung, DDS                  10  Offered  North            95       14
11 Aerospace Education Center         11  Rejected
12 ABC Stereo Warehouse               12  Ongoing
13 WTBS Channel 5 TV                  13  Ongoing
14 Hormell Texas Chili Company        14  Offered  East             53        5
15 Children's Museum                  15  Ongoing
16 FBI                                16  Ongoing
17 Mosteq Computer Company            17  Ongoing
18 Nephi's Hopi Crafts                18  Offered  East             47       14
19 Kelly Construction Company         19  Ongoing
20 Jana's Management Consultants      20  Rejected
```

FIGURE 3.30
Changing "Ongoing" to "Rejected" for WTBS Channel 5 TV

```
Q8: 2                                                                READY

                     A                            O          P           Q
1           Company Name              1      Health    Retirement Preference
2  -----------------------------------2   ----------------------------------
3  Johnson Instruments, Inc.          3     $354.00    $3,333.00          3
4  Johnson Instruments, Inc.          4     $354.00    $3,333.00          4
5  Johnson Instruments, Inc.          5     $354.00    $3,333.00          5
6  Champion Cowboy Supply             6
7  General Electronics, Inc.          7
8  First State National Bank          8     $325.00    $2,950.00          2
9  Lewis & Melts Mortgage Co.         9     $600.00    $4,400.00          1
10 Ethyl & Jung, DDS                  10    $950.00    $6,000.00          1
11 Aerospace Education Center         11
12 ABC Stereo Warehouse               12
13 WTBS Channel 5 TV                  13
14 Hormell Texas Chili Company        14    $320.00    $2,202.20          1
15 Children's Museum                  15
16 FBI                                16
17 Mosteq Computer Company            17
18 Nephi's Hopi Crafts                18    $425.00    $1,333.00          4
19 Kelly Construction Company         19
20 Jana's Management Consultants      20
```

FIGURE 3.31
Entering new values for the First State National Bank

WTBS Channel 5 TV from "ongoing" to "rejected," simply move the cell pointer to cell I13 and type the new entry, as shown in Figure 3.30.

To add new information into the database (spreadsheet), simply move to the row you want to contain the additional information, and enter the values into one cell at a time. Thus, when new information is received about the job offer from First State National Bank, simply go to row 8 and begin entering the values for "Location," "Offer," "Life Insurance," and so on. Figure 3.31 shows these values added to the database in row 8.

Performing Search Operations on the Database — Finding Rejected Companies

Your next problem is to locate all companies in the database containing "Rejected" as the job "Status." Then you are to remove the offer information from the database. However, you do wish to retain some information about the company, such as the company name, address, and so on.

Before you begin a search operation, it is necessary to set up a Search Criterion. Note that cell I25 in Figure 3.32 contains the value STATUS, and cell I26 contains "Rejected." These two values could be placed anywhere in the spreadsheet but have been placed below the Status column for convenience.

```
I28: ^Status                                                          READY

                  A                             G         H        I        J
9  Lewis & Melts Mortgage Co.       9      11/30     01/15    Offered  Mid-cities
10 Ethyl & Jung, DDS                10     11/15     11/30    Offered  North
11 Aerospace Education Center       11     11/16     12/13    Rejected
12 ABC Stereo Warehouse             12     11/16     02/22    Ongoing
13 WTBS Channel 5 TV                13     12/03     01/06    Rejected
14 Hormell Texas Chili Company      14     12/05     01/31    Offered  East
15 Children's Museum                15     11/30     01/06    Ongoing
16 FBI                              16     01/03     01/21    Ongoing
17 Mosteq Computer Company          17     12/31              Ongoing
18 Nephi's Hopi Crafts              18     12/09     01/06    Offered  East
19 Kelly Construction Company       19     12/09              Ongoing
20 Jana's Management Consultants    20     01/06              Rejected
21 Bar Four Ranch                   21     12/28     02/03    Refused
22 Matt's Films, Inc.               22     12/31     01/07    Offered  North
23 Roger, Roger & Ray, Inc.         23     12/15              Rejected
24                                  24
25 Search Criterion                 25                        Status
26                                  26                        Rejected
27                                  27
28          Company Name            28  Responded  Interview  Status
```

FIGURE 3.32
Setting up the database for query operations

These two values represent the basis of a future search operation. Also note that row 28 now contains a set of headings (field names). These headings signify the data values to be copied when a match for the Search Criterion is found; that is, data that has matching headings can be copied. Although these headings are shown in the same order as the original headings, they may be in any order, some may be eliminated, and others may be added.

The next operation is to provide a Range Name for the set of data to be searched. In Figure 3.33, the Range function is selected from the primary menu. Next, the Name option is selected, followed by the Create option. Finally, the column of data containing all the job status entries (column I) is identified by the name STATUS; it begins in I1 and ends in I23. Since only a single Name can be provided, this limits the size of column headings.

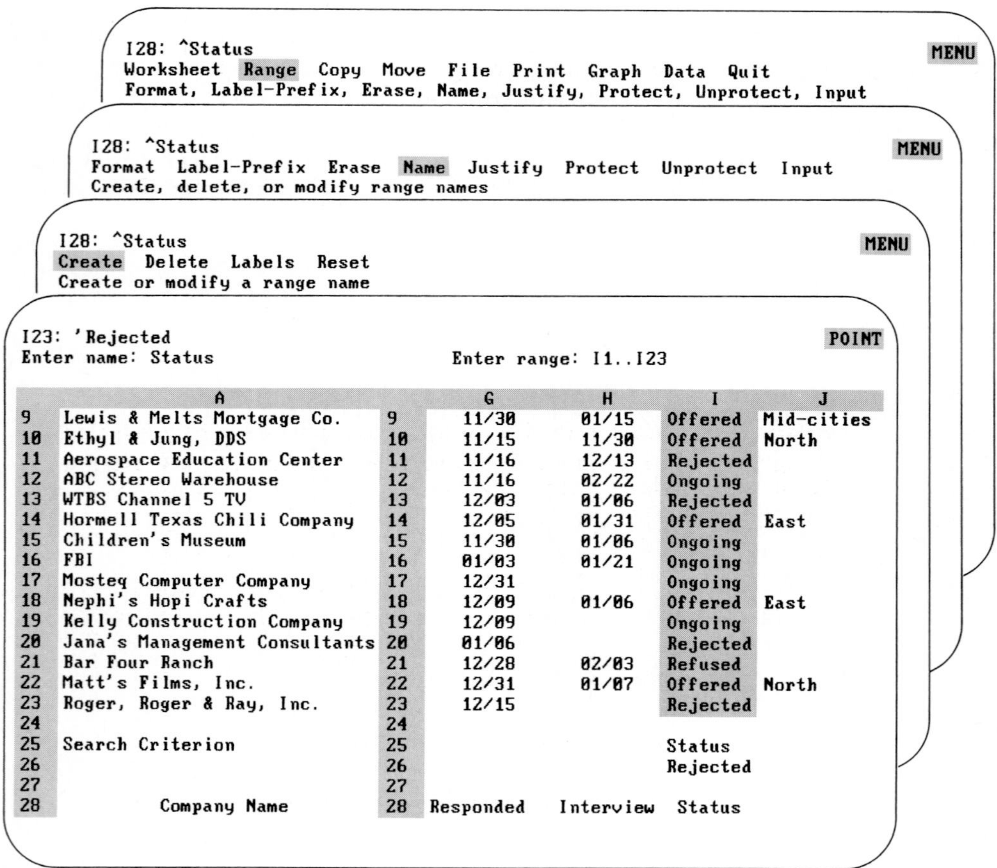

FIGURE 3.33
Providing a name for a range of data values

```
I28: ^Status                                                              MENU
Input  Criterion  Output  Find  Extract  Unique  Delete  Reset  Quit
Copy all records that match criteria to Output range
```

```
I28: ^Status                                                              MENU
Input  Criterion  Output  Find  Extract  Unique  Delete  Reset  Quit
Delete all records that match criteria
            A                              G         H         I         J
9   Lewis & Melts Mortgage Co.      9    11/30     01/15     Offered   Mid-cities
10  Ethyl & Jung, DDS               10   11/15     11/30     Offered   North
11  Aerospace Education Center      11   11/16     12/13     Rejected
12  ABC Stereo Warehouse            12   11/16     02/22     Ongoing
13  WTBS Channel 5 TV               13   12/03     01/06     Rejected
14  Hormell Texas Chili Company     14   12/05     01/31     Offered   East
15  Children's Museum               15   11/30     01/06     Ongoing
16  FBI                             16   01/03     01/21     Ongoing
17  Mosteq Computer Company         17   12/31               Ongoing
18  Nephi's Hopi Crafts             18   12/09     01/06     Offered   East
19  Kelly Construction Company      19   12/09               Ongoing
20  Jana's Management Consultants   20   01/06               Rejected
21  Bar Four Ranch                  21   12/28     02/03     Refused
22  Matt's Films, Inc.              22   12/31     01/07     Offered   North
23  Roger, Roger & Ray, Inc.        23   12/15               Rejected
24                                  24
25  Search Criterion                25                       Status
26                                  26                       Rejected
27                                  27
28          Company Name            28 Responded  Interview  Status
```

FIGURE 3.34
Selecting and performing database query operations on *next two pages)*

Now you have completed all of the preparation that is necessary before performing a search operation. You have (1) created a Search Criterion, (2) identified the data to be copied (which is optional), and (3) identified by name and range the data to be searched.

To execute the search, select the Data function from the primary menu. The next selection is the Query option from the second menu. This provides the final menu that controls the search process. Note that this menu contains the key words *Input*—identifies all the data to be affected by the search (and move), *Criterion*—specifies the cells in which the Search Criterion appears, *Output*—indicates where copied records are to be placed, *Find*—locates only the records matching the criterion, *Extract*—locates and copies the records matching the criterion from the input area to the output area, *Unique*—locate only a single match, *Delete*—removes records in the input area matching the Search Criterion, *Reset*—establishes a new set of conditions, and *Quit*—returns to the previous menu.

As shown in Figure 3.34, the first choice is to select the Input area, consisting of all cells from A1 to Q23—the entire original database. Next, the Search

```
I26: 'Rejected                                                          POINT
Enter Criterion range: I25..I26

                  A                            G        H        I        J
9   Lewis & Melts Mortgage Co.     9       11/30    01/15    Offered  Mid-cities
10  Ethyl & Jung, DDS              10      11/15    11/30    Offered  North
11  Aerospace Education Center     11      11/16    12/13    Rejected
12  ABC Stereo Warehouse           12      11/16    02/22    Ongoing
13  WTBS Channel 5 TV              13      12/03    01/06    Rejected
14  Hormell Texas Chili Company    14      12/05    01/31    Offered  East
15  Children's Museum              15      11/30    01/06    Ongoing
16  FBI                            16      01/03    01/21    Ongoing
17  Mosteq Computer Company        17      12/31             Ongoing
18  Nephi's Hopi Crafts            18      12/09    01/06    Offered  East
19  Kelly Construction Company     19      12/09             Ongoing
20  Jana's Management Consultants  20      01/06             Rejected
21  Bar Four Ranch                 21      12/28    02/03    Refused
22  Matt's Films, Inc.             22      12/31    01/07    Offered  North
23  Roger, Roger & Ray, Inc.       23      12/15             Rejected
24                                 24
25  Search Criterion               25                        Status
26                                 26                        Rejected
27                                 27
28           Company Name          28  Responded  Interview  Status
```

```
I37:                                                                POINT
Enter Output range: A28..I37

                  A                            G        H        I        J
18  Nephi's Hopi Crafts            18      12/09    01/06    Offered  East
19  Kelly Construction Company     19      12/09             Ongoing
20  Jana's Management Consultants  20      01/06             Rejected
21  Bar Four Ranch                 21      12/28    02/03    Refused
22  Matt's Films, Inc.             22      12/31    01/07    Offered  North
23  Roger, Roger & Ray, Inc.       23      12/15             Rejected
24                                 24
25  Search Criterion               25                        Status
26                                 26                        Rejected
27                                 27
28           Company Name          28  Responded  Interview  Status
29                                 29
30                                 30
31                                 31
32                                 32
33                                 33
34                                 34
35                                 35
36                                 36
37                                 37
```

FIGURE 3.34
(continued)

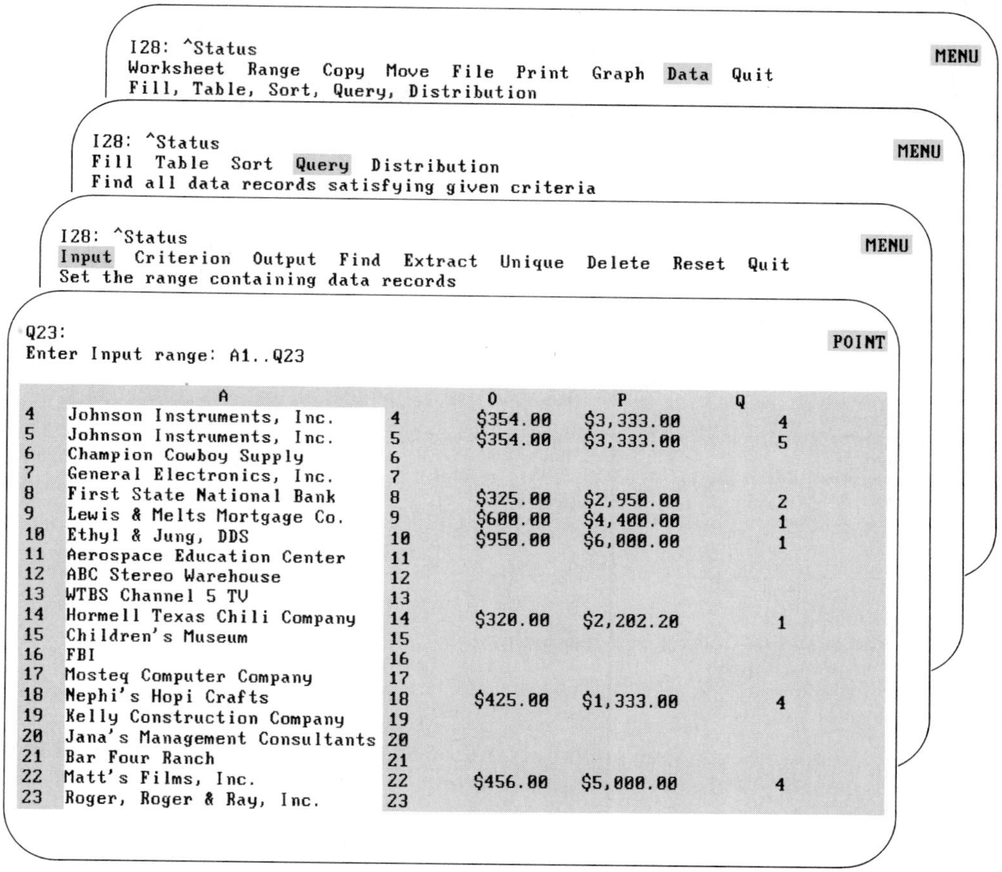

```
I28: ^Status                                                          MENU
Worksheet  Range  Copy  Move  File  Print  Graph  Data  Quit
Fill, Table, Sort, Query, Distribution
```

```
I28: ^Status                                                          MENU
Fill  Table  Sort  Query  Distribution
Find all data records satisfying given criteria
```

```
I28: ^Status                                                          MENU
Input  Criterion  Output  Find  Extract  Unique  Delete  Reset  Quit
Set the range containing data records
```

```
Q23:                                                                  POINT
Enter Input range: A1..Q23

            A                          O          P            Q
4  Johnson Instruments, Inc.    4    $354.00   $3,333.00          4
5  Johnson Instruments, Inc.    5    $354.00   $3,333.00          5
6  Champion Cowboy Supply       6
7  General Electronics, Inc.    7
8  First State National Bank    8    $325.00   $2,950.00          2
9  Lewis & Melts Mortgage Co.   9    $600.00   $4,400.00          1
10 Ethyl & Jung, DDS            10   $950.00   $6,000.00          1
11 Aerospace Education Center   11
12 ABC Stereo Warehouse         12
13 WTBS Channel 5 TV            13
14 Hormell Texas Chili Company  14   $320.00   $2,202.20          1
15 Children's Museum            15
16 FBI                          16
17 Mosteq Computer Company      17
18 Nephi's Hopi Crafts          18   $425.00   $1,333.00          4
19 Kelly Construction Company   19
20 Jana's Management Consultants 20
21 Bar Four Ranch               21
22 Matt's Films, Inc.           22   $456.00   $5,000.00          4
23 Roger, Roger & Ray, Inc.     23
```

FIGURE 3.34
(continued)

Criterion is identified as being cells I25 and I26. Then the Output area is identified as cells A28 through I37—the second set of headings and an additional nine rows. (You do not anticipate that any more than nine companies have a "Rejected" status.) Extract is now selected. This selection completes the "search and copy" operation. Data values for all of the rejected companies have now been copied below the second set of headings. Finally, to remove the rejected companies from the primary part of the database, select the Delete option.

Your screen should now look like the one in Figure 3.35. First, note that Matt's Films, Inc., originally in row 22, is now in row 19. When the Delete operation was performed, all rows that were below the deleted rows were

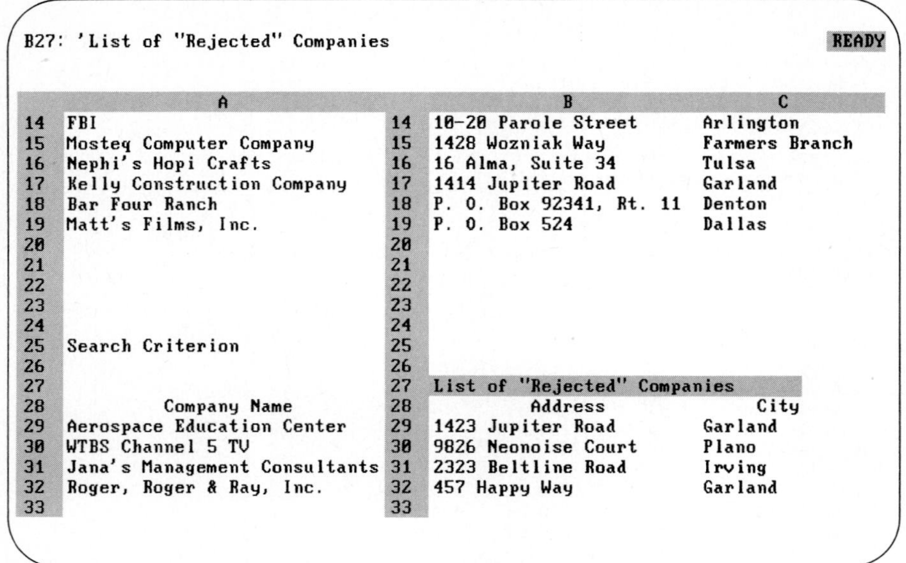
B27: 'List of "Rejected" Companies READY

	A	B	C
14	FBI	10-20 Parole Street	Arlington
15	Mosteq Computer Company	1428 Wozniak Way	Farmers Branch
16	Nephi's Hopi Crafts	16 Alma, Suite 34	Tulsa
17	Kelly Construction Company	1414 Jupiter Road	Garland
18	Bar Four Ranch	P. O. Box 92341, Rt. 11	Denton
19	Matt's Films, Inc.	P. O. Box 524	Dallas
20			
21			
22			
23			
24			
25	Search Criterion		
26			
27		List of "Rejected" Companies	
28	Company Name	Address	City
29	Aerospace Education Center	1423 Jupiter Road	Garland
30	WTBS Channel 5 TV	9826 Neonoise Court	Plano
31	Jana's Management Consultants	2323 Beltline Road	Irving
32	Roger, Roger & Ray, Inc.	457 Happy Way	Garland
33			

FIGURE 3.35
The result of finding and removing "Rejected" jobs

moved up. Second, as previously indicated, only the rejected companies now appear below the second set of headings.

Producing a Report Containing Only Offered Jobs

You have already been introduced to most of the operations that Lotus database is capable of performing. However, the job hunting problem does involve a few additional situations in which the database function can be useful. Your task now is to locate all of the jobs with a "Status" of "Offered" and produce a report containing only those companies and a count of the total.

As shown in Figure 3.36, your first step is to alter the Search Criterion so that you find only offered jobs. Thus, cell I26 now contains a new value. Next, select Data from the primary menu and Query from the second menu. Then, check the Criterion selection to make sure it has not changed. You should also recheck the Input range. (These items should have been retained from the previous use of the Query function, but it is always a good idea to check that the correct setup is being used.)

Your next operation is to establish a new Output area. Note that in Figure 3.37, a new set of headings is visible in row 40. These were placed there before entering the Data function but up to now have not been visible. Row 40 is below the companies that were previously "removed" from the primary database, as can be determined by the company names. To complete the process of retrieving "Offered" jobs, select the Extract option, which causes all records matching the Search Criterion to be copied to the Output area.

Now it is time to produce the report. The easiest way to print only those records containing an "Offered" job status value is to save the current database into another file. Then you can delete all rows that precede row 40. This leaves you with only the list of company offers shown in Figure 3.38. Note that a COUNT of the number of records has been placed in cell C14. (An alternate method of achieving this report that doesn't require producing another file is simply to indicate the part of the database to be printed via Print function options.)

Finally, using the standard Print function, print out the report shown in Figure 3.39. Note that the heading "Companies Making An Offer" has been

```
I26: 'Offered                                                      READY

I26: 'Offered                                                      POINT
Enter Criterion range: I25..I26

             A                          G         H         I         J
8  First State National Bank      8   11/30     01/05     Ongoing   North
9  Lewis & Melts Mortgage Co.     9   11/30     01/15     Offered   Mid-cities
10 Ethyl & Jung, DDS              10  11/15     11/30     Offered   North
11 ABC Stereo Warehouse           11  11/16     02/22     Ongoing
12 Hormell Texas Chili Company    12  12/05     01/31     Offered   East
13 Children's Museum              13  11/30     01/06     Ongoing
14 FBI                            14  01/03     01/21     Ongoing
15 Mosteq Computer Company        15  12/31               Ongoing
16 Nephi's Hopi Crafts            16  12/09     01/06     Offered   East
17 Kelly Construction Company     17  12/09               Ongoing
18 Bar Four Ranch                 18  12/28     02/03     Refused
19 Matt's Films, Inc.             19  12/31     01/07     Offered   North
20                                20
21                                21
22                                22
23                                23
24                                24
25 Search Criterion               25                      Status
26                                26                      Offered
27                                27
```

FIGURE 3.36
Setting up the database to find "Offered" jobs

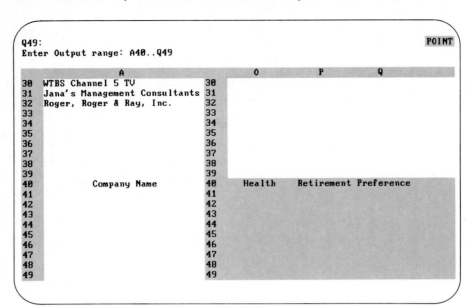

```
Q49:                                                        POINT
Enter Output range: A40..Q49

              A                        O          P         Q
30  WTBS Channel 5 TV            30
31  Jana's Management Consultants 31
32  Roger, Roger & Ray, Inc.     32
33                               33
34                               34
35                               35
36                               36
37                               37
38                               38
39                               39
40          Company Name         40    Health    Retirement Preference
41                               41
42                               42
43                               43
44                               44
45                               45
46                               46
47                               47
48                               48
49                               49
```

FIGURE 3.37
Establishing an output area for "offered" jobs

```
C14: @COUNT(C5..C12)                                        READY

              A                         C          D      E
1                                1
2                                2
3          Company Name          3    City       State   Zip
4  ------------------------------4  ----------------------------
5  Johnson Instruments, Inc.     5  Dallas         TX    76234
6  Johnson Instruments, Inc.     6  Dallas         TX    76234
7  Johnson Instruments, Inc.     7  Dallas         TX    76234
8  Lewis & Melts Mortgage Co.    8  Denton         TX    76202
9  Ethyl & Jung, DDS             9  Dennison       OK    79034
10 Hormell Texas Chili Company   10 Ft. Worth      TX    76907
11 Nephi's Hopi Crafts           11 Tulsa          OK    79345
12 Matt's Films, Inc.            12 Dallas         TX    76341
13                               13
14                               14              8
15                               15
16                               16
17                               17
18                               18
19                               19
20                               20
```

FIGURE 3.38
List of job offers

Companies Making An Offer

Company Name	Contact	City	State	Zip
Johnson Instruments, Inc.	Personnel Department	Dallas	TX	76234
Johnson Instruments, Inc.	Personnel Department	Dallas	TX	76234
Johnson Instruments, Inc.	Personnel Department	Dallas	TX	76234
Lewis & Melts Mortgage Co.	Mrs. Roberta Accure	Denton	TX	76202
Ethyl & Jung, DDS	Dr. Emil Franz Jung	Dennison	OK	79034
Hormell Texas Chili Company	Mr. Foster Brooks	Ft. Worth	TX	76907
Nephi's Hopi Crafts	Mrs. Carletta Whitecloud	Tulsa	OK	79345
Matt's Films, Inc.	Personnel Office	Dallas	TX	76341
	Total Number of Offers	8		

FIGURE 3.39
A report on Companies Making An Offer

added to row 1, and the message "Total Number of Offers" has been added to row 14. In addition, only a limited portion of the database is printed by controlling the cell area to be printed (A1 to E14).

Producing a Report for Companies Offering More Than $19,000

Your final task is to create a report for all the companies who have offered you more than $19,000. This report is to include a net amount and should be sorted by job preference.

Your first requirement is to establish a new Search Criterion. As shown in Figure 3.40, the new criterion is OFFER, where +M2>19000. Although the contents of cell M25 are easy to determine, you must check the status area at the upper-left corner of the screen to determine the actual contents of cell M26. What is shown in cell M26 is the result of the logical condition +M2>19000. Zero means the result is false, whereas 1 means the result is true. The character string +M2>19000 is interpreted to mean "is the value in cell M2 greater than 19000." Your final step in this phase is not only to provide a Name for the column of data representing offers, but also to make the cells in the "Offer" column a relative range.

The second requirement is to enter the Data function and select the Query option. Check the Input area designation, and, as shown in Figure 3.40, change the Criterion to identify cells M25 and M26. Next, identify the Output area, as shown in Figure 3.41. Finally, the Extract operation is performed, and the records matching the Search Criterion are moved to the output area.

Again, it is easiest to proceed from here by saving the original database and then deleting all but those records to be reported. As shown in Figure 3.42, unneeded fields have been eliminated, a "Net Offer" field has been added, and

```
M26: +OFFER>19000                                                    POINT
Enter Criterion range: M25..M26
```

```
M19: (C2) 18950                                                      POINT
Enter label range: M1..M19

                   A                        K        L        M            N
7   General Electronics, Inc.        7
8   First State National Bank        8      25       14  $22,000.00     $210.00
9   Lewis & Melts Mortgage Co.       9      35       14  $22,000.00     $500.00
10  Ethyl & Jung, DDS                10     95       14  $20,000.00     $325.00
11  ABC Stereo Warehouse             11
12  Hormell Texas Chili Company      12     53        5  $19,300.00     $164.00
13  Children's Museum                13
14  FBI                              14
15  Mosteq Computer Company          15
16  Nephi's Hopi Crafts              16     47       14  $15,670.00     $250.00
17  Kelly Construction Company       17
18  Bar Four Ranch                   18
19  Matt's Films, Inc.               19     33        6  $18,950.00     $155.00
```

```
M26: +M2>19000                                                       MENU
Right  Down  Left  Up
Each label in range names cell below it
```

```
M26: +M2>19000                                                       MENU
Create  Delete  Labels  Reset
Create names from a range of labels
                   A                        K        L        M            N
7   General Electronics, Inc.        7
8   First State National Bank        8      25       14  $22,000.00     $210.00
9   Lewis & Melts Mortgage Co.       9      35       14  $22,000.00     $500.00
10  Ethyl & Jung, DDS                10     95       14  $20,000.00     $325.00
11  ABC Stereo Warehouse             11
12  Hormell Texas Chili Company      12     53        5  $19,300.00     $164.00
13  Children's Museum                13
14  FBI                              14
15  Mosteq Computer Company          15
16  Nephi's Hopi Crafts              16     47       14  $15,670.00     $250.00
17  Kelly Construction Company       17
18  Bar Four Ranch                   18
19  Matt's Films, Inc.               19     33        6  $18,950.00     $155.00
20                                   20
21                                   21
22                                   22
23                                   23
24                                   24
25  Search Criterion                 25                  Offer
26                                   26                           0
```

FIGURE 3.40
Finding offers that are greater than $19,000

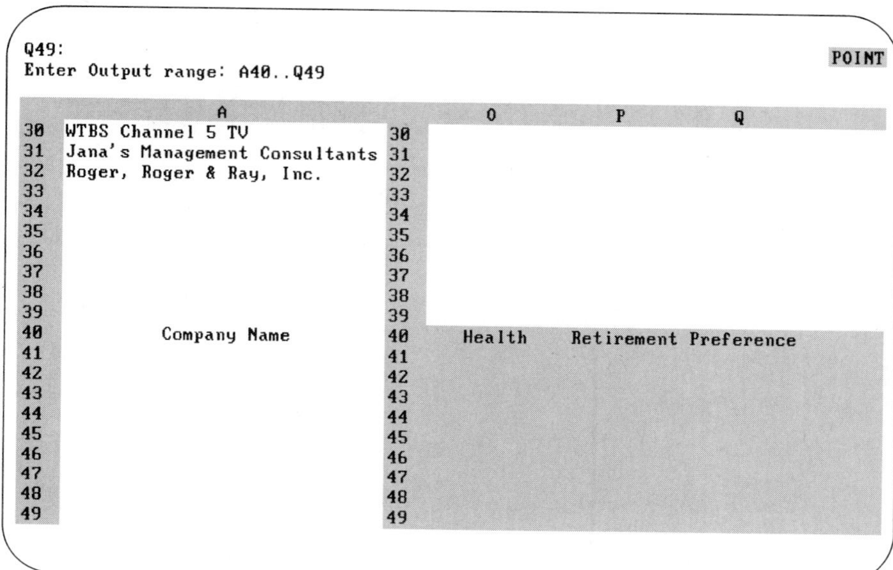

FIGURE 3.41
Output area for offers greater than $19,000

C3: (C2) +B3+E3+F3+G3

READY

	A	B	C	D
1	Company Name	Offer	Net Offer	Preference
2	----------------------------	----------	----------	----------
3	Lewis & Melts Mortgage Co.	$22,000.00	$27,500.00	1
4	Ethyl & Jung, DDS	$20,000.00	$27,275.00	1
5	Hormell Texas Chili Company	$19,300.00	$21,986.20	1
6	First State National Bank	$22,000.00	$25,485.00	2
7	Johnson Instruments, Inc.	$19,200.00	$23,022.00	4
8	Johnson Instruments, Inc.	$19,100.00	$22,922.00	5
9				
10				
11				
12				
13				
14				
15				
16				
17				
18				
19				
20				

FIGURE 3.42
Sorted list of offers greater than $19,000

```
                    Current Job Offers

      Company Name                Offer      Net Offer  Preference
-------------------------------------------------------------------
Lewis & Melts Mortgage Co.     $22,000.00  $27,500.00           1
Ethyl & Jung, DDS              $20,000.00  $27,275.00           1
Hormell Texas Chili Company    $19,300.00  $21,986.20           1
First State National Bank      $22,000.00  $25,485.00           2
Johnson Instruments, Inc.      $19,200.00  $23,022.00           4
Johnson Instruments, Inc.      $19,100.00  $22,922.00           5
```

FIGURE 3.43
Current Job Offers report

the records have been ordered by "Preference." Finally, by selecting (and controlling) the Print option, you can produce the report illustrated in Figure 3.43.

Other Features of Lotus Database

This section has explained each of the functions available through Lotus 1-2-3 database; no other features are available. However, Lotus does permit the use of *compound search criteria* for more complicated search requests: Search criteria in separate cells are identified, and multiple sets of criteria are designated through the Criteria option of the Data menu. (However, Criterion cells must be adjacent to one another.) For example, you may decide to search the database shown in Figure 3.42 for "Net Offer" values greater than $27,000 and jobs that you ranked above three. First, you would establish the search criteria —cell C10 would contain "Net Offer," cell C11 would contain +C2>27000, cell D10 would contain "Preference," and cell D11 would contain +D2<3. Next, you would make sure that the data in columns C and D was identified as range names. Then, you would enter the Data Query procedure and identify the Criterion cells as C10 through D11. After these steps have been completed, other database operations proceed normally.

Finally, Lotus provides a series of special mathematical functions that are related only to database processing. Thus, normal spreadsheet mathematical functions, such as COUNT and SUM, are provided in an additional form (for example, DCOUNT and DSUM) that is related to database operations.

Automating Lotus Commands—Keyboard Macros

Your final problem using the Lotus database of companies to which you have applied is to create a macro (procedure) that will print mailing labels for all the companies. Note that a keyboard macro is not a database function; it is a feature of Lotus that can be used whenever you are in the 1-2-3 mode.

A keyboard macro is nothing more than a collection of keystrokes that have been saved in a worksheet. For example, if you placed the cursor in cell A26 and entered the sequence '/PPAQ, as shown in Figure 3.44, and then stored this in a named range, execution of that range would enter the commands:

/ Get Main Menu
P Select the Print Menu
P Select PRINTER
A Align the top of the paper
Q Quit

Note that when you are entering these command sequences you must enter a ' first, otherwise pressing the / key will cause the Main Menu to appear on the screen rather than enter the slash (/) in the cell.

In addition to commands entered from the keyboard as normal keystrokes, you can use commands called *Special Key Indicators* (see Table 3.4) and special /X commands (see Table 3.5).

The following three rules apply to executing a set of macro instructions:

1. The instructions must be entered into the spreadsheet.
2. The set of instructions must be a "named" range.
3. The "named" range must be executed.

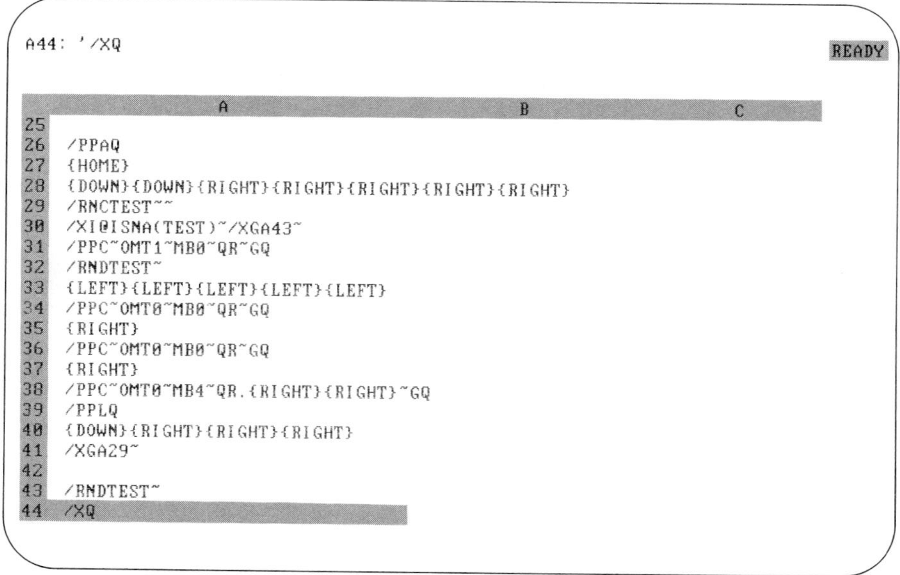

FIGURE 3.44
The Command Sequence for a Mailing Label Macro

TABLE 3.4 Special Key Indicators

Command	Key	Command	Key
{DOWN}	Down arrow	{EDIT}	F2
{UP}	Up arrow	{NAME}	F3
{RIGHT}	Right arrow	{ABS}	F4
{LEFT}	Left arrow	{GOTO}	F5
{HOME}	Home key	{WINDOW}	F6
{PGDN}	Page down	{QUERY}	F7
{PGUP}	Page up	{TABLE}	F8
{END}	End key	{CALC}	F9
{DEL}	Delete key	{GRAPH}	F10
{BS}	Backspace	{?}	Pause for input
{ESC}	Escape	~	Return

TABLE 3.5 /X Commands

Command	Function
/XIcondition	Processes an IF-THEN condition.
/XGlocation	Processes a Go To specified location.
/XClocation	Calls a subroutine at the specified location.
/XR	Returns from a subroutine to line after the /XC used to call the subroutine.
/XQ	Quit the macro execution.
/XMlocation	Processes the user-defined menu at the specified location.
/XLmessage~location~	Displays a message and places the text response at the specified location.
/XNmessage~location~	Displays a message and places the numeric response at the specified location.

To build a set of macro instructions for your company records that will print mailing labels, enter the instruction sequence shown in Figure 3.44. Now, follow the command sequence in Figure 3.45 to name the first macro instruction (cell A26) as \P. The \ followed by a letter is used to name a macro instruction set; a single spreadsheet may have up to 26 different sets of macro instructions. A special macro instruction name, \0, is automatically executed whenever you enter the command sequence /File Retrieve.

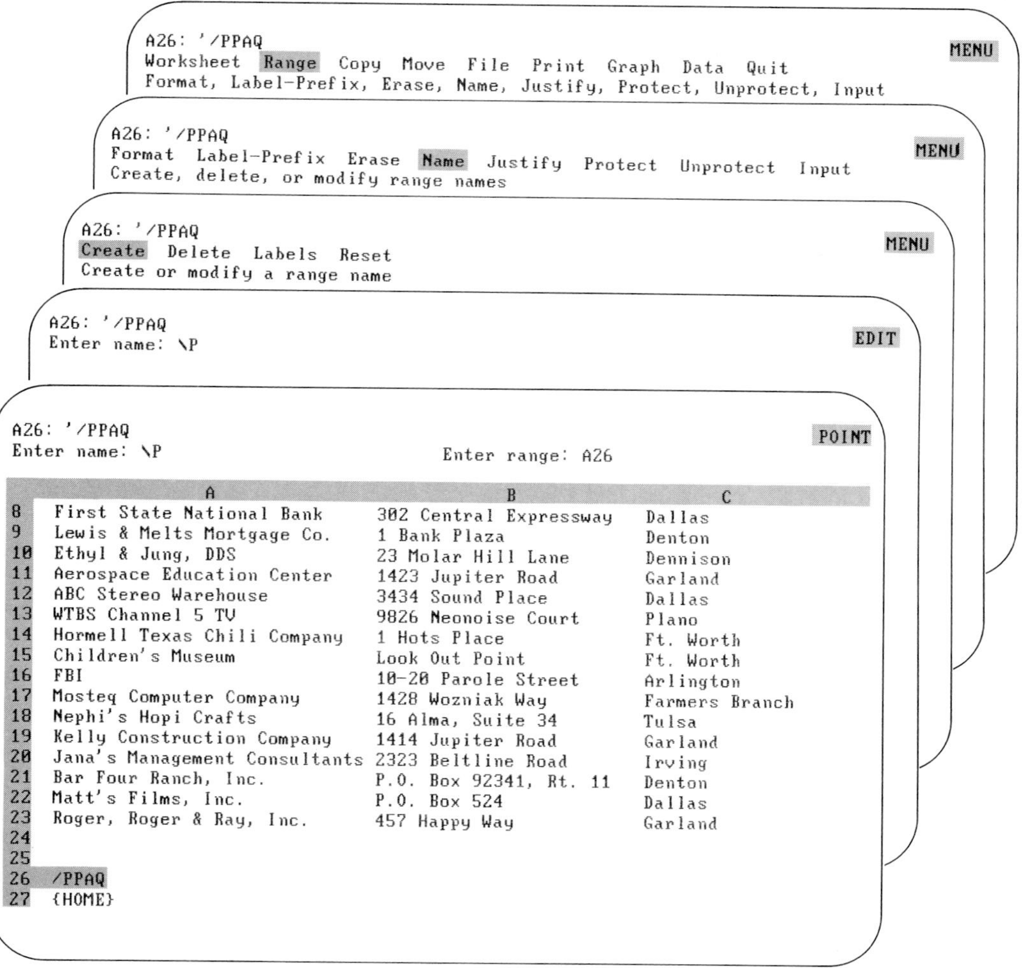

FIGURE 3.45
Giving a Range Name to the Macro

```
Personnel Department
Johnson Instruments, Inc.
P.O. Box 1234
Dallas               TX   76234
```

```
Personnel Department
Johnson Instruments, Inc.
P.O. Box 1234
Dallas               TX   76234
```

⋮

```
Mrs. Canada Strong
Bar Four Ranch, Inc.
P.O. Box 92341, Rt. 11
Denton               TX   76205
```

```
Personnel Office
Matt's Films, Inc.
P.O. Box 524
Dallas               TX   76341
```

```
Personnel Department
Roger, Roger & Ray, Inc.
457 Happy Way
Garland              TX   75242
```

FIGURE 3.46
The Printed Mailing Labels

To produce the mailing labels shown in Figure 3.46, enter the function @NA in cell F24. This function declares a cell as "not available" and is used in the instructions in cell A30 to test for the end of your data. Finally, press the ALTernate and P keys at the same time to execute the macro named \P and print the labels.

Introduction to Graphics

The two previous sections dealt with methods of calculating (spreadsheets) and storing (databases) large amounts of related data. You are now capable of overwhelming yourself and others with volumes of numbers! For example, suppose you are the manager of an amusement park, and for the past three years you have been recording, on a monthly basis, the average daily gate receipts and the average daily receipt totals for the entire park. At the end of the three years, you would have the data presented in Table 3.6.

Obviously, the data could supply you with some useful information, but the table is hard to read. However, if you present the same data in a graph, as in Figure 3.47, you can quickly see the changes that are taking

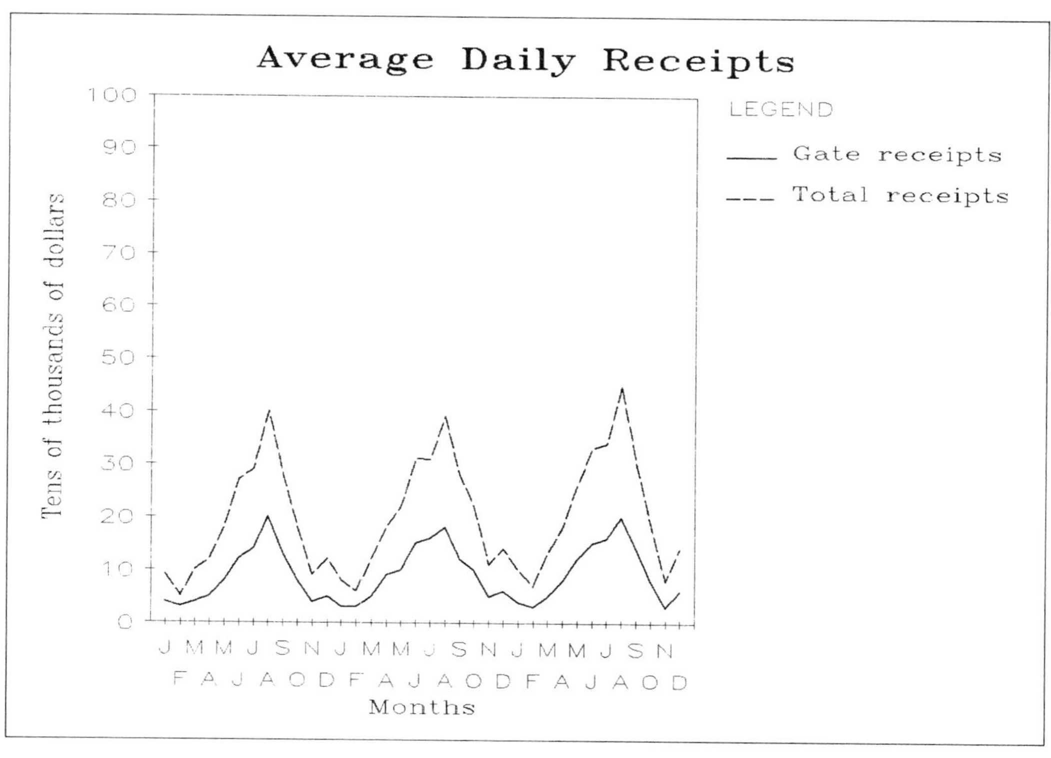

FIGURE 3.47
Graph of average daily receipts

TABLE 3.6 Amusement Park Revenues

Month/ Year	Gate Receipts	Total Receipts	Week	Gate Receipts	Total Receipts
1/83	40,000	90,000	7/84	160,000	310,000
2/83	30,000	50,000	8/84	180,000	390,000
3/83	40,000	100,000	9/84	120,000	280,000
4/83	50,000	120,000	10/84	100,000	220,000
5/83	80,000	180,000	11/84	50,000	110,000
6/83	120,000	270,000	12/84	60,000	140,000
7/83	140,000	290,000	1/85	40,000	100,000
8/83	200,000	400,000	2/85	30,000	70,000
9/83	130,000	280,000	3/85	50,000	130,000
10/83	80,000	180,000	4/85	80,000	180,000
11/83	40,000	90,000	5/85	120,000	260,000
12/83	50,000	120,000	6/85	150,000	330,000
1/84	30,000	80,000	7/85	160,000	340,000
2/84	30,000	60,000	8/85	200,000	450,000
3/84	50,000	120,000	9/85	140,000	310,000
4/84	90,000	180,000	10/85	80,000	190,000
5/84	100,000	220,000	11/85	30,000	80,000
6/84	150,000	310,000	12/85	60,000	140,000

place from month to month. To put into words the information in Figure 3.47 would take several pages.

Defining Business Graphics

The days of **"stand-alone" graphics packages** (software that produces only charts and graphs) are rapidly disappearing. Graphics is becoming a part of existing spreadsheet and integrated packages. However, the stand-alone packages for computer graphics are not going to disappear. They will simply become more versatile and include additional capabilities and flexibility not found in most of the current stand-alone graphics packages.

Despite the increase in the capability of graphics packages and the movement to in-

TABLE 3.7 Best Use of Chart Types

Display	Chart Type		
	Bar Chart	Line Chart	Pie Chart
Relationship	X		X
Movement		X	
Data values clearly and accurately represented	X	X	
Data values quickly understood			X

clude business graphics as a part of other packages (for example, spreadsheets), the basic functions of business graphics will remain the same. This section will cover the standard features of a graphics package. Although most of the work involved in creating graphics will be handled for you by the software package, you will be required to make some decisions yourself, and you will need to understand what the computer is doing in order to take full advantage of a package's capabilities.

There are five basic functions of graphics: charting and chart selection; scaling; drawing and painting; doing circles and lines; and labeling. The functions may be done differently by different software packages, but their purpose and results are the same.

Charting and Chart Selection

Charts are graphic or pictorial representations of data. They are used to show relationships or movements in the data values. The selection of the chart type can be critical to the information being presented.

There are three basic types of charts available to the users of a graphics package: **bar charts, line charts,** and **pie charts.** Some special variations of these charts are also available, depending on the software package you are using. Although each of these chart types can be used to show both relationships and movement, some are more suitable than others for each type of display. Table 3.7 provides an overview of each basic chart type and the type of presentation for which it is best suited.

Bar charts show relationships among data elements better than any other type of chart. For this reason, and because they are easily understood, they are most often used for management displays. A simple bar chart of the amusement park revenue data is shown in Figure 3.48.

Line charts are the most common type of chart. They communicate movement better than any other type of chart, and they convey the greatest level of detail. Line charts are often called *graphs* because they are built by connecting a set of plotted points. Figure 3.49 illustrates the use of a line chart to display the amusement park

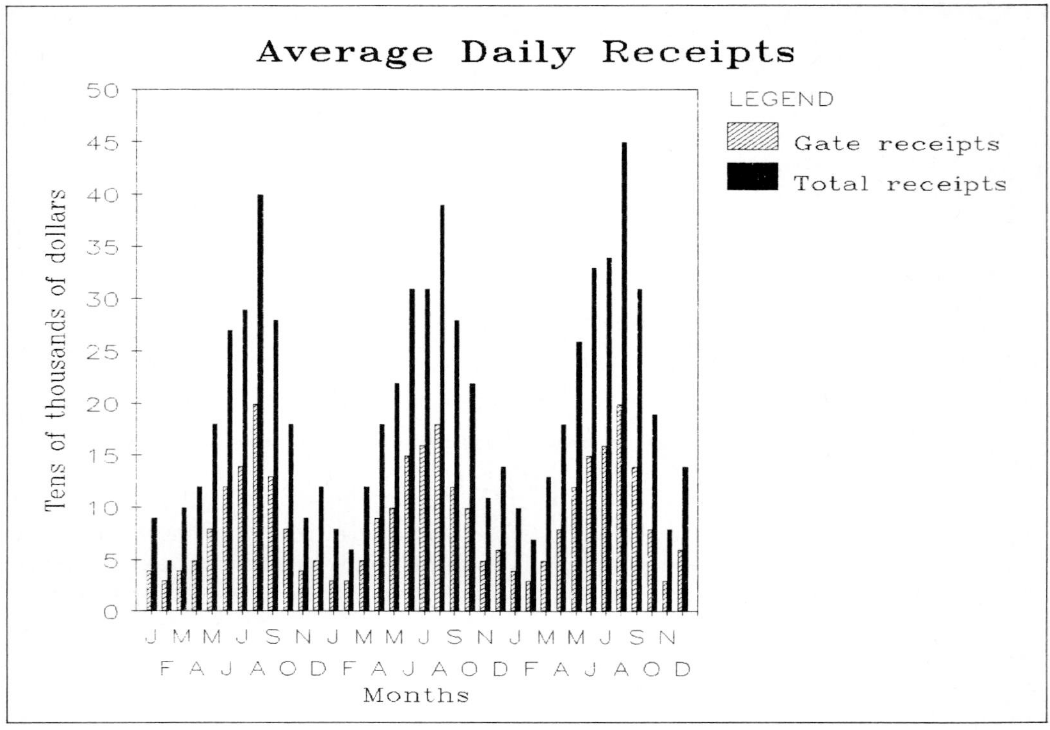

FIGURE 3.48
Bar chart of average daily gate receipts and total receipts

data. There are two types of commonly used line charts: The first is a **scatter chart,** shown in Figure 3.50. A scatter chart uses unconnected data points. The second is an **area chart,** as shown in Figure 3.51, which is a line chart with a shaded area under the line.

Pie charts are used to show quantitative data as a percentage of the whole. They are used to show relationships between parts and are primarily used for comparisons. Figure 3.52 is a pie chart showing a comparison of the total annual amusement park revenues for the last three years.

A special option that is frequently available in graphics software packages is the ability to plot more than one set of data values on the same graph. The ability to chart more than one set of data may also allow you to mix the types of charts or stack your charts. Figure 3.53 is an example of a **stacked bar chart.**

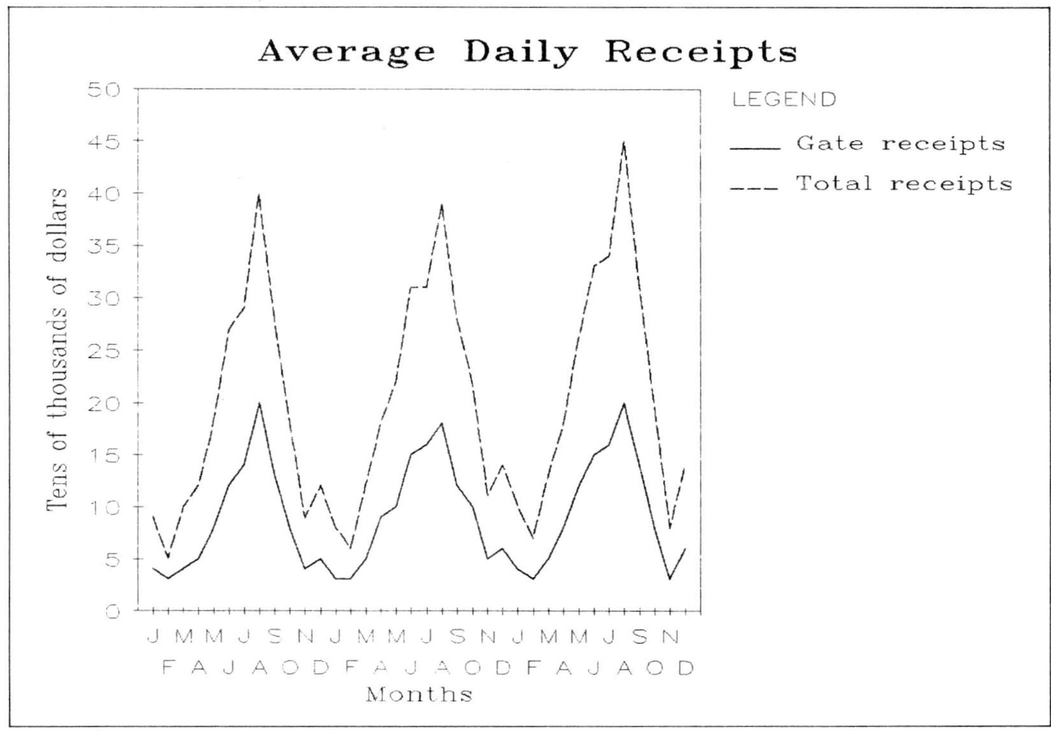

FIGURE 3.49
Line chart of average daily gate receipts and total receipts

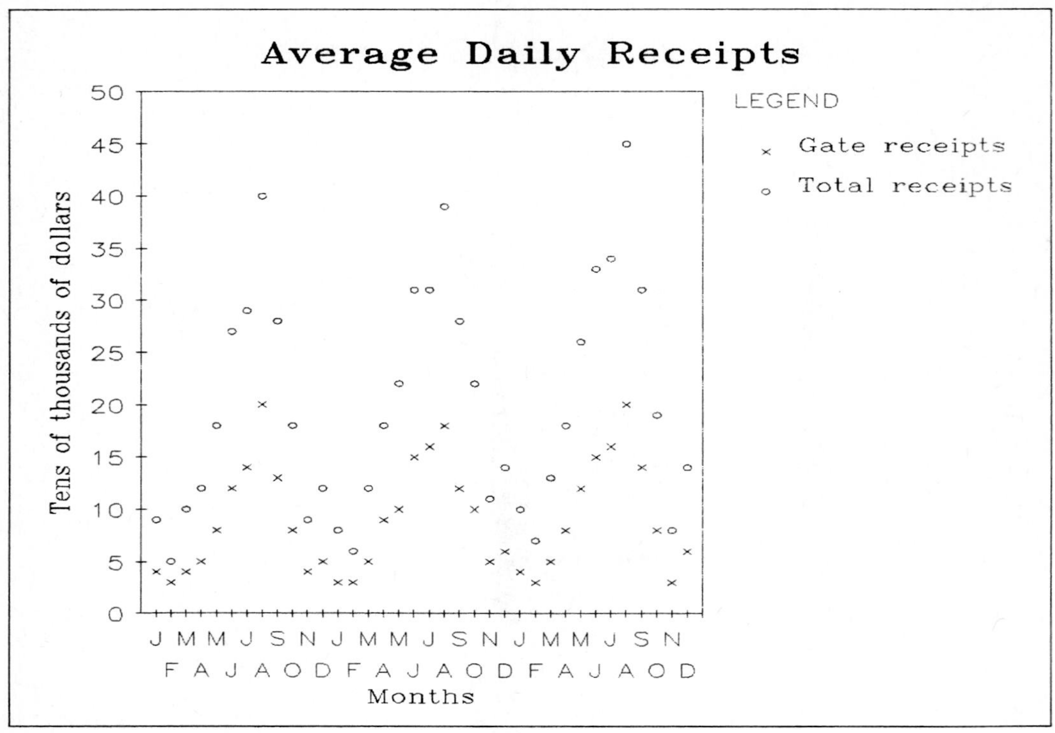

FIGURE 3.50
Scatter chart of average daily gate receipts and total receipts

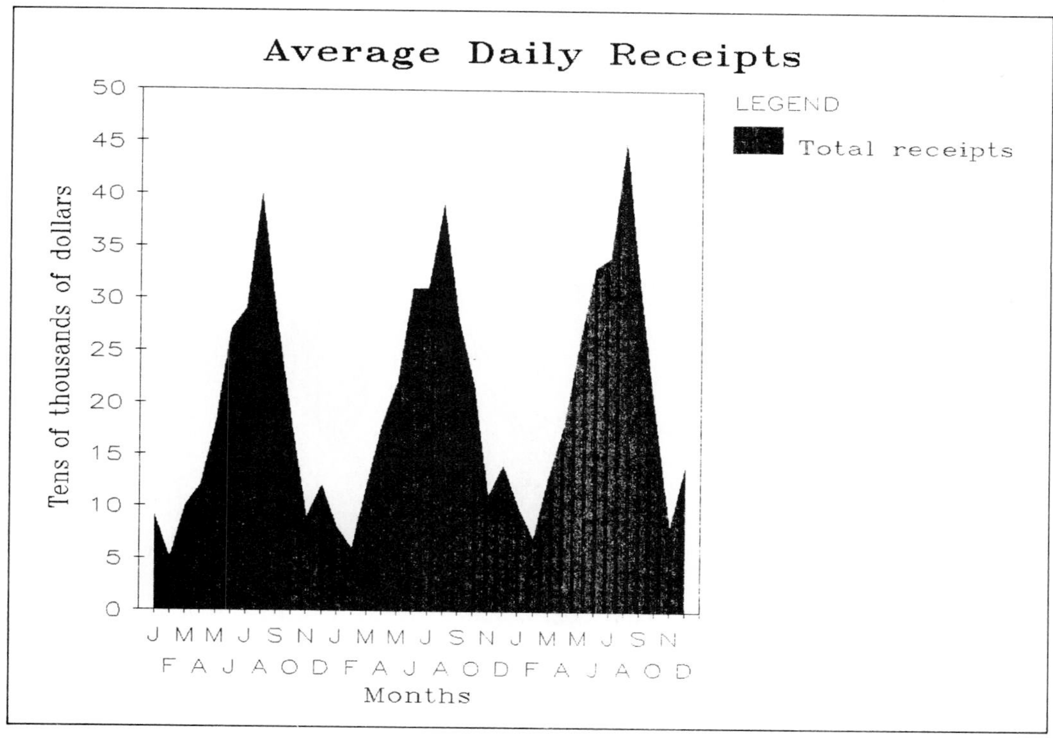

FIGURE 3.51
Area chart of average daily total receipts

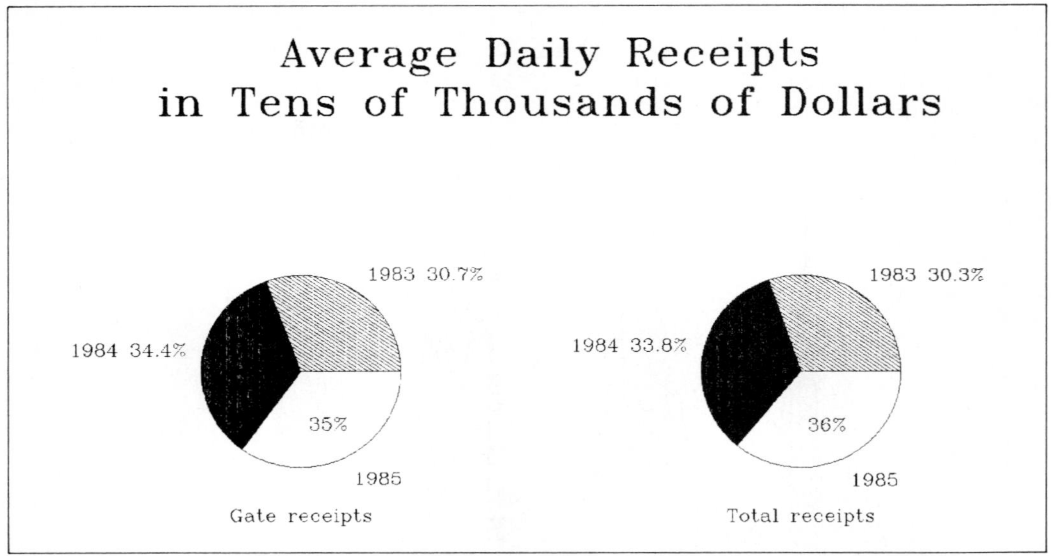

FIGURE 3.52
Pie chart of average daily gate receipts and total receipts

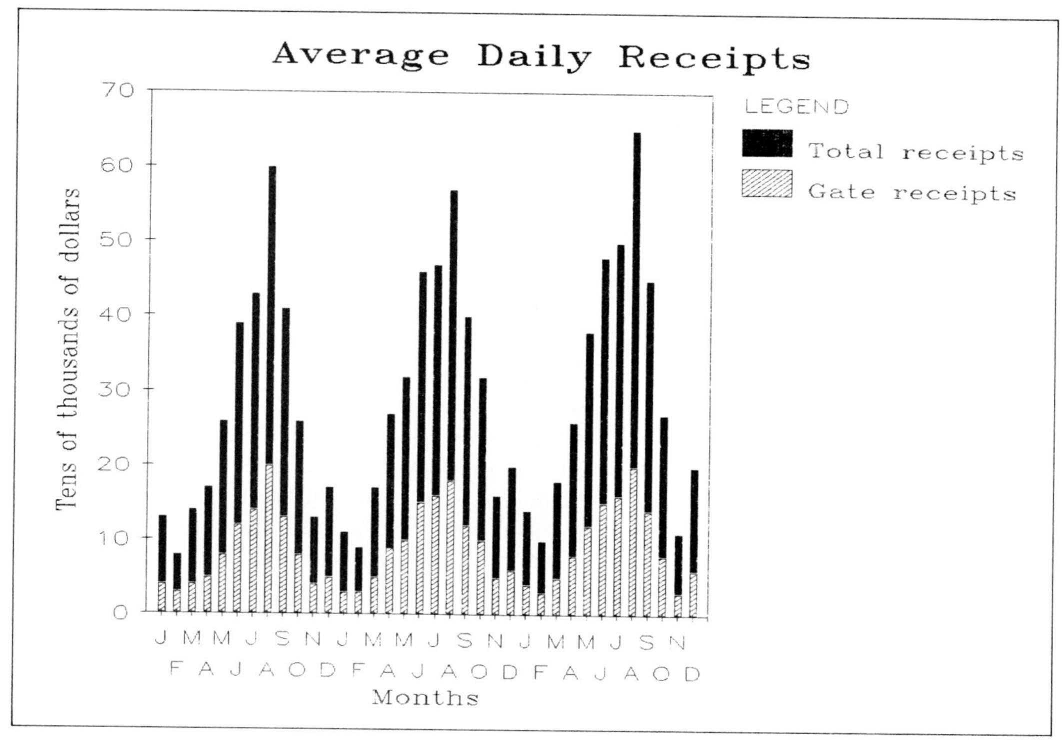

FIGURE 3.53
Stacked bar chart of average daily gate receipts and total receipts

Lotus 1-2-3 Graphics

Learning to Use Lotus 1-2-3 Graphics

This is your third opportunity to examine the capabilities of Lotus 1-2-3. In this section, you will investigate the graphics functions available in Lotus. Because the primary operations of Lotus stem from the spreadsheet capabilities of the package, you should have worked through the first section of this module. The data on which the graphs in this module are based was produced using the database functions of Lotus in the second section. Thus, it is recommended that you review both of these sections before you proceed.

To begin, enter LOTUS and select the 1-2-3 option from the initial screen. After the spreadsheet skeleton appears, retrieve the complete database con-

```
I25: 9                                                                  MENU
Worksheet  Range  Copy  Move  File  Print  Graph  Data  Quit
Create a graph
                  A                              G          H        I          J
9   Lewis & Melts Mortgage Co.       9      11/30      01/15    Offered   Mid-cities
10  Ethyl & Jung, DDS                10     11/15      11/30    Offered   North
11  Aerospace Education Center       11     11/16      12/13    Rejected
12  ABC Stereo Warehouse             12     11/16      02/22    Ongoing
13  WTBS Channel 5 TV                13     12/03      01/06    Ongoing
14  Hormell Texas Chili Company      14     12/05      01/31    Offered   East
15  Children's Museum                15     11/30      01/06    Ongoing
16  FBI                              16     01/03      01/21    Ongoing
17  Mosteq Computer Company          17     12/31               Ongoing
18  Nephi's Hopi Crafts              18     12/09      01/06    Offered   East
19  Kelly Construction Company       19     12/09               Ongoing
20  Jana's Management Consultants    20     01/06               Rejected
21  Bar Four Ranch                   21     12/28      02/03    Refused
22  Matt's Films, Inc.               22     12/31      01/07    Offered   North
23  Roger, Roger & Ray, Inc.         23     12/15               Rejected
24                                   24
25                                   25  Counts:    Ongoing           9
26                                   26             Offered           8
27                                   27             Rejected          3
28                                   28             Refused           1
```

FIGURE 3.54
Entering the Lotus graph function

taining all companies and their present status. Then add the entries shown in the lower right corner—rows 25 through 28—as illustrated in Figure 3.54. You are now ready to proceed with the graphics operations.

Solving the Job Hunting Problem

The remaining sections of this module are devoted to solving the job hunting problem. Once again, you will use the job hunting problem—this time to learn about graphics packages. You will create and print (or plot) graphs to represent pictorially the data you have been collecting about the companies.

Everyone is interested in keeping track of how well the job hunting process is going and comparing the offers that have been received from the different companies. With this in mind, the following activities were designed to enable you to create charts that can be useful in evaluating the job hunting activities. The data you need for this problem is presented below. (The data is also found in Appendix A.)

1. Create a pie chart that compares the number of companies in each of the "Status" categories in your collection of data. You currently have 21 companies (including the three offers from Johnson Instruments) in your files: negotiations are still ongoing for nine companies, three have rejected your application, you have refused the offer from one, and eight companies have made you an offer.
2. (a) Create a bar chart showing the offers you received from the eight companies. The companies should be listed in alphabetical order.
   (b) Create a stacked bar chart showing the Actual Offer from each of the companies. The Actual Offer is the Salary Offer plus the Life Insurance Contribution, the Health Insurance Contribution, and the Retirement Contribution.
3. Create a line chart that charts the Actual Offers (companies listed in alphabetical order) and the Average Actual Offer ($23,470.00.)

The numbers that follow were used in the spreadsheet section. The data is summarized as follows:

		Contributions			
Company Name	Salary Offer	Life	Health	Retirement	Actual Offer
Ethyl & Jung, DDS	$20,000	$320	$950	$6,000	$27,275
Hormell Texas Chili Co.	19,300	164	320	2,202	21,986
Johnson Instruments, Inc. (mid-cities)	19,200	135	354	3,333	23,022
Johnson Instruments, Inc. (south)	19,000	135	354	3,333	22,822

Company Name	Salary Offer	Contributions			Actual Offer
		Life	Health	Retirement	
Johnson Instruments, Inc. (north)	19,100	135	354	3,333	22,922
Lewis & Melts Mortgage Co.	22,000	500	600	4,400	27,500
Matt's Films, Inc.	18,950	155	456	5,000	24,561
Nephi's Hopi Crafts	15,670	250	425	1,333	17,678

What Is the Distribution of Job Status Values?—Producing a Pie Chart

To enter the graphics mode, select Graph from the Lotus 1-2-3 primary menu (see Figure 3.54). Then select the Type of graph to be created, as illustrated in Figure 3.55. You are then presented with a choice of graph types, including

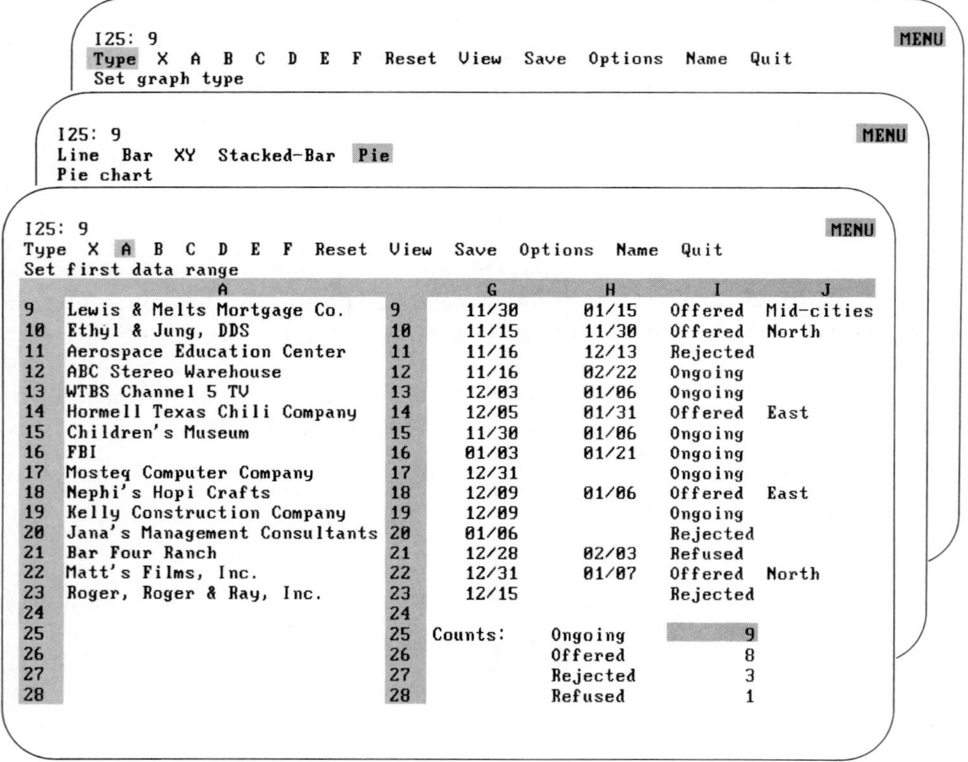

FIGURE 3.55
Beginning a pie chart

I28: 1
Enter first data range: I25..I28 POINT

	A	G	H	I	J
9	Lewis & Melts Mortgage Co.	11/30	01/15	Offered	Mid-cities
10	Ethyl & Jung, DDS	11/15	11/30	Offered	North
11	Aerospace Education Center	11/16	12/13	Rejected	
12	ABC Stereo Warehouse	11/16	02/22	Ongoing	
13	WTBS Channel 5 TV	12/03	01/06	Ongoing	
14	Hormell Texas Chili Company	12/05	01/31	Offered	East
15	Children's Museum	11/30	01/06	Ongoing	
16	FBI	01/03	01/21	Ongoing	
17	Mosteq Computer Company	12/31		Ongoing	
18	Nephi's Hopi Crafts	12/09	01/06	Offered	East
19	Kelly Construction Company	12/09		Ongoing	
20	Jana's Management Consultants	01/06		Rejected	
21	Bar Four Ranch	12/28	02/03	Refused	
22	Matt's Films, Inc.	12/31	01/07	Offered	North
23	Roger, Roger & Ray, Inc.	12/15		Rejected	
24					
25		Counts:	Ongoing	9	
26			Offered	8	
27			Rejected	3	
28			Refused	1	

FIGURE 3.56
Specifying a data range for job status values

Line, Bar, XY, Stacked-Bar, and Pie charts. For your first chart, select the Pie type either by moving the cursor to that position and pressing RETURN or simply by pressing P. You will then return to the primary graphics menu. To select the data to be presented in the pie chart, select data range A. You will then be asked to specify the beginning and ending cell locations of the first data range. If necessary, move the cell pointer to cell I25, press the period key (Lotus will show ..), move the cursor to cell I28, and press the RETURN key. Figure 3.56 shows the data to be presented in a pie chart form.

Titles for the Pie Chart — An Initial Look at Labeling

The next step is to provide a series of titles to be presented with the pie chart. Select the X option from the primary menu, and you will be asked to supply the x-axis data values for the pie chart. Because there are no x- and y-axes for pie charts, these values are interpreted to be titles for the individual wedges of the pie. As shown in Figure 3.57, the range of these values is H25 through H28.

Last, give your pie chart a chart title. To do this, select Options from the primary menu, Titles from the next menu, and First from the final menu. You will then be asked to enter the title for the chart. As shown in Figure 3.58, you have chosen to name it "Status of Companies in Job Hunt."

```
I25: 9                                                              MENU
Type  X  A  B  C  D  E  F  Reset  View  Save  Options  Name  Quit
Set X-range
                 A                             G          H          I        J
9   Lewis & Melts Mortgage Co.     9       11/30      01/15     Offered  Mid-cities
10  Ethyl & Jung, DDS              10      11/15      11/30     Offered  North
11  Aerospace Education Center     11      11/16      12/13     Rejected
12  ABC Stereo Warehouse           12      11/16      02/22     Ongoing
13  WTBS Channel 5 TV              13      12/03      01/06     Ongoing
14  Hormell Texas Chili Company    14      12/05      01/31     Offered  East
15  Children's Museum              15      11/30      01/06     Ongoing
16  FBI                            16      01/03      01/21     Ongoing
17  Mosteq Computer Company        17      12/31                Ongoing
18  Nephi's Hopi Crafts            18      12/09      01/06     Offered  East
19  Kelly Construction Company     19      12/09                Ongoing
20  Jana's Management Consultants  20      01/06                Rejected
21  Bar Four Ranch                 21      12/28      02/03     Refused
22  Matt's Films, Inc.             22      12/31      01/07     Offered  North
23  Roger, Roger & Ray, Inc.       23      12/15                Rejected
24                                 24
25                                 25  Counts:     Ongoing              9
26                                 26              Offered              8
27                                 27              Rejected             3
28                                 28              Refused              1
```

```
H28: 'Refused                                                       POINT
Enter X-axis range: H25..H28

                 A                             G          H          I        J
9   Lewis & Melts Mortgage Co.     9       11/30      01/15     Offered  Mid-cities
10  Ethyl & Jung, DDS              10      11/15      11/30     Offered  North
11  Aerospace Education Center     11      11/16      12/13     Rejected
12  ABC Stereo Warehouse           12      11/16      02/22     Ongoing
13  WTBS Channel 5 TV              13      12/03      01/06     Ongoing
14  Hormell Texas Chili Company    14      12/05      01/31     Offered  East
15  Children's Museum              15      11/30      01/06     Ongoing
16  FBI                            16      01/03      01/21     Ongoing
17  Mosteq Computer Company        17      12/31                Ongoing
18  Nephi's Hopi Crafts            18      12/09      01/06     Offered  East
19  Kelly Construction Company     19      12/09                Ongoing
20  Jana's Management Consultants  20      01/06                Rejected
21  Bar Four Ranch                 21      12/28      02/03     Refused
22  Matt's Films, Inc.             22      12/31      01/07     Offered  North
23  Roger, Roger & Ray, Inc.       23      12/15                Rejected
24                                 24
25                                 25  Counts:     Ongoing              9
26                                 26              Offered              8
27                                 27              Rejected             3
28                                 28              Refused              1
```

FIGURE 3.57
Creating a legend for wedges of the pie

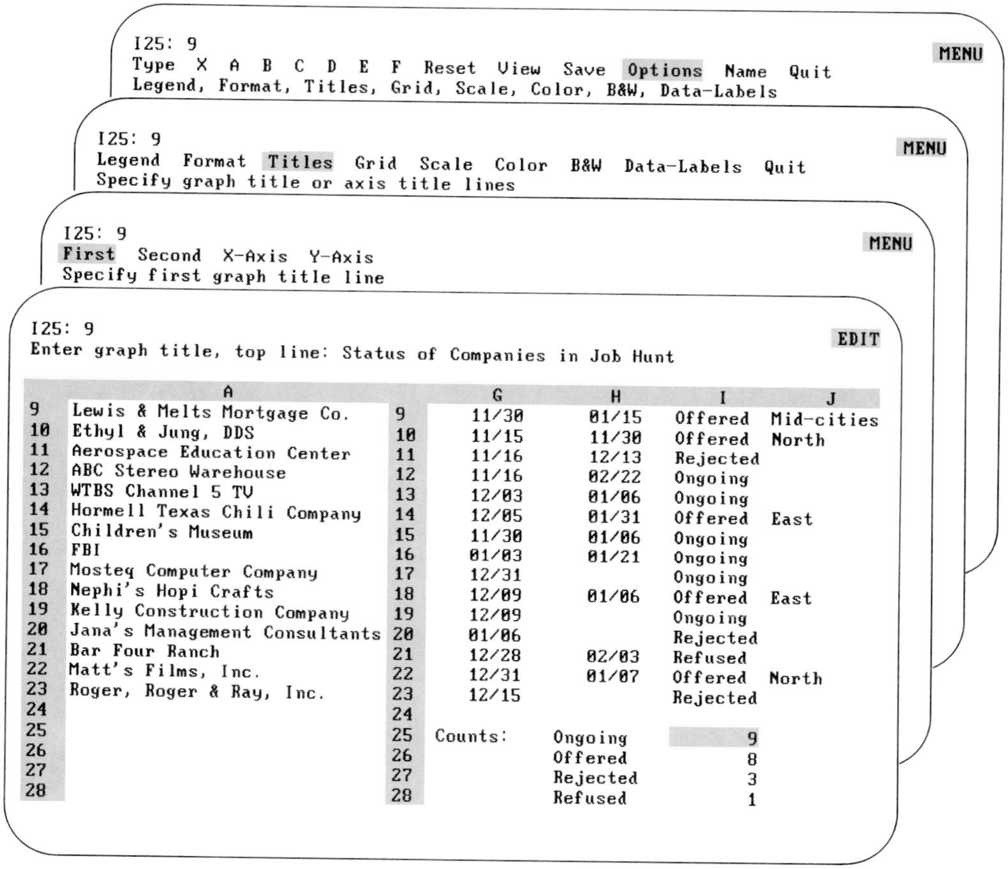

```
I25: 9                                                              MENU
Type  X  A  B  C  D  E  F  Reset  View  Save  Options  Name  Quit
Legend, Format, Titles, Grid, Scale, Color, B&W, Data-Labels

I25: 9                                                              MENU
Legend  Format  Titles  Grid  Scale  Color  B&W  Data-Labels  Quit
Specify graph title or axis title lines

I25: 9                                                              MENU
First  Second  X-Axis  Y-Axis
Specify first graph title line

I25: 9                                                              EDIT
Enter graph title, top line: Status of Companies in Job Hunt
```

	A		G	H	I	J
9	Lewis & Melts Mortgage Co.	9	11/30	01/15	Offered	Mid-cities
10	Ethyl & Jung, DDS	10	11/15	11/30	Offered	North
11	Aerospace Education Center	11	11/16	12/13	Rejected	
12	ABC Stereo Warehouse	12	11/16	02/22	Ongoing	
13	WTBS Channel 5 TV	13	12/03	01/06	Ongoing	
14	Hormell Texas Chili Company	14	12/05	01/31	Offered	East
15	Children's Museum	15	11/30	01/06	Ongoing	
16	FBI	16	01/03	01/21	Ongoing	
17	Mosteq Computer Company	17	12/31		Ongoing	
18	Nephi's Hopi Crafts	18	12/09	01/06	Offered	East
19	Kelly Construction Company	19	12/09		Ongoing	
20	Jana's Management Consultants	20	01/06		Rejected	
21	Bar Four Ranch	21	12/28	02/03	Refused	
22	Matt's Films, Inc.	22	12/31	01/07	Offered	North
23	Roger, Roger & Ray, Inc.	23	12/15		Rejected	
24		24				
25		25	Counts:	Ongoing	9	
26		26		Offered	8	
27		27		Rejected	3	
28		28		Refused	1	

FIGURE 3.58
Producing titles on the pie chart

Chart Manipulations—Viewing, Clearing, and Saving

Now that you have provided all of the necessary entries, Quit the Options menu and select View from the primary menu. You will then see the chart shown in Figure 3.59. When you have finished viewing the chart, press any key, and you will return to the primary graphics menu. If you decide to enter changes, all unchanged values (data, titles, and so on) are retained until you change the graph Type or Reset the graph. However, you will probably want to print this graph later, so you should select the Save option from the menu and supply a file name for the chart, as illustrated in Figure 3.60. Printing graphs is another function that will be discussed later.

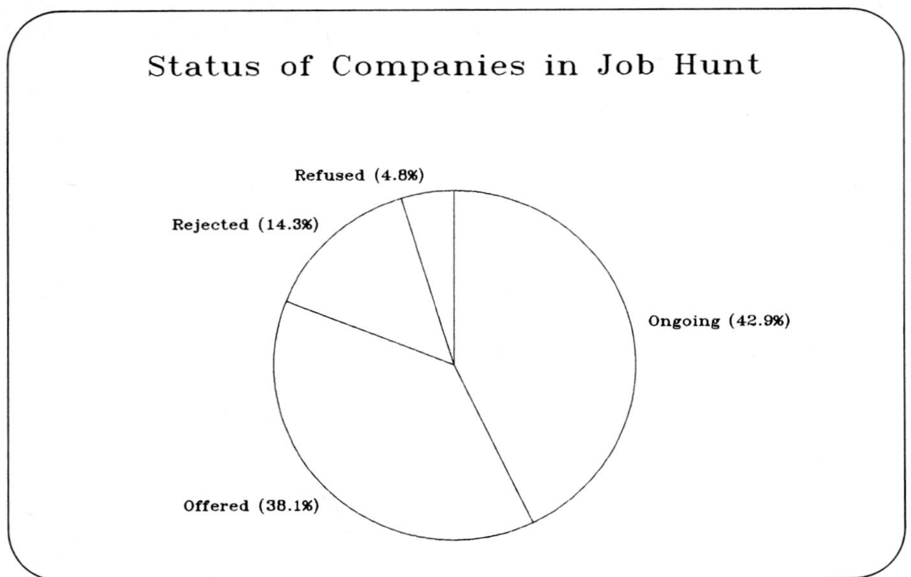

FIGURE 3.59
The pie chart—distribution of job status values

```
I25: 9                                                              EDIT
Enter graph file name: PIE

              A                           G          H        I          J
9   Lewis & Melts Mortgage Co.     9    11/30      01/15   Offered   Mid-cities
10  Ethyl & Jung, DDS              10   11/15      11/30   Offered   North
11  Aerospace Education Center     11   11/16      12/13   Rejected
12  ABC Stereo Warehouse           12   11/16      02/22   Ongoing
13  WTBS Channel 5 TV              13   12/03      01/06   Ongoing
14  Hormell Texas Chili Company    14   12/05      01/31   Offered   East
15  Children's Museum              15   11/30      01/06   Ongoing
16  FBI                            16   01/03      01/21   Ongoing
17  Mosteq Computer Company        17   12/31              Ongoing
18  Nephi's Hopi Crafts            18   12/09      01/06   Offered   East
19  Kelly Construction Company     19   12/09              Ongoing
20  Jana's Management Consultants  20   01/06              Rejected
21  Bar Four Ranch                 21   12/28      02/03   Refused
22  Matt's Films, Inc.             22   12/31      01/07   Offered   North
23  Roger, Roger & Ray, Inc.       23   12/15              Rejected
24                                 24
25                                 25 Counts:   Ongoing          9
26                                 26           Offered          8
27                                 27           Rejected         3
28                                 28           Refused          1
```

FIGURE 3.60
Saving the pie chart for later printing

How Do the Offers Measure Up?—Producing a Bar Chart

Now you want to turn your attention to the companies that have made you an offer. Return to the Lotus spreadsheet by entering Quit from the primary graphics menu. Your next problem deals only with companies for which the job status is "Offered." Eliminate all other companies from the spreadsheet. Then re-enter the Graph mode from the primary spreadsheet menu and select Type. Again, your choices are Line, Bar, XY, Stacked-Bar, and Pie. This time, select Bar to produce a bar chart, as indicated in Figure 3.61. Next, select data range A and enter the range for Offer, as shown in Figure 3.62.

Titles for the Bar Chart—More on Labeling

After you have supplied the data to be graphed, you should provide titles. Choose Options from the primary menu and Titles from the second menu. As before, select First and enter the title for the chart, which is "Amount of Company Job Offers." This title will appear at the top of the bar chart. Then, choose the X-Axis option and enter the title "Companies in Alphabetical Order." The x-axis title will appear at the bottom of the bar chart. This is followed by selecting a title for the y-axis, which should be "Offers in Dollars." The y-axis title will appear along the left edge of the bar chart.

```
M3: (C2) 20000                                                        MENU
Line  Bar  XY  Stacked-Bar  Pie
Bar graph
                  A                            M          N         O          P
1          Company Name              1     Offer       Life     Health    Retirement
2  ------------------------------2  -------------------------------------------
3  Ethyl & Jung, DDS                 3   $20,000.00  $325.00  $950.00    $6,000.00
4  Hormell Texas Chili Company       4   $19,300.00  $164.00  $320.00    $2,202.20
5  Johnson Instruments, Inc.         5   $19,000.00  $135.00  $354.00    $3,333.00
6  Johnson Instruments, Inc.         6   $19,100.00  $135.00  $354.00    $3,333.00
7  Johnson Instruments, Inc.         7   $19,200.00  $135.00  $354.00    $3,333.00
8  Lewis & Melts Mortgage Co.        8   $22,000.00  $500.00  $600.00    $4,400.00
9  Matt's Films, Inc.                9   $18,950.00  $155.00  $456.00    $5,000.00
10 Nephi's Hopi Crafts               10  $15,670.00  $250.00  $425.00    $1,333.00
11                                   11
12                                   12
13                                   13
14                                   14
15                                   15
16                                   16
17                                   17
18                                   18
19                                   19
20                                   20
```

FIGURE 3.61
Selecting a bar chart

```
M10: (C2) 15670                                                    POINT
Enter first data range: M3..M10

                      A                                M          N         O          P
1           Company Name                 1        Offer       Life     Health    Retirement
2   ---------------------------------2   ----------------------------------------------------
3   Ethyl & Jung, DDS                    3    $20,000.00  $325.00  $950.00    $6,000.00
4   Hormell Texas Chili Company          4    $19,300.00  $164.00  $320.00    $2,202.20
5   Johnson Instruments, Inc.            5    $19,000.00  $135.00  $354.00    $3,333.00
6   Johnson Instruments, Inc.            6    $19,100.00  $135.00  $354.00    $3,333.00
7   Johnson Instruments, Inc.            7    $19,200.00  $135.00  $354.00    $3,333.00
8   Lewis & Melts Mortgage Co.           8    $22,000.00  $500.00  $600.00    $4,400.00
9   Matt's Films, Inc.                   9    $18,950.00  $155.00  $456.00    $5,000.00
10  Nephi's Hopi Crafts                  10   $15,670.00  $250.00  $425.00    $1,333.00
11                                       11
12                                       12
13                                       13
14                                       14
15                                       15
16                                       16
17                                       17
18                                       18
19                                       19
20                                       20
```

FIGURE 3.62
Specifying a data range for offers

Finally, as shown in Figure 3.63, you wish to produce a legend for the job offer amount. Select Legend from the Options menu and select data range A. The title for this legend item is "Dollars Offered." After the legend is in place, you are ready to look at your bar chart. Select Quit from the Options menu and then select View from the primary menu. The bar chart will be produced as shown in Figure 3.64. Finally, save this chart so that it can be printed later.

Looking at the Actual Offers—Creating a Stacked Bar Chart

You need to examine further the offers made by each of the companies. First, select the Stacked-Bar chart from the Type option. You already have a beginning for this chart because you have just completed the a bar chart. To create the stacked bar chart, simply add the elements that represent additional data to each stack. As shown in Figure 3.65, you may begin this process by selecting the B data range and entering the data values from the "Life" column. Then select the C range and enter the data values from the "Health" column. Finally, select the D range and enter the data values from the "Retirement" column.

Now provide titles and legends. Select Options and then Titles. You can keep the x- and y-axis titles previously specified. However, you should change the First title to "Amount of Company Actual Offers." Next, you should provide new legend information. Select Legend from the Options menu and

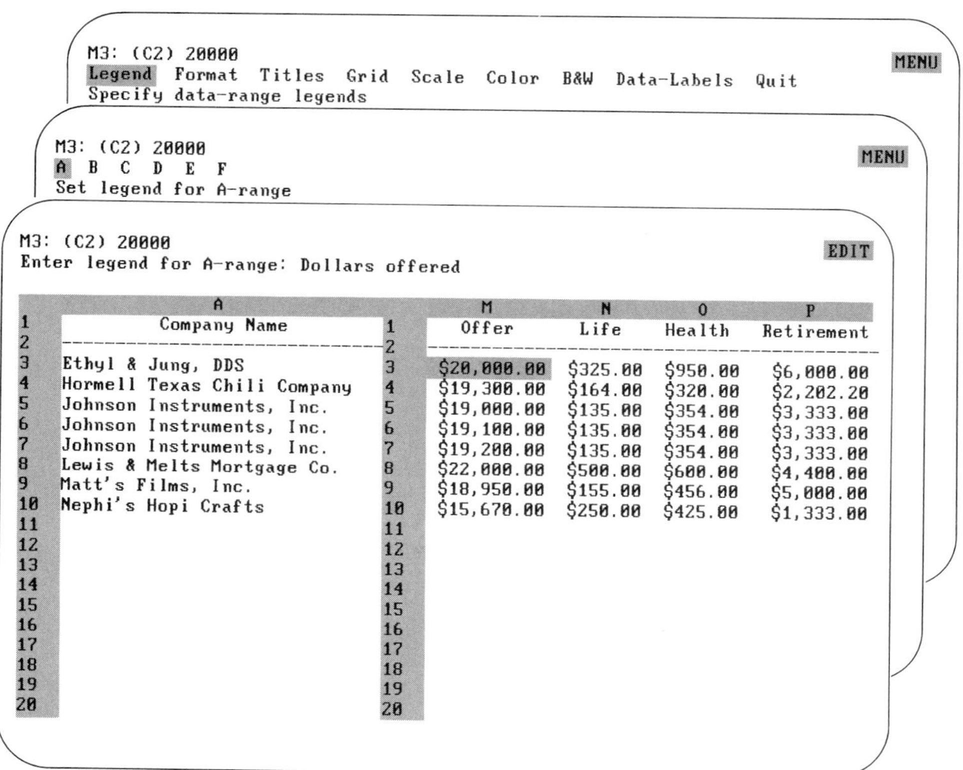

FIGURE 3.63
Creating a legend for dollars offered

select data range A. The new legend title for this item is "$ Offer." The legend titles for data ranges B, C, and D are "Life," "Health," and "Retirement," respectively. Now that the chart is complete, Quit the Options menu and select View from the primary menu. After viewing the stacked bar chart, illustrated in Figure 3.66, save it for later printing.

Comparing Actual Offers with the Average Offer — Creating a Line Chart

Before you create the line chart, you need to return to the spreadsheet and create two new columns of information — "Actual" and "Average," as shown in Figure 3.67. The actual offer is the total of the offer, life, health, and retirement cells for each company. The values for the average offer are computed for all the actual job offers and simply copied to the cells in the "Average" column. Now return to the Graph function.

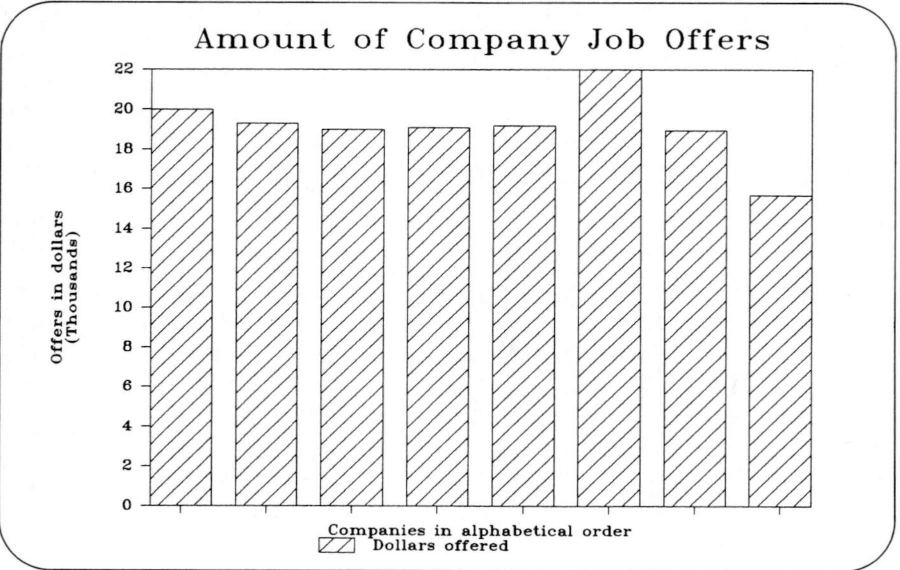

FIGURE 3.64
The bar chart — amount of company job offers

N10: (C2) 250 POINT
Enter second data range: N3..N10

	A		M	N	O	P
1	Company Name	1	Offer	Life	Health	Retirement
2	------------------------------	2	----------	----------	----------	----------
3	Ethyl & Jung, DDS	3	$20,000.00	$325.00	$950.00	$6,000.00
4	Hormell Texas Chili Company	4	$19,300.00	$164.00	$320.00	$2,202.20
5	Johnson Instruments, Inc.	5	$19,000.00	$135.00	$354.00	$3,333.00
6	Johnson Instruments, Inc.	6	$19,100.00	$135.00	$354.00	$3,333.00
7	Johnson Instruments, Inc.	7	$19,200.00	$135.00	$354.00	$3,333.00
8	Lewis & Melts Mortgage Co.	8	$22,000.00	$500.00	$600.00	$4,400.00
9	Matt's Films, Inc.	9	$18,950.00	$155.00	$456.00	$5,000.00
10	Nephi's Hopi Crafts	10	$15,670.00	$250.00	$425.00	$1,333.00
11		11				
12		12				
13		13				
14		14				
15		15				
16		16				
17		17				
18		18				
19		19				
20		20				

FIGURE 3.65
Adding data ranges to the stacked bar chart

To begin the creation of the line chart, select Type and then Line. Next, select data range A and identify the "Actual" data values, as shown in Figure 3.67. Repeat this sequence for data range B and the "Average" column. Then select Legend from the Options menu. Provide the legend "Actual Offer" for data range A and "Average Offer" for data range B. Now you are ready to view your chart. The line chart is shown in Figure 3.68. Save this chart for later printing.

Printing Your Charts

The spreadsheet function of Lotus does not include an option to print graphs. To produce a graph on a printer, you must Quit the spreadsheet function and return to the Lotus Access System. As shown in Figure 3.69, one of the choices from this menu is PrintGraph. Once you have made this selection, Lotus will produce a message on the screen asking you to place the Print Graphics disk in drive A. Once this has been done and you have pressed any key on the keyboard, you will see the screen presented in Figure 3.70. This screen controls the printing of graphs. First, Select a graph for printing. This choice will produce the screen shown in Figure 3.71. The graph files are indicated along the left side of this screen; mark the one to be printed with the # symbol by pressing the SPACE BAR. In this illustration, the PIE file—the pie chart developed earlier

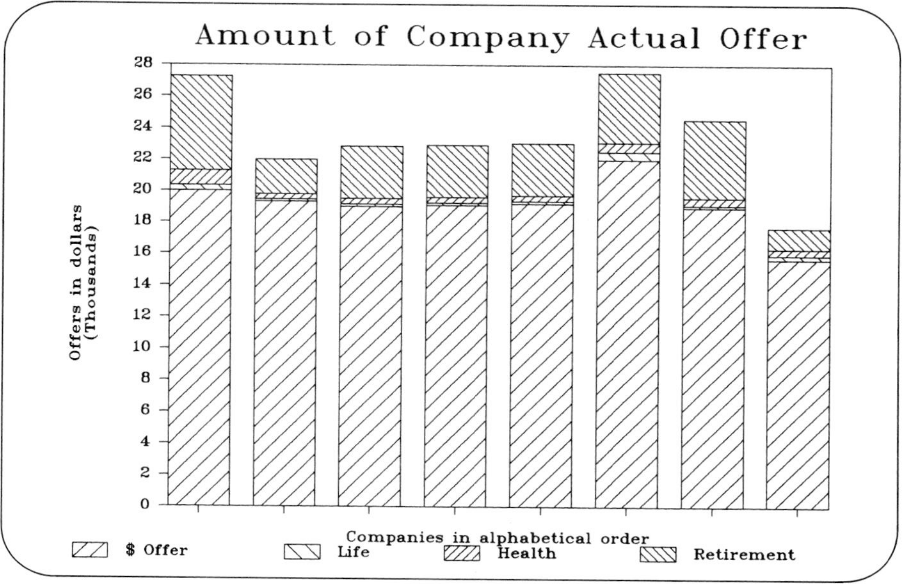

FIGURE 3.66
The stacked bar chart—amount of actual offers

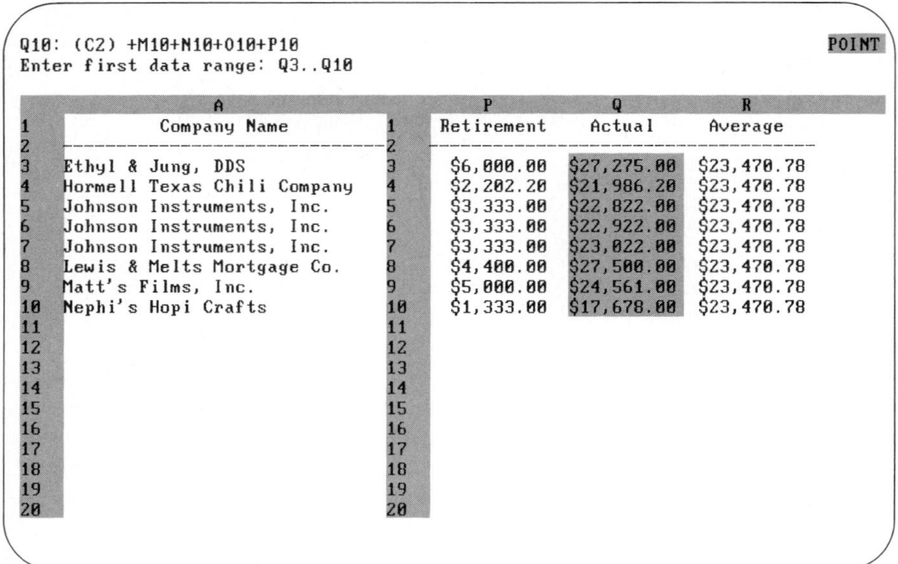

Q10: (C2) +M10+N10+O10+P10 POINT
Enter first data range: Q3..Q10

	A		P	Q	R
1	Company Name	1	Retirement	Actual	Average
2		2			
3	Ethyl & Jung, DDS	3	$6,000.00	$27,275.00	$23,470.78
4	Hormell Texas Chili Company	4	$2,202.20	$21,986.20	$23,470.78
5	Johnson Instruments, Inc.	5	$3,333.00	$22,822.00	$23,470.78
6	Johnson Instruments, Inc.	6	$3,333.00	$22,922.00	$23,470.78
7	Johnson Instruments, Inc.	7	$3,333.00	$23,022.00	$23,470.78
8	Lewis & Melts Mortgage Co.	8	$4,400.00	$27,500.00	$23,470.78
9	Matt's Films, Inc.	9	$5,000.00	$24,561.00	$23,470.78
10	Nephi's Hopi Crafts	10	$1,333.00	$17,678.00	$23,470.78
11		11			
12		12			
13		13			
14		14			
15		15			
16		16			
17		17			
18		18			
19		19			
20		20			

FIGURE 3.67
Entering a data range for a line chart

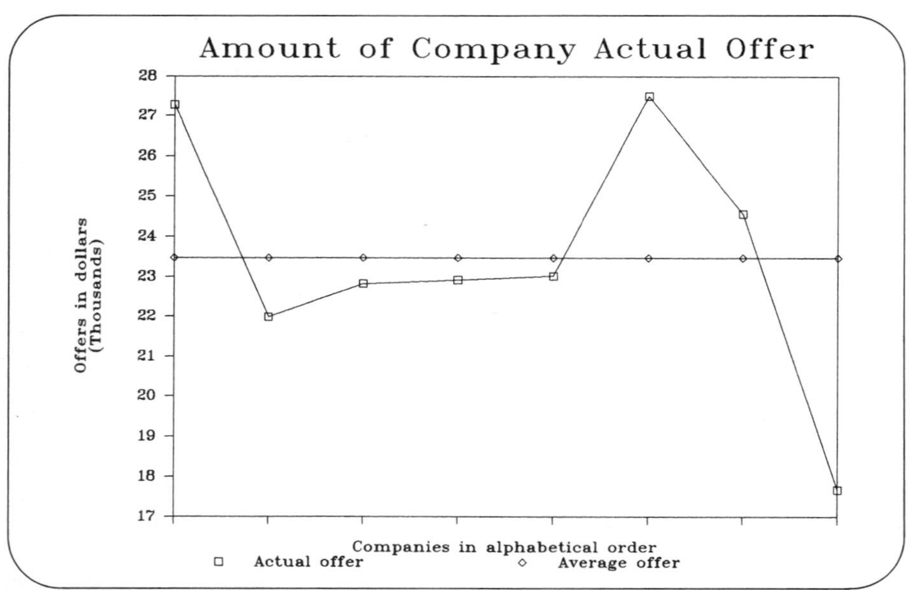

FIGURE 3.68
The line chart—comparing actual offers to average offer

```
Lotus Access System  V.1A  (C)1983 Lotus Development Corp.          MENU
--------------------------------------------------------------------------------
1-2-3  File-Manager  Disk-Manager  PrintGraph  Translate  Exit
Enter Lotus Graphics Printing system
================================================================================



                              Thu  01-Jan-87
                                 9:19:36am






        Use the arrow keys to highlight command choice and press [Enter]
 Press [Esc] to cancel a choice; Press [F1] for information on command choices
```

FIGURE 3.69
Selecting the PrintGraph function

```
Copyright 1982, 1983 Lotus Development Corp.  All Rights Reserved.        MENU
--------------------------------------------------------------------------------
Select  Options  Go  Configure  Align  Page  Quit
Select pictures
================================================================================
 SELECTED GRAPHS  COLORS              SIZE    FULL          DIRECTORIES

                  Grid:     Black     Left Margin:    .500  Pictures
                  A Range:  Black     Top Margin:     .250  B:\
                  B Range:  Black     Width:         6.852  Fonts
                  C Range:  Black     Height:        9.445  C:\LOTUS
                  D Range:  Black     Rotation:     90.000
                  E Range:  Black                           GRAPHICS DEVICE
                  F Range:  Black     MODES
                                                            IBM/4
                  FONTS               Eject: No             Parallel
                                      Pause: No
                  1: ROMAN2                                 PAGE SIZE
                  2: ROMAN2
                                                            Length   11.000
                                                            Width     8.000
```

FIGURE 3.70
Controlling the printing of graphs

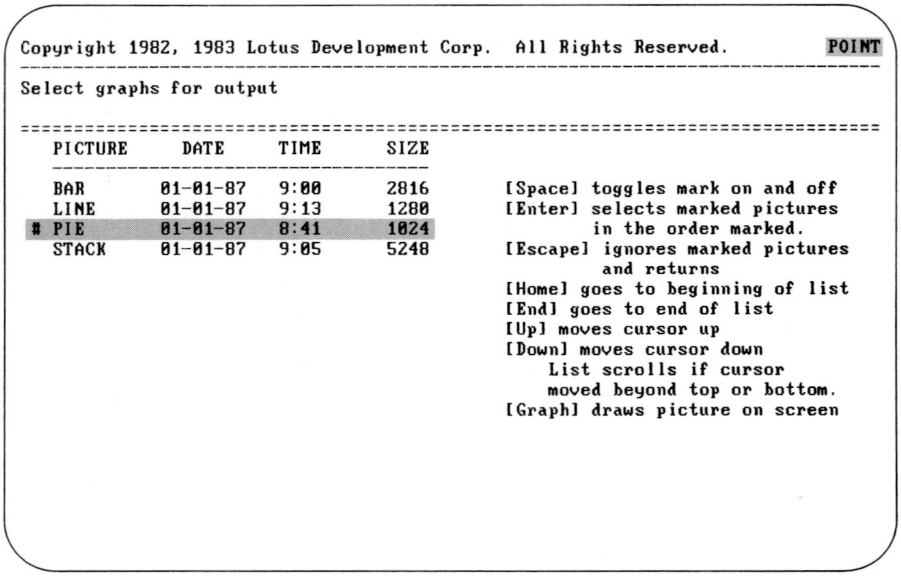

```
Copyright 1982, 1983 Lotus Development Corp.  All Rights Reserved.        POINT
--------------------------------------------------------------------------------
Select graphs for output

================================================================================
   PICTURE      DATE      TIME      SIZE
   ------------------------------------
   BAR        01-01-87   9:00      2816        [Space] toggles mark on and off
   LINE       01-01-87   9:13      1280        [Enter] selects marked pictures
 # PIE        01-01-87   8:41      1024                in the order marked.
   STACK      01-01-87   9:05      5248        [Escape] ignores marked pictures
                                                        and returns
                                               [Home] goes to beginning of list
                                               [End] goes to end of list
                                               [Up] moves cursor up
                                               [Down] moves cursor down
                                                   List scrolls if cursor
                                                   moved beyond top or bottom.
                                               [Graph] draws picture on screen
```

FIGURE 3.71
Selecting a graph file to be printed

—is to be printed. Then return to the previous screen (Figure 3.70). From this screen, you are permitted to change the Options (shown below the menu), Configure the printer, Align the paper, advance to a new Page, and so on. To produce the graph on the printer, select the Go option. Once the graph has been printed, you may Select another graph for printing. When Quit is selected from the menu, you will be returned to the Lotus Access System screen, from where you may Exit Lotus or re-enter one of the other functions. Remember, you will probably have to change disks to get to most of the other Lotus functions.

Summary

Lotus 1-2-3 is an extremely powerful spreadsheet package with the added capabilities of limited database operations and graphics features. The HELP command (F1) is very useful to the beginning user trying to learn the commands as well as the experienced user who needs a quick reminder. Table 3.8

presents a summary of the Lotus 1-2-3 menus; Table 3.9 lists the options available through the Lotus Access System Menu; and Table 3.10 lists the functions available in Lotus.

The remainder of this section is devoted to the uses of spreadsheets and business graphics. For a similar discussion of database uses, read the summary material in Module 2. This section also presents guidelines for evaluating spreadsheet and graphics packages. For evaluation guidelines of database packages, again read the summary material in Module 2.

Uses of Spreadsheets

Because spreadsheets are designed to make arithmetic using large amounts of data easier to handle, many of the initial uses of these types of packages were accounting related. However, the purposes for which the packages were written and the purposes for which they are actually used can be very different. In general, you could say that the use of spreadsheet packages is limited only by the imagination limitations of the user's.

Perhaps the easiest and most common use of spreadsheet packages is for personal checkbook balancing. When your checking account statement arrives in the mail and you start to reconcile the bank's records with what you have recorded in your checkbook, there always seem to be problems. Some checks you have written have not cleared the bank, the bank has added service charges for checks written, deposits have been processed, and charges may have been posted for the use of the bank's ATM (Automatic Teller Machine). In addition, you may have made errors in arithmetic over the last month. Spreadsheets can quickly be set up to record all deposits, checks, and service charges and do the arithmetic required to balance your checkbook. If you create a separate column to keep a running balance, much like in your checkbook, you can even find the arithmetic errors that usually take hours to locate manually.

Another common use of the spreadsheet is as a teacher's grade book. Although entering grades into a spreadsheet package takes as long (or slightly longer) as entering grades in a grade book, there are several advantages for the teacher. The students can be recorded in any order the teacher wants (usually alphabetically by the students' names) and later changed to another order (may be ordered by course average). The average grade on an assignment or test can be calculated automatically. The student records can be sorted by student number, assignment grade, or test grade for printed reports. Finally, at the end of the term, the students' final averages and grades can be calculated automatically, saving the teacher a great deal of time and work. Another advantage to the teacher, which the student can share, is the ability of a spreadsheet package to calculate automatically a student's average after each grade is entered. This

TABLE 3.8 Lotus 1-2-3 Menus

Worksheet	Range	File	Print	Graph	Data
Global	Format	Retrieve	Printer	Type	Fill
Format	Fixed	Save	Range	Line	1 2
(see Range	Scientific		Line	Bar	Reset
Format option)	Currency	Combine	Page	XY	
Label-Prefix	'	Copy	Options	Stacked -Bar	Table
Left	General	Entire File	Header	Pie	Sort
Right	+/−	Named Range	Footer	X	Data-Range
Center	Percent	Add	Margins		Primary-Key
Column-Width	Date	Entire File	Left	A B C D E F	Secondary-Key
Set	1(DD-MMM-YY)	Named Range	Right		Reset
Reset	2(DD-MMM)	Subtract	Top	Reset	Go
Recalculation	3(MMM-YY)	Entire File	Bottom	Graph	Quit
Natural	Text	Named Range	Borders	X	
Columnwise			Columns	A B C D E F	Query
Rowwise	Label-Prefix	Xtract	Rows	Quit	Input
Automatic	Left	Formulas	Setup	View	Criterion
Manual	Right	Values	Page-Length		Output
Iteration	Center	Erase	Other	Save	Find
Protection	Erase	Worksheet	As-Displayed	Options	Extract
Enable		Print	Cell-Formulas	Legend	Unique
Disable	Name	Graph	Formatted	A B C D E F	Delete
Default	Create		Unformatted	Format	Reset
Printer	Delete	List	Quit	Graph	Quit
Interface	Labels	Worksheet	Clear	Lines	Distribution
Auto-LF	Right	Print	All	Symbols	
Left	Down	Graph	Range	Both	
Right	Left	Import	Borders	Neither	
Top	Up	Text	Format	A B C D E F	
Bottom	Reset	Numbers	Align	Lines	
Page-Length	Justify		Go	Symbols	
Wait		Directory	Quit	Both	
Setup	Protect			Neither	
Quit	Unprotect		File	Quit	
			(see Printer options)		

- Directory
- Status
- Update
- Quit

- Insert
  - Column
  - Row
- Delete
  - Column
  - Row
- Column-Width
  - Set
  - Reset
- Erase
- Titles
  - Both
  - Horizontal
  - Vertical
  - Clear
- Window
  - Horizontal
  - Vertical
  - Sync
  - Unsync
  - Clear
- Status

Input

- Title
  - First
  - Second
  - X-Axis
  - Y-Axis
- Grid
  - Horizontal
  - Vertical
  - Both
  - Clear
- Scale
  - Y Scale
    - Automatic
    - Manual
    - Lower
    - Upper
    - Format
      - (see Range)
    - Quit
  - X Scale
    - (see Y Scale)
- Skip
- Color
- B&W
- Data-Labels
  - A B C D E F
  - Quit
- Quit

- Name
  - Use
  - Create
  - Delete
  - Reset
  - Quit

Copy, Move, and Quit Functions do not produce submenus.

TABLE 3.9 Lotus Access System Menu

File-manager	Disk-manager	PrintGraph	Translate
Copy	Disk-copy	Select	VC to WKS
Erase	Compare	Options	DIF to WKS
		Color	
Rename	Prepare	Font	WKS to DIF
Archive	Status	Size	DBF to WKS
		Full	
Disk-drive	Quit	Half	WKS to DBF
A		Manual	Quit
B		Quit	
C		Pause	
D		Eject	
E		Quit	
Sort		Go	
Primary			
Secondary		Configure	
Reset		Files	
Go		Pictures	
Quit		Fonts	
Quit		Quit	
		Device	
		Page	
		Length	
		Width	
		Quit	
		Interface	
		Save	
		Reset	
		Quit	
		Align	
		Page	
		Quit	

Exit function does not produce a submenu.

TABLE 3.10 Lotus 1-2-3 Functions

Function Type and Format

Mathematical Functions:

@ABS(x)	@INT(x)
@MOD(x,y)	@PI(x)
@RAND	@SQRT(x)
@ROUND(x,digits)	@LN(x)
@LOG(x)	@SIN(x)
@EXP(x)	@TAN(x)
@COS(x)	@ACOS(x)
@ASIN(x)	@ATAN2(x,y)
@ATAN(x)	

Special Functions:

@NA @ERR
@IF(x, true_value, false_value)
@CHOOSE(t,v0,v1,v2,...,vn)
@HLOOKUP(x,table_range,row#)
@VLOOKUP(x,table_range,column#)

Logical Functions:

@FALSE	@TRUE
@ISNA(x)	@ISERR(x)

Financial Functions:

@NPV(x,range)
@IRR(guess,range)
@PMT(prn,int,term)
@FV(pmt,int,term)
@PV(pmt,int,term)

Statistical Functions:

@COUNT(list)	@SUM(list)
@AVG(list)	@STD(list)
@MIN(list)	@MAX(list)
@VAR(list)	

Date Functions:

@DATE(yr,mnth,dy)

@TODAY	@DAY(x)
@MONTH(x)	@YEAR(x)

Database Statistical Functions:

@DCOUNT(inp_rng,offset,crit_rng)
@DSUM(inp_rng,offset,crit_rng)
@DAVG(inp_rng,offset,crit_rng)
@DMIN(inp_rng,offset,crit_rng)
@DMAX(inp_rng,offset,crit_rng)
@DSTD(inp_rng,offset,crit_rng)
@DVAR(inp_rng,offset,crit_rng)

way both teacher and student can determine what the student's grade is at any time during the term.

The owner of a mountain resort uses a spreadsheet to keep track of sales and cash flow. Profits depend on a high volume of small sales ($50 to $200) at several profit centers, such as restaurant, boat dock, gift shop, and landing strip. When all the accounting was done by hand, the owner got reports on a monthly basis only and then often after several weeks' delay. Using a spreadsheet package, daily reports with year-to-date and month-to-date sales figures in 23 different categories are produced on demand. The package also produces monthly sales tax and alcohol tax reports. The use of a spreadsheet package has shortened the reporting time between the owner and the resort's accountant and allowed for better cash-flow control, which means that excess funds can be quickly identified and invested in certificates of deposit to maximize profits.

A specialty print shop also uses spreadsheets to control its profits. Because of the many variables involved, it used to take the owner of the print shop several hours to estimate the cost of printing jobs. Job prices would vary based on the amount of art work and the number of colors used, the type of press used, and the grade of paper, as well as several other factors. Using a spreadsheet package and a series of formulas and functions developed over a weekend, the owner now enters the data into the spreadsheet and can quote a price that includes the profit margin in a matter of seconds.

Banks and savings and loan companies use spreadsheets in a similar manner. When a customer applies for a loan to buy a house or a car, the loan application information is entered into a spreadsheet package. The analysis done by the spreadsheet package determines whether the customer is qualified for the loan and the amount of the monthly payments needed to pay off the loan. Although the loan approval process still takes a couple of days, the customer now has immediate information about the terms of the loan.

City governments use spreadsheets to help their citizens. A small town in Ohio used a spreadsheet package to analyze the effects of a rate increase for a natural gas company on the company's profits and on the company's customers. As a result of the analysis, the amount of the rate increase was reduced, and methods of billing the customers were changed. This action resulted in only small increases in the citizens' gas bills, while at the same time it improved the company's ability to meet its expenses.

A financial planner uses a spreadsheet to investigate investment alternatives and strategies. The financial analyst determines the current value of an investment, such as the market price and quantity of stocks, and determines at what point, as the price falls, it would be worthwhile to change to another investment, discounting the amount of brokerage fees. In the same fashion, the analyst uses the spreadsheet to determine when investments should be altered as stock prices increase. Thus, the analyst uses the spreadsheet to solve "what if" problems, such as "what if the value of commodity A rises and that of commodity B remains the same?" By using a spreadsheet, the analyst improves the performance of the investment portfolio.

These are just some of the ways to use spreadsheets. There are many others. In fact, several books have been written on spreadsheet application. The number and variety of applications will increase as these packages continue to evolve and become even more powerful. However, spreadsheets cannot solve *all* numeric data manipulation problems. The more mathematically elaborate and logically complex the process, the more likely the solution of the problem lies with programs written in a developmental language. Although you might find someone using a spreadsheet to perform payroll processing, this type of application is still better suited to more specific software produced in a developmental language.

Uses of Graphics

Now that you are acquainted with the capabilities of Lotus graphics, let's look at how graphics are being used today.

Movies

Hollywood has been using computer graphics in special effects for years. *Tron* and *Star Trek II* are classic examples of movies that have used computer graphics. Although still in its infancy, computer graphic imaging can create simulated "worlds" that have never existed before. Movies are no longer limited by the physical characteristics of reality; instead, they are limited only by the imagination of the movie maker.

Industry

"Drafting Dan" is a cross between a typewriter and a drafting board and is used to develop engineering designs for new products. Although "Drafting Dan" has never been built anywhere except in Robert Heinlein's book *Door into Summer,* copyright 1956, a lot of its relatives have been. "Drafting Dan's" relatives are known as **CAD/CAM (computer-aided design/computer-aided manufacturing)** machines. In the mid-1950s, General Motors was one of the first companies to attempt to use computer-aided design. However, CAD/CAM did not become generally available until the late 1960s. Today, this type of system is used to help design parts, products, and structures from roller bearings to buildings to sophisticated jets, including the space shuttle.

Business

Business graphics are generally divided into two areas: information and presentation. **Information graphics** is the term used to refer to charts and graphs that help one see detailed data in an easy-to-read format. **Presentation graphics** are of higher resolution, usually in color, and more expensive. Although the distinction between the two can be difficult to determine, information graphics are usually too detailed to be used for presentations.

The Wharton School of the University of Pennsylvania in Philadelphia conducted a study that found that speakers were perceived more favorably when they used graphics. Business graphics, therefore, could have a significant effect on your ability to present your ideas successfully.

Guidelines for the Evaluation of Spreadsheet Packages

Before you select a spreadsheet package for your own use, try to answer the following questions:

- **Completeness of documentation** Are the manuals well written, understandable, and easy to use? Are tutorials on package use available?
- **Operating characteristics** What is the maximum size of the spreadsheet supported by the package? How fast does the package perform calculations on a small, a medium, and a large spreadsheet? Is the speed affected by particular combinations of formulas and functions? How fast does it save and retrieve files? What flexibility do you have in terms of file storage?
- **Ease of setup** When using the package, how easy is it to enter data? How do you address cells, and how easy is it to reference a cell or a range of cells? Are range labels available?
- **Command structure** Is the package command or menu driven? How easy is it to select and execute a command? Are menus understandable and given in a logical sequence?
- **Internal help facility** Is the Help option available? How easy is it to use? How complete is it? How quickly can you find the information you need?
- **Cursor movement** Can you easily move around the spreadsheet using the arrow keys? Can you scroll easily? Are additional keys or key combinations available to move around the spreadsheet more quickly?
- **Cell formatting** Can you format a single cell, or must you format a complete column or section? What are the minimum and maximum cell widths? What kinds of text formatting are available (for example, left-justified, right-justified, centered)? Can the contents of cells be adjusted to cell lengths? What kinds of number format options are available? Are standard formats (integer, floating point, and so on) available? Are special formats (dates, percentages, and so forth) available?
- **Editing cell values** Is an editing feature available? How easy is it to use? What kinds of editing operations can be performed (for example, character insertion and deletion)?
- **Windows** How many windows are available? What controls do you have on synchronized versus unsynchronized scrolling? Are these controls assigned by window or to the whole spreadsheet? How easy is it to go from one window to another?
- **Printing flexibility** What controls do you have on printing? Can you "print" to a file as well as to a printer? Can you print only a portion of the spreadsheet? Do you have page controls, including top and bottom mar-

gins, left and right margins, headings, footings, and page numbering? Can you print formulas and functions as well as cell values? Are special routines available to take advantage of special printer features?

- **Completeness of functions** Do you have adequate mathematical and logical functions? How easy are the functions to use? How flexible are they? Are any of the functions related to identifying and interpreting errors?
- **Interfacing characteristics** Are the files produced by the package directly compatible with any other software? Can the package produce print files? DIF files? SYLK files? Are there any special interfacing provisions, like automatic conversion of data from another package? Does this version of the package accept data produced by a previous version, or is there a translation process?
- **Other characteristics** Can the package produce graphics on the screen and on the printer? What, if any, provisions have been made for word processing? Database uses? Communications?

Guidelines for the Evaluation of Graphics Packages

Before you select a graphics package for your own use, try to answer the following questions:

- **Help facility** Is a Help feature available, and, if so, how extensive is it? Does it describe processes such as chart selection, scaling, data entry, and so on? Can it be accessed when needed?
- **Documentation** How complete is the documentation? Is it well written and understandable? Is it well organized? Does it provide helpful tips and suggestions? Does the package have a tutorial?
- **Organization** Is the package command driven or menu driven? Do the commands seem "natural" to use? Are the menus complete and logically arranged? Do you have any difficulty getting from one menu to another? Are there any "holes" in the charting process that are not adequately explained?
- **Graph types** Can you create pie charts? Bar charts? Line charts? Can you pull a "wedge" from a pie chart? Can you produce multiple sets of bars on one bar chart? Can you produce stacked bar charts? Scatter charts? Area charts? What are the limitations on these charts? Is the charting process logical, flexible, and well defined? How easy is the charting process? Can multiple charts be placed into a single viewing area (screen or printer)? Side-by-side? Are the charts relatively accurate and free from distortions?
- **Data entry** Is this graphics function a direct part of a multi-function package? Does the data directly transfer from other functions? Does the

package interface with other packages? Do you have the option of entering data into the package directly, even if it interfaces with other software in some way? How difficult is the data entry process? Can you easily modify data that has been previously entered? Can you easily add data? Delete data? Is data entered as pairs (sets) or individually? Can the data be saved? Separated from the chart? Is it retained when creating multiple charts from the same data?

- **Chart modification and storage** Once a chart has been created, can it be easily altered or added to? Is the chart automatically "updated" with each change? Is the chart redrawn from "scratch" each time a change is made? Can one chart be used as an "overlay" for another? Are storage and retrieval of charts easy and natural? What is the process for retrieving and viewing an existing chart? Are charts stored in a form that can be transmitted to other types of packages?
- **Labeling** What kinds of charting labels are available? Titles? x- and y-axis? Legends? Are any of the labels automatically supplied? Do you have a choice of plotting symbols for scatter charts? Do you have any "floating" labels that can be placed where you want them? Are the labels saved as you move from chart to chart?
- **Drawing and painting** Does the package have either of these capabilities? How precise are the drawing controls? Can circles be drawn automatically? Rectangles? Other shapes? Do you have control over line widths? What controls do you have over text production? Do you have any font selections? Can you paint with patterns? Colors? How many colors? How are they selected?
- **Producing output** Can your graphics be produced on a printer? Plotter? Both? Do you have the right kind of printer to interface with the package? Plotter? Do you have separate size controls when producing a chart on these output devices? Can the charts be rotated? What is the effect of printing colors on a standard printer? On a single-pen plotter? Is the resolution of the printed result similar to that viewed on the screen? How fast is the printing process? Plotting process?
- **Interfaces with other packages** Does the package directly interface with other software packages? Can the chart be stored in an alternate format (for example, DIF, ASCII, SYLK)? Is it directly integrated with other functions? Can charts be transmitted in a communications environment?
- **Special features** Can the package produce three-dimensional charts? Drawings? Can the charts or drawings be rotated? Is there a "zoom" feature? An "invert" feature? Can you "cut and paste" a chart or drawing? Can you produce a "slide show?" What are the timing characteristics? How difficult is it to produce a slide show? How easy it to change? Do you have extended mathematical features? Built-in geometric functions?

APPENDIX A

Job Hunting Data

For even the most experienced person, job hunting can be a confusing time. This is particularly true of a student who is looking for a job that he or she hopes will turn into a career. The student in this problem has decided to organize a record of all the activities involved in looking for and evaluating job offers.

The problem presented here will be used in each module to give you an introduction to each of the software packages covered in the text. All of the data needed to solve the problems presented in the Module Introductions is presented in Table A.1, Companies Applied To, and Table A.2, Offers From Companies.

The problem situation is this: The following information is collected for each company to which an application is made.

Company Name	Date the Résumé Was Submitted
Address	Date the Company Responded
City	Date the Interview Is Set for
State	The Status of Negotiations
Zip Code	Contact Person

When a company makes you an offer, the following data is added:

Work Site
Salary Offered
Life Insurance Paid by the Company
Health Insurance Paid by the Company
Retirement Benefits Paid by the Company
Commuting Distance
Number of Vacation Days
Subjective Rank (Job Preference) of How Well the Student Likes the Offer

You will be asked to initiate contact with the company (word processing), evaluate the various offers (spreadsheets), organize the information in a database, and graphically display information needed in the job hunting process.

TABLE A.1 Companies Applied To

Company Name	Address	City	State	Zip Code	Contact Person	Date Résumé Sent	Date Company Responded	Job Status	Date of Interview
Johnson Instruments, Inc.	P.O. Box 1234	Dallas	TX	76234	Personnel Department	11/01	12/15	Offered	01/23
Champion Cowboy Supply	126 Hollyhill Road	Garland	TX	75342	Mr. Joe Garcia	11/02	01/10	Ongoing	
General Electronics, Inc.	87634 Dynamics Way	Ft. Worth	TX	76908	Mr. Robert LeTrec	11/02	11/15	Ongoing	12/24
First State National Bank	302 Central Expressway	Dallas	TX	76243	Ms. Judith Welpit	11/02	11/30	Ongoing	01/15
Lewis & Melts Mortgage Company	1 Bank Plaza	Denton	TX	76202	Mrs. Roberta Accure	11/03	11/30	Offered	01/15
Ethyl & Jung, DDS	23 Molar Hill Lane	Dennison	OK	79034	Dr. Emil Franz Jung	11/04	11/15	Offered	11/30
Aerospace Education Center	1423 Jupiter Road	Garland	TX	75342	Personnel Department	11/06	11/16	Rejected	12/13
ABC Stereo Warehouse	3434 Sound Place	Dallas	TX	76342	Ms. Alice Faye Kong	11/06	11/16	Ongoing	02/22
WTBS Channel 5 TV	9826 Neonoise Court	Plano	TX	76851	Dr. Jana Willoughby	11/06	12/03	Ongoing	01/06
Hormell Texas Chili Company	1 Hots Place	Ft. Worth	TX	76907	Mr. Foster Brooks	11/10	12/05	Offered	01/31
Children's Museum	Look Out Point	Ft. Worth	TX	76908	Personnel Director	11/10	11/30	Ongoing	01/06
FBI	10–20 Parole Street	Arlington	TX	76745	Mr. H. Daniel Hoover	11/10	01/03	Ongoing	01/21
Mosteq Computer Company	1428 Wozniak Way	Farmers Branch	TX	76331	Mr. Peter Hoague	11/15	12/11	Ongoing	
Nephi's Hopi Crafts	16 Alma, Suite 34	Tulsa	OK	79345	Mrs. Carletta Whitecloud	11/17	12/09	Offered	01/06
Kelly Construction Company	1414 Jupiter Road	Garland	TX	75242	Personnel Division	11/17	12/09	Ongoing	
Jana's Management Consultants	2323 Beltline Road	Irving	TX	75061	Ms. Jana Davidson	12/03	01/06	Rejected	
Bar Four Ranch, Inc.	P.O. Box 92341, Rt. 11	Denton	TX	76205	Mrs. Canada Strong	12/03	12/28	Refused	02/03
Matt's Films, Inc.	P.O. Box 524	Dallas	TX	76341	Personnel Office	12/03	12/31	Offered	01/07
Roger, Roger & Ray, Inc.	457 Happy Way	Garland	TX	75242	Personnel Department	12/03	12/15	Rejected	

TABLE A.2 Offers From Companies

Company Name	Location	Salary Offer	Contributions: Life Insurance	Contributions: Health Insurance	Contributions: Retirement	Commute Distance	Vacation Days	Job Preference
Johnson Instruments, Inc.	South	19000.00	135.00	354.00	3333.00	45	5	3
Johnson Instruments, Inc.	Mid-cities	19200.00	135.00	354.00	3333.00	35	5	4
Johnson Instruments, Inc.	North	19100.00	135.00	354.00	3333.00	25	5	5
Matt's Films, Inc.	North	18950.00	155.00	456.00	5000.00	33	6	4
Lewis & Melts Mortgage Company	Mid-cities	22000.00	500.00	600.00	4400.00	35	14	1
Ethyl & Jung, DDS	North	20000.00	325.00	950.00	6000.00	95	14	2
Hormell Texas Chili Company	East	19300.00	164.00	320.00	2202.20	53	5	1
Nephi's Hopi Crafts	East	15670.00	250.00	425.00	1333.00	47	14	4
First State National Bank	North	22000.00	210.00	325.00	2950.00	25	14	2

APPENDIX B

Questions and Activities

WordStar

1. Is WordStar command driven or menu driven? Does it have a help function? How is the help function used?
2. What is the maximum size of a document that WordStar can handle? What is the "word processing hierarchy"?
3. Check the documentation. What are the additional features available to you? How do you select and use them?
4. How are the control characters handled?
5. What other word processing packages (besides WordStar) can be used on your microcomputer? (*Note:* Use the library or your local computer store to find the answer to this question.)

dBASE II and III

As you answer the following questions, keep the differences between dBASE II and dBASE III in mind.

1. Describe the creation process for this database structure. What are the limitations on attribute names? What data types are available?
2. Are one-to-one relationships supported by the package? One-to-many? Many-to-many?
3. What command(s) can be used to query the database? Do you have control over which attributes are listed as a result of a query? How? What is the name of the option that indicates the relational conditions to be supplied?
4. How do you go about changing an attribute value? What commands are involved? What do you do to add an entity to the database? To delete an entity? Can you "mark" and "recall" deleted entities?
5. What is the process involved in producing a report? How do you control how a report looks? What "extended" controls do you have (for example, page length and width, headings, totals)?

6. You are still not happy with the job offers you have received. Use the COMPANY database to find all the companies for which negotiations are still "Ongoing" and for which no interview data has been established. You want the list to include company name, address, contact person, and the date on which your résumé was acknowledged.
7. Set up a database of the books you have in your personal library. (Include textbooks, as well as books you read for personal enjoyment; however, do not include more than 20 books.) This database should contain the following attributes:

   Author (last name first)
   Title
   Edition (1st, 2nd, and so on)
   Publisher
   Publication date (copyright date)
   Length (number of pages)
   Type (textbook, fiction, nonfiction, and so on)
   Subject area (major topic—for example, "Computers")
   Comments on the content of the book (no more than 50 characters per book)

   Now generate three reports. The first report should list, in alphabetical order by author, all the books in your library. The second report should list all the books in your library that have been published since 1980. This report should include only author, title, and publication date and should be ordered chronologically by publication date. The final report should list author, title, subject area, and comments. This report should be sorted by subject area and include the total number of pages for each subject area. All reports should include a count of the number of books in the list.

Lotus 1-2-3

1. Is Lotus 1-2-3 command driven or menu driven? Does it have a help function? How is the help function used?
2. Compare the capabilities of each of the functions in Lotus 1-2-3 with the capabilities of the "stand-alone" packages you have used? Which has the greatest capability?
4. Check Lotus 1-2-3's documentation to find out what additional features are available. How do you use them (separate programs or parts of the integrated system)?
5. What other integrated software systems (besides Lotus 1-2-3) can be used on your microcomputer? (*Note:* Use the library or your local computer store to find the answer to this question.)

INDEX

Absolute address, 119
Activity specification process, 8
Address, absolute or relative, 119
Alphanumeric data, 121
Applications software, 5, 6–9
  developmental tasks in, 8
  source code versus object code in, 6–8
Area chart, 185
Arithmetic operations, 5
  scalar, 119
Assembly languages, 5
Attribute, 54

Bar charts, 183, 184, 185
  stacked, 185
BASIC, 8
Branching operations, 5
Byron, Augusta Ada, 2

Cell, 118
Cell-referencing system, 118
Character data, 119, 121
Charts, 183–185
Code (*see also* Software)
  object, 6–7, 8
  operation, 5, 9
  source, 6–7
Command driven software, 9
Commands (tables of):
  in dBASE II and III, 102–112
  in Lotus 1-2-3, 125–126, 180
  in WordStar, 46, 47
Compiler, 7
Computer-aided design/Computer-aided manufacturing (CAD/CAM), 197
Conceptual view of data, 51–52, 53
Copy protection, 8
Cursor movement codes:
  in dBASE II, 73
  in Lotus 1-2-3, 126–128
  in WordStar, 19

Data:
  alphanumeric, 121
  character, 119, 121
  collection of, 54
  conceptual view of, 51–52, 53
  independence of, 51, 54
  integrity of, 51
  logical view of, 52–53
  numeric, 121
  physical view of, 53–54
  redundancy of, 50, 51, 54
  types of, in spreadsheets, 119–121
Data element, 54
Data item, 54
Data management systems (DMS), 50
Database management system (DBMS), 49, 50 (*see also* Databases)
Databases, 1, 49–58
  dBASE II and III, 59–98, 102–115
  definition of, 54
  evaluation of, 99–102
  history of, 49–50
  types of, 56–58
  uses of, 98–99
dBASE II, 59–97, 102
  activity tracking, 67–70
  adding records, 75–77
  commands in, 102–112
  creating, 61–67
  cursor movement codes, 73
  eliminating records, 81–83
  examining databases, 77–81
  field types, 63
  help functions, 59–60
  indexing, 83–84
  joining databases, 91–94
  modifying contents, 71–75
  printing, 87–91
  scope options, 79
  sorting records, 84–87
  starting and stopping, 67

dBASE III, 59–98, 102
  commands in, 102–112
  functions in, 113–115
Developmental software, 5–6
Direct access, 49
Domain/key normal form, 58

Entity, 54
Entity record, 54
Evaluation:
  of databases, 99–102
  of graphics software, 199–200
  of spreadsheet software, 197–199
  of word processing software, 45, 48

Field, 54
  types of, in dBASE II, 63
File management systems (FMS), 49
Firmware, 5
Function keys:
  in Lotus 1-2-3 spreadsheet, 127, 180
  in WordStar, 47
Functions:
  in dBASE III, 113–115
  in Lotus 1-2-3 spreadsheet, 147–151
  in Lotus 1-2-3, 195
  mathematical, in Lotus 1-2-3 database, 178
  in spreadsheets, 121
  table, in Lotus 1-2-3 spreadsheet, 156–160
  window, in Lotus 1-2-3 spreadsheet, 137–139

Garbage in, garbage out (GIGO), 54
Graphics, 183–185
  evaluation of, 199–200
  functions of, 183
  for information and presentation, 197
  Lotus 1-2-3 graphics, 186–190
  uses of, 197
Graphs, 184

Help functions:
  in dBASE II, 59–60
  in Lotus 1-2-3, 128
  in WordStar, 13, 15, 20–21
Hierarchical database model, 56
Hierarchical structures, 50

Input-output operations, 5
Install programs, 8
Instructions, *see* Software
Integrated software packages, 122
Integrity, 51
Interpreter, 7

Jacquard, Joseph, 2

Keys:
  primary/secondary, 54
  in relational databases, 58

Languages:
  assembly, 5
  macro, 8
  meta, 8
  package command, 8–9
  procedural, 5
  third-generation, 5
Line charts, 183, 184, 185
Logic operations, 5
Logical operators, 81
Logical view of data, 52–53
Lotus 1-2-3 database, 163–182
  compound search criteria in, 178
  entering data, 165–167
  headings, 165
  macros in, 178–182
  mathematical functions, 178
  printing, 173
  search operations, 167–178
  special key indicators in, 180
Lotus 1-2-3 graphics, 186–190
  creating charts, 188–190
  labeling, 188–189
  printing, 190
  viewing, clearing, saving charts, 188

Lotus 1-2-3 spreadsheet, 122–162
  adding rows, 151–153
  changing column widths, 131
  characteristics of, 122–126
  commands, 125–126
  copying, 144–146
  cursor movement in, 126–128
  entering headings and labels, 130–131
  entering numeric values, 139
  entering text, 137
  formatting numeric cells, 134
  formatting text cells, 132–134
  formulas, 143–144
  function key designations in, 127
  functions, 147–151
  help functions, 128
  inserting columns, 141–142
  printing, 160–161
  quitting, 161
  saving, 140
  sorting, 153–156
  table functions, 156–160
  window functions, 137–139
Lotus 1-2-3, 190–191
  access system menu options, 194
  functions in, 195
  menus, 192–193

Macro languages, 8
Macros, 178–182
Mailmerge functions, 37–43
Many-to-many (m : m) relationships, 55–56
Matrix, 118
Menus, 9
  in Lotus 1-2-3, 192–194
  software driven by, 9
  in WordStar, 46
Meta languages, 8

Network database model, 56, 57
Neumann, John von, 2
Numeric data, 121

Object code, 6–7, 8
Occupations, software
 applications for, 3–4
One-to-many (1 : m) relationships, 55
One-to-one (1 : 1) relationships, 54–55
Operands, 5, 9
Operating system software, 5, 6
Operation code, 5, 9

Package command languages, 8–9
Packaged software, 8
Physical view of data, 53–54
Pie charts, 183, 185
Primary keys, 54
Procedural languages, 5
Program, *see* Software
Programming languages, 5–6

Random access, 49
Read-only memory (ROM), 5
Record, entity, 54
Redundancy, 50, 51, 54
Relational database model, 57, 58
Relational operators, 80
Relationships, 54–56
Relative address, 119
Reserved word, 5, 9
Ruler, 19–20

Scalar arithmetic operations, 119
Scatter chart, 184–185
Scope options, 79
Scratchpads, *see* Spreadsheets
Scrolling, 118
Secondary keys, 54
Software:
 developmental, 5–6
 historical development of, 2
 integrated, 122
 menu driven, 9
 stand-alone, 183
 system, 5, 6
 user friendly, 8
Sort functions:
 in dBASE II, 84–87
 in Lotus 1-2-3, 153–156
Source code, 6–7
Spelling checker, 29–34
Spreadsheets, 1–2, 116–121
 data types in, 119–121
 evaluation of, 197–199
 Lotus 1-2-3, 122–162
 terminology in, 118–119
 uses of, 191, 195–196
Stand-alone software, 183
Stored-program concept, 2, 5
Supervisor, 5
System software, 5
 working structure of, 6

Tree structures, 50
Tuples, 58

User friendly software, 8

Word processing programs, 1
 evaluation of, 45, 48
 uses of, 44–45
 WordStar, 13–43, 45
WordStar, 13–43, 45
 commands and function keys, 47
 cursor movement chart, 19
 editing, 26–29
 entering text, 23–26
 find and replace functions, 35–36
 help function, 13, 15, 20–21
 mailmerge, 37–43
 opening menu commands, 46
 page reformatting, 28–29
 printing, 36–37
 spelling checker, 29–34
Work space, 118
Worksheets, *see* Spreadsheets